NetTravel:
How Travelers Use
the Internet

NetTravel: How Travelers Use the Internet

Michael Shapiro

NetTravel: How Travelers Use the Internet
by Michael Shapiro

Copyright © 1997, Songline Studios, Inc. and Michael Shapiro. All rights reserved. No part of this book may be reproduced or transmitted in any form or by any means without prior written permission from Songline Studios. Printed in the United States of America.

Published by Songline Studios, Inc. and O'Reilly & Associates, Inc., 101 Morris Street, Sebastopol, CA 95472.

Series Editor: Melissa Koch

Editor: Stephen Pizzo

Printing History: April 1997:   First Edition.

Songline Guides is a trademark of Songline Studios, Inc.

Many of the designations used by manufacturers and sellers to distinguish their products are claimed as trademarks. Where those designations appear in this book, and Songline Studios, Inc., was aware of a trademark claim, the designations have been printed in caps or initial caps.

Specific copyright notices and restrictions for software on the CD-ROM accompanying this book are included on that CD-ROM. All of the programs described in this book and provided on the CD-ROM are subject to change without notice.

While every precaution has been taken in the preparation of this book, the publishers take no responsibility for errors or omissions, or for damages resulting from the use of information in the book.

 This book is printed on acid-free paper with 85% recycled content, 15% post-consumer waste. The publishers are committed to using paper with the highest recycled content available consistent with high quality.

ISBN: 1-56592-172-0

Cover Design: Edie Freedman   [3/98]
Production Services: Thomas E. Dorsaneo

Contents

Foreword

Will the Internet have a major impact on travel, on the traveling consumer, on our effort to travel more efficiently? I'm one of those foolish optimists you hear about who is convinced it will. And yet my views are sharply at odds with those of many of my travel colleagues.

In the travel industry trade press, scarcely a week goes by without a letter to the editor expressing cynical boredom with all the talk about cyberspace and the Web. The public, they say, demands to speak with a human being when booking their trips and tours, and will always be so inclined. These doubters believe the Internet will—at best—account for one percent of ticket sales, even less for travel advice. Every other prediction about the eventual mechanization of travel purchases has not come true, they continue, and traditional methods will still prevail for planning and purchasing a trip.

With all respect, these doubters seem very much like the world-weary types who predicted in the late 1940s that television would not be widely adopted. They are expressing a hope, not a prediction. Already, in its very infancy as it applies to travel, the Internet accounts for hundreds of millions of dollars of travel transactions, and for untold instances of travel advice and information.

With the crudest tools at hand—slow modems, limited computer memory capacity, as yet imperfect Internet travel programs—and with limited penetration of computer technology into the average home, millions of people are nevertheless accessing Internet travel programs in their eagerness to improve the way they book their trips. Imagine the growth that will occur when the Internet is perfected to allow for instant responses and greater ease of use.

The first reason the Internet's use for travel will grow has to do with the growing complexity of travel information. Two thousand tour operators now assault us with their brochures and catalogs. Air fares change hourly. Secret discounts abound. Hundreds of destinations make special offers, institute special programs. One hundred and thirty cruise ships, with many more to come, set out on varying

Online spending for travel services will reach $1 billion by the end of 1997, almost 50 percent of the $2.3 billion that will be spent online in 1997, according to a 1997 report from Jupiter Communications, a leading online analyst, based in New York.

itineraries each week. Upstart airlines come and go. Air fare sales to here and there break out almost weekly.

No individual alive, no travel counselor, no walking encyclopedia, can properly keep up with these developments using traditional media for their information. And the public is becoming increasingly aware of these human limitations. Only a tool like the Internet can enable a successful search for all the possibilities.

Computer programs now in existence or in construction permit people, including travel agents, to tap into a vast library of daily changing information, and make a reasonably well-informed decision about their own imminent travel plans or the travel plans of others.

The second reason for the eventual success of the Internet in travel has to do with the procedures for booking a trip once the dates and destinations have been chosen (a fairly simplistic process), as opposed to assessing the travel information relating to those decisions (which is difficult and complex).

Most of the time, in the final booking process, travel professionals are simply placing human bodies into airplane seats on particular flights, or into hotel rooms or cruiseship cabins for particular dates, or into automobiles at various airports. Many members of the public—wisely or not, for good or ill—have concluded that the actual booking process can just as easily be accomplished by travelers themselves, using reservations programs on the Internet. Some find it pleasant or engrossing to do so.

Many of them—again wisely or not, for good or ill—have concluded that the actual booking process does not require telephone conversations with a third party. They also believe—wisely or not—that the purely mechanical task of assigning bodies to seats, rooms, and cabins can be handled so easily on the Internet as to result in savings to the airlines, cruiselines, car rental companies, and hotel chains with which they deal.

Sooner or later one of the major airlines, cruiselines, car rental companies, or hotel chains will offer cheaper prices to people who "book it themselves" on the Internet. Already some of those companies have been making such offers in veiled terms, almost subliminally, paying lip service to traditional modes. But sooner or later some big company will do so openly and boldly. And when that happens there will be a further rush to the Internet.

The major retailers, foreseeing this development, have now begun to ally themselves with the Internet, to use it, perfect it, make it into a marketing tool for themselves. These extremely canny retail companies will benefit from the Internet. The cynics and nay-sayers will be hurt by it. My own Internet site, Arthur Frommer's Outspoken Encyclopedia of Travel (*http://www.frommer.com*) is already being used by a great many dynamic retail travel agents. They find that it enables them to keep up far better with important developments in travel.

Michael Shapiro has performed an important service to both the travel industry and the traveling public with the publication of this guide to the many Internet services for travel. It is well researched, thorough, and imaginatively presented. I'm proud to have been asked to provide the foreword to such a pioneering book.

Arthur Frommer

New York, NY

February 1997

Arthur Frommer's Outspoken Encyclopedia of Travel
http://www.frommer.com
or
http://www.frommers.com
Daily travel news, secret bargains, and insider tips.

About the Author

Michael Shapiro, a producer for CNET in San Francisco, has worked as a journalist and travel writer since 1984. Before joining the staff of O'Reilly & Associates' Global Network Navigator in 1994, he worked for daily newspapers in the San Francisco Bay Area. His first online stories appeared in GNN's Travelers' Center, and included a series on Guatemala, a piece on bicycling through Denmark, and a story about a nightmare rafting misadventure on California's American River. His travel features often appear in the *San Francisco Examiner*. Michael also writes for print magazines covering the Net, including *Internet Underground*.

Michael Shapiro

In 1995, he became a founding editor of *Web Review* (*http://webreview.com*), an online magazine devoted to covering the nascent world of the Net. Working with veteran investigative reporter Steve Pizzo, he helped launch *Net Daily News*, a daily online journal that covered just about everything that was engaging or illuminating where news and the Net intersect.

In his spare time, Michael leads whitewater rafting adventures and sea kayak trips for disabled people. A native of New York, he now lives near Sebastopol, California, about an hour's drive north of San Francisco.

Acknowledgments

My journey to the region where the Internet meets the travel world began in April 1994, when I saw Allen Noren demonstrate a startlingly new Web-based service from O'Reilly & Associates. Allen, then editor of GNN's Travelers' Center, showed how the Internet could be the ideal jumping-off point for a real-world journey. After that fateful night in April, I stayed in touch with Allen for more than six months until I landed a job at GNN. Throughout the conception and writing of this book, Allen has served as a reservoir of useful advice, and I appreciate the direction he has given this project.

I'd like to thank my editor, Steve Pizzo, who helped shape and mold this book and who was always ready—if I got off track—to slap me in the face and guide me back to the path I needed to follow. Songline Studios' publisher Dale Dougherty lent his wise counsel and fine editing skills to this project, and the time he gave to *NetTravel* helped make it a much better book. Dave Sims helped me conceive and outline this project, and I value the sharp insight he offered. Richard Koman and Bob Schmitt also helped me answer key questions along the way.

I'd also like to thank all the people who read early versions of the manuscript: Morris Dye, Marc-David Seidel, Edward Hasbrouck, Andres Edwards, and Phyllis Shapiro. Arthur Frommer enhanced this project with his extensive knowledge of the travel industry and clear vision of how it is evolving. I appreciate his graciousness and willingness to write the foreword of my book. Copy editing and production was handled expertly by Lunaea Hougland and Tom Dorsaneo.

And of course I deeply appreciate the community of travelers who shared their experiences using the Net. You are the ones who are showing how it's done, and the trails you have blazed will make it easier for others to create their own pathways through the Net.

A broad network of friends and family helped keep me going during the six months it took to write and edit this book. Jeffrey Seligson, my good friend and yoga guru, helped keep my body limber after too many long days of sitting in front of a computer. Shawn and Bruce pulled me away to watch 49ers' games and enjoy the company of their beautiful baby Will Kindred; and Ralph and Joanne lent me their canoe so I could paddle to work as a flood of biblical proportions surrounded Songline's offices as my deadline approached.

Larry, Phyllis, and Andy Shapiro were there to share family dinners and listen to me rant. And they kept passing on useful articles from the mainstream press that I might have missed as I kept my eyes focused on online stories. My grandparents, Corinne and Stanley Kreutzer, had valuable suggestions that have enriched the book, and I raise a toast to them as they reach their tenth decade on the planet.

Ultimately, I greatly appreciate the kindness, love, and sunny presence of Willow Taraja, who kept me going with hugs, miso soup, and chai tea.

It's true that every book is the work of many people. I've learned a great deal from all the people with whom I have worked and communicated in the past few months. Thank you for broadening my horizons.

Michael Shapiro
shapiro@songline.com
http://nettravel.com
Sebastopol, California
March, 1997

Introduction

PLUG IN, TURN ON, TAKE OFF

The Internet is revolutionizing the way people travel. It has thrown open travel resources that were previously accessible only to professional travel agents. Airlines, hotels, and tour companies have rushed to set up reservation sites on the World Wide Web, which offers a direct channel to their customers. And the Net is a way to connect with people in distant locales, people who will offer recommendations of what to see, where to go, and where to stay. Many serious travelers already consider the Net indispensable, and some of these travelers will tell their stories in the pages ahead, offering examples of how to best use this magnificent resource.

- ▶ Becoming Your Own Travel Planner
- ▶ A Bright Future for Online Travel
- ▶ Who Is this Book For?
- ▶ You Can Get There from Here
- ▶ Connecting with People Worldwide
- ▶ A Virtual Roadmap
- ▶ A Traveler's Toolbox

BECOMING YOUR OWN
TRAVEL PLANNER

NetTravel explains in concrete terms how travelers can use the Internet to become informed travel consumers. The Net allows all kinds of travelers, whether they travel for business or pleasure, to become personally involved in their own travel planning. Travelers can now choose from a larger pool of resources, and save money by searching the Net's rapidly expanding inventory of travel sites.

Until the advent of online booking agents, travel agents controlled access to reservation systems. So it used to be easier to call a travel agent, tell him or her what kind of trip you had in mind, let the agent sort through all the airline schedules and fares, and make the necessary arrangements. For most travelers, this system may offer desired conveniences. But the times, they are a-changin', and lots of travelers, corporate travel planners, and business people want to take trip planning—or at least some parts of travel arranging—into their own hands.

The Net has matured and evolved to the point where travelers can now use it as a personal travel planner. With search engines and database-powered sites that can match a traveler's needs with online resources, the same information swamp that once sent a traveler to a professional agent can now be navigated easily. Airline fares and schedules are sorted and served up in seconds, last-minute travel bargains are emailed directly to you, and corporate travel planners can find sites that let them plug their company's travel needs into a customized travel program. Even travelers who are not ready or inclined to jettison their trusty travel agent can use the Net to plan their trips and establish itineraries, and then let the agent handle the final booking.

AN END RUN AROUND CLOGGED SWITCHBOARDS

The best way to get a sense of what is possible on the Net is to demonstrate how travelers are using this new tool to take the hassle out of booking their trips. The Southwest Airlines sale during the summer of 1996 is a good example of how travelers used the Net to get the deals they wanted. On July 14, 1996, Southwest announced one of the most extraordinary bargains in airline history: $25 per flight segment, wherever Southwest flies. As word spread about the deal (and other airlines matched it), airline phone switchboards were soon overwhelmed, and lines at airport counters stretched longer than football fields.

TIP

Southwest Airlines is not available through all airline reservation systems. To buy Southwest tickets online, it's most efficient to go directly to the company's Web site (*http://www.iflyswa.com*).

But savvy Internet travelers made an end-run around the bottleneck. While most customers were still on hold, Net travelers had their cheap tickets in hand. Robert De Vries was one of those who bagged his Southwest ticket using easySABRE on CompuServe. Robert's prize: $25 tickets from San Francisco to Seattle.

By responding to a series of prompts, Robert told the reservation system what dates he wanted to travel and instructed it to look for the cheapest flights. Robert could see the same information that a travel agent or airline salesperson could punch up. He soon found the $25 flights on the days he wanted, entered his credit card number, and the ticket confirmation was delivered to his door within two days.

"It was smooth, easy, no hassle," Robert says. The online reservation system he was using clearly showed him which days were still

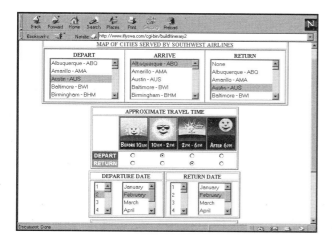

FIGURE INTRO-1

Travelers can use Southwest's Web site (http://www.iflyswa.com) to check flight schedules and prices.

available and also which of the competing airlines were matching the $25 dollar fare. (For a full discussion of booking flights, see Chapter 2, "Planes, Trains, and Automobiles.")

A BRIGHT FUTURE FOR ONLINE TRAVEL

Most analysts believe the future of the Net-based travel industry is very bright. According to Jupiter Communications, a leading analyst of Internet-related trends, online travel sales reached $326 million in 1995 and were projected to almost double to $608 million in 1996. By 2000, that figure is expected to reach more than $3 billion, a tenfold increase in just five years. Various forecasts predict that the travel market will make up nearly one-half of online sales by the turn of the century.

This optimistic forecast makes sense. The Net offers significant advantages to both buyers and sellers in the travel arena. The consumer, for the first time, is able to access a dynamic database of information (such as what airline flights or hotel rooms are currently available) and evaluate destinations with online multimedia tools— for example, a video of a sailing trip in Hawaii.

For travel service suppliers, the benefits are also potentially huge, allowing them to reach travel buyers without having to go through layers of intermediaries. For example, an airline such as TWA can sell directly to passengers, without having to pay travel agents. As more people buy online, the airline can reduce the number of operators employed at its traditional reservation phone banks. Another advantage for travel suppliers is that for the first time, they can tightly target travelers who have specified needs or interests. So if American Airlines has a special deal between Dallas to Chicago, it can target business customers who have expressed interest in this route. Or if a hotel can project that it will only be half full during an upcoming weekend, it can publicize steep discounts on the Net to help fill those rooms. While this is a boon for travel suppliers, it's also great for consumers because it makes it easier to find the kind of travel desired at the best price possible.

According to a 1996 survey by YP&B/Yankelovich Partners National Leisure Travel Monitor, 50 percent of travelers say they are interested in using the Net to get information about travel packages or book a trip. Among family travelers, 12 percent said they had already used the Net to research pleasure trips in the past year, and 5 percent said they had actually booked a trip online. And this was some time ago, so the numbers have certainly increased since this study was conducted.

AN EMOTIONAL CONNECTION

Travel suppliers are employing the Net to extend their reach and convey content in an emotional way that was never possible with the standard brochure. Richard Bangs, former head of the adventure tour company Mountain Travel Sobek (*http://www.mtsobek.com/*), worked for years to bring more detailed information about the company's trips to his clients.

"To think that travelers made a major travel decision based on a single image and a few paragraphs of text is now astonishing—today people can learn so much more and better target their wants," he says. "The catalog was static. It was always somewhat out of date as soon as it was printed. The Net is convenient—you can ask a question in the middle of the night. Or a new trip to Korea can be posted immediately."

Until the Net came along, Richard felt that adventure tour companies couldn't adequately convey what they had to offer. "We'd always been frustrated with the lack of a suitable communications tool. To have a two-week trek through the Himalayas and try to convey that with one photo wasn't good enough," he says. "The question was how could we bring the experience closer. As soon as the Net started to show its hand, we knew this is the tool we wanted—not just because the Net can deliver more text and images. On the Net we can

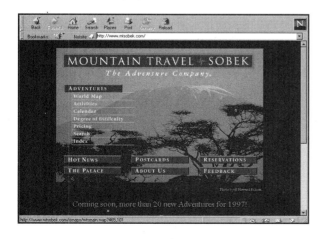

FIGURE INTRO-2
Mountain Travel Sobek (http://www. mtsobek.com) uses the Web to give travelers a better sense of what they can expect on their trips.

deliver sound—the trumpet of an elephant, groan of a shifting glacier, or the gamelan of Indonesia—and distribute this globally. It's not just that you can provide infinitely more material, you can provide emotional material."

WHO IS THIS BOOK FOR?

Before writing a book, an author must answer the question: "Who is this book for?" The answer came to me during an interview with Ken Orton, president of Preview Travel, one of the main airline reservations site on the Web. Ken said he designed his site to reflect the wishes of a particular kind of traveler he described as the person "who always wanted to turn the travel agent's computer screen around."

That remark hit home for me. How many times have I sat at a travel agent's desk or stood at an airline ticket counter staring at the back of a terminal while the agent tapped the keys, frowned at the screen—tapped the keys again, groaned—and tapped the keys some more? I always had to resist the urge to just reach out, turn the terminal around, and say, "Look, let me see what my options are."

This book will help you find the tools now available on the Internet to do just that. Many travelers will still use travel agents to make reservations for them, at least until they feel more confident in this new medium. Similar to patients who read about their illnesses to become more informed, travelers use the Net become more knowledgeable before embarking on a journey. And better travelers have better trips. In the pages ahead, you'll read about some Net-enhanced trips and even a few Net-inspired journeys.

Preview Travel

Destination information is at *http://www.vacations.com*. For airline schedules and hotel bookings, see *http://www.reservations. com*.

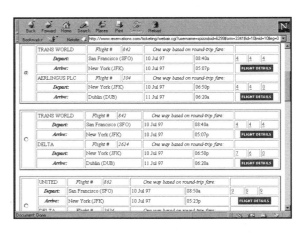

FIGURE INTRO -3

Preview Travel (http://www.reservations. com) lets you turn the screen around to see your travel options.

Maybe you're standing in a bookstore right now, reading this introduction and wondering whether this book is worth buying. Perhaps you're thinking, I could just get online, search for some travel sites, and find what I need on my own. If you've been on the Net for years and are very familiar with travel resources and the travel industry, you may be right. Put it down and save yourself a few bucks.

What Can this Book Do for You?

But if you haven't spent years poring over travel sites on the Web, watching them evolve, and testing them to see what's most valuable, you will learn to be a more efficient and effective travel planner by reading this book. *NetTravel* goes beyond showing you how to use online resources; it offers an inside view into how the travel industry works. And the more you know about the travel business, the better equipped you'll be to get good deals and find the options that best suit your travel needs.

In brief, here's what *NetTravel* offers:

- Tips for how to search and find the resources you need. This book can show you how to use Net resources to create your own guidebook, selecting the information you need from Web sites to compile a packet of information that will be more up-to-date, relevant, and tailored to your needs than any printed guidebook.

- Guidelines for planning your vacation or business trip. *NetTravel* offers a virtual toolbox of some of the best resources on the Web: places you can find maps, weather forecasts, train schedules, and much more.

- Profiles of veteran travelers. *NetTravel* shares the stories of people who have blazed trails on the Net and who offer their journeys as examples. Some even offer their email address, inviting you to seek their advice if you want some help navigating.

YOU CAN GET THERE FROM HERE

NetTravel is about choices and convenience. Today's connected travelers have more options than ever before, and they can access these options on their terms. These are not necessarily new travel destinations or modes of transportation. Most of them were always there, just not accessible to the typical traveler. The Net has thrown open the world's travel inventory, and any traveler with a Net connection can explore these options 24 hours a day, seven days a week.

Travel editor Morris Dye notes that before the dawn of online travel services, agents sold two things: access to reservation systems and knowledge about travel planning. With the increasing availability of the Net, selling access—for example, to an airline's computerized reservations system (CRS)—becomes less important. What agents will continue to sell is their expertise—people will always need informed travel counselors.

Sally Lewis, a single, working mother with three children, says Net access to travel reservation systems and destination information offers her unparalleled convenience:

> I don't have time to sneeze, let alone sit in a travel agent's office to plan a trip. I can, however, log on at 11 p.m. on a Sunday night and make all my arrangements by myself.
>
> I use the Net for basically everything. Work, fun, conversation, free phone calls, the kids' homework, shopping, you name it. For a trip to England, I booked the airfare through one of our online agents and saved over $250 on a Virgin Atlantic Airways flight. I'll be staying with a friend I met online, and I planned my entire sightseeing itinerary online (rates, hours of operation, history, etc.). I made car reservations, printed driving maps, and registered for the travel trade show that I will be attending, and I'll be meeting with several of our clients I have worked with online.
>
> While I am away, I will be connected with my kids via email. As far as I am concerned, you can do anything easily online. People just have to get in the habit of using it, that's all.

Voice on the Net
http://www.von.com
Net phone software is available for about $50. You can talk for free to anyone who has the same software. The sound quality isn't as good as a normal telephone line—but the price can't be beat. This site has links to leading Net phone companies.

Sally discovered that using the Net to plan her travels could lead to unexpected and rewarding encounters. Through an Internet chat group, Sally became friends with a man in London who offered to show her around the city. To get better acquainted, they hooked up through their Internet phones, talking for hours without having to pay a dime to Ma Bell.

> We hooked up over an Internet phone service so we could make free phone calls and chat for hours. When I told him I was coming over, he asked to visit me. It'll be a fun trip. Rather than do the touristy things, we'll do what the locals do—maybe we'll even close a pub one night.

CONNECTING WITH PEOPLE WORLDWIDE

Using the Net skillfully means much more than peering into the soul of a machine and extracting information. In front of every terminal is a live person, and many of these people are willing to help you. People are connecting through the Net via email and through Usenet newsgroups, which are electronic bulletin boards. (We'll discuss these in Chapter 8.)

There's a newsgroup or mailing list for just about every area and type of travel. And, just as the best travel experiences are often the connections made with other people, the best travel planning often involves getting in touch with others and gleaning wisdom from their tips and advice.

Following links on the Net or threads in newsgroups can lead travelers to people they might never have met and places they would never have found if they'd planned their trip through a travel agent or tour service. Often talking to people in online discussion groups leads to real-world connections that can greatly enrich your journey.

Edward Hasbrouck, a travel agent who specializes in around-the-world packages, was planning to go to Indonesia and wondered where he could find English books in the city of Bandung (Indonesia's third largest city, on the island of Java). He posted a query in a newsgroup called *soc.culture.indonesia* and received several responses recommending bookstores.

One person who responded said, "You can talk to my former English teacher from high school when you get to Bandung." During his trip, Edward used the tips to find the books he needed. "After I found the books, I thought, what the heck, I'd look him up (the English teacher). He was a little confused as to how I knew his former student, but he invited me to be a guest speaker in his classroom. I got to ask his students questions, and they got to ask me what life is like in the West."

A VIRTUAL ROADMAP

NetTravel is written for travelers who want to save money and time, directing them to the most useful resources on the Net and showing them how to best use these resources. This book lists many of the best sites on the Web, but also offers much more. *NetTravel* is an instructional guide to help you find the resources you need and connect with people who can add to your travel experience.

No book about the Internet that simply lists sites is relevant for more than a few months. The Net is changing too fast for any listing of sites to remain comprehensive. The goal of *NetTravel* is to familiarize you with the basics of Internet travel planning, introduce key resources, and help you get more comfortable and familiar with the methods of planning and arranging your own travel.

The first three chapters of *NetTravel* focus on the nuts and bolts of travel planning: how to find a destination, book a flight, and reserve a hotel room. The middle section of the book (Chapters 4-8) highlights the many niches of the travel market where the Net is so useful, from getting a good deal to finding the right cruise. This section also shows how certain groups—from business travelers to adventurers—can best employ the Net while on the road. The final section shows how to use the Net to connect with other people and how to stay in touch while you're traveling. The last chapter is a guide for travel agents, showing how those in the travel business can use the Net to their greatest advantage. The appendices provide a quick reference guide and can help you get online and get started.

Chapter 1, "Destination Anywhere," starts with a mini-course in how to use the Net to research trip options, choose a destination, and learn what you need to know before you go.

Chapter 2, "Planes, Trains, and Automobiles," discusses how to reserve flights, find train schedules, and rent a car, all over the Net. Here we demonstrate the advantages of booking over the Net—for example, the ability to evaluate options on your own and get discounts available only to those who book online.

Chapter 3, "Room and Board," explains how the Net helps travelers research and choose accommodations anywhere in the world. Many hotel and resort sites post photos of their facilities, letting travelers preview rooms so there are no unpleasant surprises upon arrival. Restaurant guides include dining recommendations and even full menus.

Travel may broaden the intellect, but it can certainly diminish the bank account. For most travelers, saving money is a top priority, so Chapter 4, "Finding the Best Deals," provides dozens of Net-based strategies to help you find the best deal, such as a site where travel companies auction empty seats and tour packages to the highest bidder. We'll show you how you can save hundreds of dollars by booking it yourself over the Web and pocketing most of the commission that would have been paid to a travel agent.

Chapter 5, "Taking Care of Business," demonstrates how business travelers can save time and money by booking travel over the Net. Business travelers, who often make repeat trips to the same location, can use corporate travel systems to plan several trips at the same time. And corporate travel managers can use these systems to direct their employees to preferred airlines and hotels, helping keep the lid on travel expenses.

One of the nicest features of the Net is that it caters to just about every traveler's special interest. Chapter 6, "The Ultimate Vacation," shows you how to find what you need for your type of trip, and highlights resources for family travel, cruise vacations, senior excursions, gay/lesbian travel, and services for disabled travelers.

Chapter 7, "Adventure Travel," shows you how to use the Net to plan an adventure and how to find information about places that printed guidebooks don't cover in great detail. This chapter discusses how to use free Web-based email services to stay in touch—from just about any locale—with friends and family at home as well as fellow travelers on the road.

Since most Web sites that provide travel resources are commercial affairs, the information they provide may not be entirely impartial. But there are places on the Net where travelers can go for unvarnished opinions from fellow travelers: newsgroups, online conferences, and mailing lists. Chapter 8, "Newsgroups and Mailing Lists," takes an in-depth look at travel newsgroups, where travelers post specific questions and get answers about planned trips, or recount the highs and lows of their trips. And since newsgroups are getting more crowded as they get more popular, this chapter shows how to make your query stand out and elicit responses from those in the know.

As seasoned travelers know, not everything goes according to plan when they're on the road. When a traveler needs to shift to Plan B, the Net can be a superb resource. Travelers can use the Net to find a hotel for the next day, change flight arrangements, or send email to others who are on the road and reachable only through email. Chapter 9, "Traveling with the Net," discusses the advantages (and a couple of disadvantages) of staying wired while on the road. In this chapter, we'll discuss the best ways to hook up, what to watch out for, and how to stay online even if you don't take a laptop with you.

Chapter 10, "How Travel Agents Use the Net," is specifically for travel professionals, such as travel agents. Rather than viewing the Net solely as a competitor, this chapter shows how successful travel agents have turned the Net into a tool and ally. Those who embrace the Net will discover that it is a better way to communicate with their clients and can lead to increased bookings from beyond the agent's home turf. This chapter shows how integrating the Net into an existing travel business can enhance the trip planning process for agents and their customers.

A TRAVELER'S TOOLBOX

Unlike other Internet guidebooks, *NetTravel* is not just a collection of Web site addresses. This book offers what is much harder to find online: instruction on using the Net as a travel resource and personal stories from those who have made successful journeys through the Net. But a list of sites can also be useful, so Appendix A rounds up the key sites for various types of travel. If you know what type of site you're seeking—for example, a site to find train schedules—you can go straight to Appendix A.

If you are new to the Internet, some of the terms used in this book may be unfamiliar to you. Perhaps you're not sure what an Internet site is or maybe you're not clear about newsgroups. If terms like URL, Usenet, and hyperlink are Greek to you, you might want to refer to Appendix B, Internet Basic Training. For those who don't yet have a Net connection, this appendix will show you how to get online. We also cover what you'll need to get on the Net, namely, a relatively new computer with a modem, an Internet connection with an email account, and a browser such a Netscape Navigator or Microsoft's Internet Explorer.

Finally, if you belong to AOL or another online service, see Appendix C, which rounds up the best travel areas on AOL, CompuServe, and MSN.

Now that we've mapped the territory, let's get started with Chapter 1, "Destination Anywhere," which shows how to use Internet resources to create a customized, personal guidebook.

Destination Anywhere

1

The majority of travelers aren't completely sure where they want to go when they start planning a vacation. They have a general idea, but are fuzzy on the specifics. Until the advent of the Internet, travelers had to make those decisions based on dated information contained in static travel brochures and the advice of a few friends. Today, however, a new world of possibilities is available online. Travelers can evaluate thousands of tour options and destinations, compare prices, and have email discussions with travel suppliers. Once travelers choose a destination, they can use the Net to find the right flights, hotel rooms, and rental cars. By intelligently mining this motherlode of information, travelers can plan their itineraries before they leave and make the best use of the time spent at the destination. Because sites on the Web can be updated anytime, travelers can use the Net to get up-to-the-minute weather forecasts, currency rates, cultural calendars, and much, much more. This chapter offers a review of these resources as well as techniques for how to best use them.

▶ The Internet Travel Landscape

▶ How to Use Online Travel Resources

▶ Preparing an Itinerary

▶ Points of Embarkation

▶ Online Guidebooks

▶ Getting Informed Before You Go

1

THE INTERNET TRAVEL LANDSCAPE

During the past couple of years, the number of options available to Net-connected travelers has skyrocketed. Because the Internet is not centrally controlled, there is no single authoritative directory of Internet travel resources. So, before trying to navigate the maze of travel sites, the intelligent traveler should first take a moment to get oriented to the types of travel resources on the Net.

Search directories

Yahoo
http://www.yahoo.com

A search directory to help you find what you seek on the Net.

One useful type of resource is a search directory such as Yahoo (*http://www.yahoo.com*). Although these directories are not specific to travel, they have travel sections with categories for airlines, hotels, tours, etc. Search directories are a good place to see what's out there, but it's often hard to find the most useful sites because these directories don't typically evaluate sites—they just list them.

Travel site directories

Travel directories, on the other hand, list primarily travel resources, and often evaluate or comment on them. An example of this type of site is Travel Weekly (*http://www.traveler.net/two/*) which has a dozen categories, including cruises, railroads, and theme travel, as well as the standards: air travel, hotels, and tours. Travelers could also check NetTravel (*http://nettravel.com*), the companion site to this book, which lists some of the links mentioned throughout the text as well as new sites that came online too late to be included here.

Major booking sites

This leads to the next category: major booking sites which maintain central databases with entries from hundreds of travel providers. An example of this type is Microsoft's Expedia (*http://www.expedia.com*), a huge site where travelers can choose from hundreds of airlines, thousands of hotels, and several rental car companies. These sites also help travelers choose a destination by providing detailed destination information.

Online guidebooks

NetTravel
http://nettravel.com

The companion site to this book. Check it for updates.

Finally, there are online guidebooks, which don't try to sell you flights or tour packages. If they're selling anything, it's usually their print guides or travel-related merchandise. Many of the best online guides were preceded by their print forerunners, such as the hugely popular Lonely Planet site (*http://www.lonelyplanet.com*) which puts much—but certainly not all—of its print guidebook information on the Net.

Of course, within each of the above categories, there are dozens of travel-related subcategories as well, such as official tourism office sites hosted by national, state, and local governments, as well as commercial sites, which range from Airlines of the Web (*http://www. itn.net/airlines/*) to highly focused personal accounts of an individual's journey.

Each of these sources can be valuable; each has a place in helping a traveler compile a custom guidebook. To use them well, however, travelers need to have a basic understanding of how to use each type of resource. While the Net offers a phenomenal array of tools, it can be a jungle out there. By spending some time reading this book and experimenting with online resources, any traveler can quickly become adept at using the Net to plan or book trips.

HOW TO USE ONLINE TRAVEL RESOURCES

Before a big trip, most travelers head to the travel section of their local bookstore and scan the shelves looking for books about interesting vacation destinations. If they already know where they're going, they try to find the right book for that place. Then they pick a book, pack it in their carry-on, and hope it has the listings they need. But much of the book is either too general, doesn't apply to the specific places they're going, or discusses activities they have no interest in pursuing. What if they could find a guidebook created specifically for them? Today, rather than heading straight to the bookstore, travelers can log onto the Net and produce their own personalized guidebooks.

As veteran Net travelers know, every journey through the Web of resources is unique. One site links to the next which leads to another useful resource. But those who are new to the Net may prefer a formula to get started. What follows is a series of steps to help travelers use the Net effectively.

START WITH A SEARCH DIRECTORY

There are two ways to find travel and destination Web sites: directories, which organize information in categories, and keyword searches, whereby the user types in a word or phrase and scans listings of sites that most closely match the search terms. There are millions of Web sites out there, so it can be difficult to find which sites are best for you. Try to be as specific as you can in naming a place or activity. If you want to spend your next vacation drinking good beer in the Northwest, type in *Seattle AND microbreweries.*

There are several different types of search directories. AltaVista (*http://www.altavista.digital.com*) lists millions of sites. Type in keywords and AltaVista returns the entries that most closely match your keywords. Yahoo can also do keyword searches, but has a more limited number of sites catalogued. The advantage of using a search directory such as Yahoo is that you can start with broad categories, move to increasingly specific categories, and explore the listings. You can, for example, click on the category Travel, then Tours, then Women's Tours and peruse the listings there, which include links to sites ranging from Wild Women Adventures to Going Places Together. The deeper you go in a search directory, the more specific the listings become.

TIP

Most search directories have clear instructions on how to best use them. It pays to spend a few minutes reading through these tips to make the best use of each search directory. Reading these notes will also help distinguish among the strengths and weaknesses of various search directories.

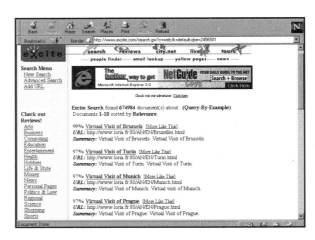

FIGURE 1-1

Excite's search directory lets users click on the "More Like This" link to see related sites (http://www.excite.com).

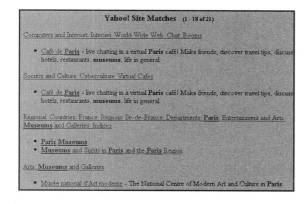

FIGURE 1-2
With Yahoo's search directory (http:/www. yahoo.com), you can search by subject or keyword.

NARROW YOUR SEARCH

When you get a list of resources, sort through them to see what looks useful and check them out. Examining what a search directory returns will give you a better idea of how to refine your search. If you use Excite (*http://www.excite.com*) as your search directory, you can click on the More Like This button next to the sites that work for you.

CULLING THE HERD

Create a bookmark folder for your trip and bookmark sites that look interesting. Later, go back and review the sites in this folder more carefully. When you find information like train schedules or restaurant and lodging information that you will need for any given leg of your tip, print it out for inclusion in your trip guidebook.

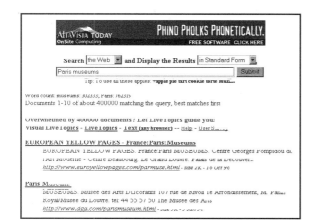

FIGURE 1-3
The AltaVista search engine (http://www. altavista.digital.com) pulls up every site it can find that matches the keywords entered. The closest matches are at the top.

TIP

A bookmark is a handy way to save the address of a Web site in your browser. In Netscape Navigator, simply click on Bookmarks and scroll down to Add Bookmark to save the site's address. When you want to go back to that site, click again on Bookmarks and you'll see the site listed as one of your bookmarks. Then just click on that bookmark to return to the site.

MINE A GOOD SITE

If you find a site that works for you, chances are that the links to other sites provided there will also be of interest and value. So mine a good site thoroughly by checking out all the links provided before you move on. Following a trail of links can be the best way to turn up useful information as well as injecting surprise and serendipity into your journey.

LOCATE THE PROPER NEWSGROUPS

DejaNews

http://www.dejanews.com

This Web site helps you find newsgroups.

Once you've narrowed your search and are at least loosely focused on a destination, it's time to begin sorting through the Usenet newsgroups. Newsgroups are giant electronic bulletin boards, where you can find fellow travelers with similar interests. Among the more than 16,000 newsgroups are many that focus on travel. Some are devoted to travel in particular countries or regions, and these are good places to post questions and get answers. To find the right newsgroup for your post, see DejaNews (*http://www.dejanews.com*), where you can enter keywords (for example, British Virgin Islands) and find out which newsgroup is the right place for your post.

BOOK IT

To create your own guidebook, print selected materials you find on the Net. If you're taking a suitcase, use a three-hole punch and put your materials into a binder where they can stay neat. If you're backpacking, at least staple your printouts together in an order that matches your itinerary and slip them into a Ziploc freezer bag. Voila, you've got your own guidebook, custom-made for your needs and interests.

What is remarkable about the Internet is that it allows the user to customize and personalize the entire process of travel planning. You can start wherever you see fit, get what you need, and compile it in a way that suits you. Now, let's see how some real-world travelers have used the Net to plan their trips.

PREPARING AN ITINERARY

To prepare her personal itinerary—complete with cost estimates—for a trip to Montreal, Kelly Jo Garner turned to the Net. Her goal was to prepare a grant proposal to study French-Canadian culture in Montreal. Kelly Jo, a student at the University of North Carolina, had to compile a detailed itinerary, including transportation costs, daily food budgets, even museum entrance fees. Kelly Jo was amazed at how many resources she found.

Kelly Jo Garner
kelly@sunsite.unc.edu
University of North Carolina

Through various Web sites (such as the official Montreal tourism information site at *http://sun2.cum.qc.ca/octgm/english/Welcome.html*) and postings to various newsgroups, "I got all the prices I needed on lodging, travel, and food," Kelly Jo says. "I could ask through a newsgroup (such as *rec.travel.usa-canada*), 'What's the price of an average meal in Montreal?'" Those who frequented that group were quick to email her the advice she needed.

Thanks to her Net research, Kelly Jo and another student won grants to spend 17 days in the world's second-largest French-speaking city. Before leaving for Montreal, Kelly Jo got back online and printed

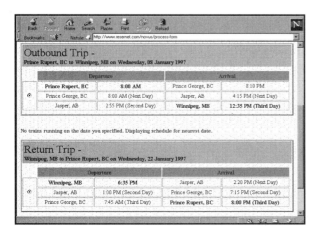

FIGURE 1-4
The VIA Rail site (http://www.viarail.ca) lets users examine railroad timetables for Canada and reserve train tickets.

Olsen and Associates
*http://www.olsen.ch/
cgi-bin/exmenu*

Check out the currency con-
verter run by this Swiss firm
to see how much your
money will be worth when
you go abroad.

train timetables from VIA, Canada's Passenger Rail Network
(*http://www.viarail.ca/e1.html*), lists of festivals from the Montreal site,
and currency rates. From travel newsgroups, Kelly Jo collected
replies to her posts to round up the last of the data she needed for the
trip. "I put all this into a three-ring binder," she says. "The information was accurate and current—most of it was posted in the week
before I left."

Kelly Jo's research illustrates one of the key advantages of using the
Net: the information is often much more current than what's found
in printed guidebooks. Traditional guidebooks can be out of date before they are printed. For up-to-date information, whether you want
to know what's playing at the Ashland Shakespeare Festival or
whether that B&B in Asheville is still open, the Net is the best place
to check. Also, a small hotel in Milan isn't likely to keep its Web page
up if it's out of business. But it will continue to appear in the guidebooks for a long time.

Kelly Jo more or less followed the strategy laid out at the beginning
of this chapter. She began by searching in a directory for the keyword
Montreal. After refining and narrowing her search to visitor information for Montreal, Kelly Jo examined the most promising sites for her
trip. Next, she checked newsgroups, such as *alt.travel.roadtrip*, and
after reading some posts in the group to see if it was the right place
for her queries, she posted some questions of her own.

AN INTERNET HONEYMOON

Many travelers are terrified by the notion of arranging their own vacations. Travel agents remain a security blanket for most travelers.
But you don't need to be an expert to plan your trip on the Net. As
travel sites become more user-friendly and intuitive, all it takes is a
little practice. For those who are unsure or uneasy about making actual reservations online, they can still use online resources to plan
their vacations. Once they have those plans sketched out they can
pick up the phone and call their trusty agent, who will be more than
happy to make the bookings.

Those who have already taken the plunge have found it easy, fun,
and unexpectedly rewarding—both financially and emotionally.
Leslie Camino-Markowitz, a public relations specialist from Santa
Rosa, California, planned her honeymoon on the Web and ended up
with more than she could have imagined.

I'm a real rookie. I just got in there and started exploring, started searching for travel in Spain. I got a list of travel agents through Webcrawler and one had a description for the island of Ibiza. I sent email to the agency that had the Web page on Ibiza.

Note: Webcrawler (*http://webcrawler.com*) is a search directory on the Web.

Webcrawler
http://webcrawler.com
A selective list of travel sites by subject.

I received a response the next day. They asked for more information and said "Tell us what your tastes are." We told them we wanted something that's adventurous, romantic, and a good deal. They responded the next day with some ideas and found a great place for us in Ibiza. They know the area and can find what you want. They made it very simple. We were blown away because it was the first time we've done anything through the Net. I'm not a techie person.

But the Net's role in Leslie and Michael's honeymoon doesn't end there. Call this part of the trip "The Net to the Rescue."

We were in the middle of getting married and forgot the paperwork about what hotel we were staying at. We couldn't find the agency in any phonebooks. Just then I remembered there was an Internet café in Barcelona. [See the Web page of El Cafe de Internet in Barcelona at http://www.cafeinternet.es/]. So we rented a computer and sent email saying we forgot our paperwork and needed to know our hotel for the island of Ibiza. We asked them to fax the information to our hotel, but we never received a fax.

FIGURE 1-5
Leslie and Michael Camino-Markowitz found unexpected benefits in planning their honeymoon on the Net.

Festive Travel

http://www.festivetravel. com/ibiza.htm

Check out this agency's Web site, specializing in trips to Ibiza, "the White Island."

When we got to Ibiza there were two gentlemen with a big sign saying "Camino-Markowitz." It was the two travel agents who made the arrangements from Ibiza, two Americans who are working from Ibiza. They met us and took us to the hotel and got us a room with a beautiful view because they wanted to make sure our honeymoon was perfect. Lots of people at the hotel had made their plans through the Net.

Leslie and Michael may have eventually found the hotel without a Net connection, but their story highlights the Net's usefulness both before and during a trip. Would they have ever learned of remote Ibiza without surfing the Net? Maybe. But then again, maybe not. And, remote as it was, their email plea for help reached the travel agents in Ibiza and solved their problem.

POINTS OF EMBARKATION

Journeys, on the Net as in the real world, begin at embarkation points. On the Net, the best points of embarkation are typically on-line travel directories. Most of the large Net directories maintain a separate travel index. Travelers can find a well-organized and manageable set of links categorized by region and subject at WebCrawler's travel area (*http://webcrawler.com/select/trav.new.html*). A nice feature about Webcrawler is that it also provides links to travel newsgroups; for example the category Europe includes links to *rec.travel.europe, soc.culture.german,* and *uk.rec.youth-hostel.*

Sites such as Webcrawler Travel and Travel Weekly select the cream of travel information skimmed off the top by travel experts. They have waded through thousands of travel sites and selected what they consider to be the best in each category. So these resources can be ideal starting points for those who don't want to sort through the millions of sites on the Web's wild range. (Note: Excite purchased WebCrawler in late 1996, but a spokesman for WebCrawler said the company would keep the WebCrawler URLs for the foreseeable future.)

These organized directories help you zero in on the kind of travel you are interested in, while whetting your appetite for the journey you're planning. In these venues, you will be exposed to ideas and destinations that may not have occurred to you and for which you would not have otherwise searched.

As mentioned earlier, another good starting point is Travel Weekly Online (*http://www.traveler.net/two/*), a clean, well-organized list of travel resources arranged by subject. You can also use Travel Weekly to find a travel agent on the Web (*http://www.traveler.net/two/twpages/twagents.html*). And any travel agent you find on the Web should have email, which will make follow-up communications much easier.

The Travel Channel (*http://www.travelchannel.com*) is a comprehensive source for city profiles and much more. A click on Vacations, Holidays & Getaways leads to the Universal Travel Resource Locator, which lists more than 25,000 travel-related Web pages. Using the Resource Locator to search for the terms Hawaii and sailing returned a list of 53 links, ranging from companies that offer tours to sites that provide information.

The Travel Channel
http://www.travelchannel.com

City profiles and links to hundreds of travel sites organized by subject.

You can browse the lists or search for your interests or for a destination. You'll also find the Vacation Store, listing bargains to more than 50 destinations. The Spotlight section considers a new destination each week and has archives of past features in City Profiles. Click on Travel Facts & Opinion for a collection of travel newsletters, such as Travelin' Woman or The Discerning Traveler.

Another good starting point for city guides, travel news, and destination information is CNN Travel (*http://www.cnn.com/TRAVEL/*). The site includes links to many other useful sources on the Web. For example, Getting Ready includes a link to How Far Is It? (*http://www.indo.com/distance*), where you can input two destinations, find the distance between them, and see maps of these areas.

For a general index of cultural events at your destination, don't miss CultureFinder (*http://www.culturefinder.com*). Just input the name of

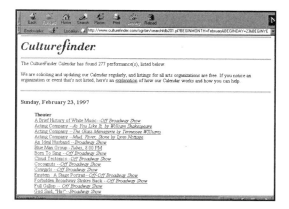

FIGURE 1-6

Use CultureFinder (http://www.culturefinder.com) to see a list of performances for any city you plan to visit.

your destination and the dates you'll be there, and it will deliver a list of events, including art exhibits, operas, plays, classical music performances, and much more. You can select the types of events you want to attend or see the whole range of listings for the time you'll be there.

THE VIRTUAL TOURIST

WebCrawler (*http://webcrawler.com*) and Lycos (*http://www.lycos.com*) were the starting points for Tony, a biochemistry professor at the University of Oxford. Tony sought unofficial sites, where he could find honest information, untainted by a seller's point of view. His search yielded a number of unofficial Web sites.

For a trip to Las Vegas, Tony used the Net to wade through the hype and find free entertainment, good restaurants, and an inexpensive but comfortable hotel room.

> *Particularly useful for this visit were the "honest" reports (for example, Las Vegas Index at* http://lvindex.com/) *about local amenities, restaurants, cabaret venues, and free entertainment, rather than the official establishment and commercial descriptions. This site really did help us plan an efficient and most enjoyable couple of days, made even more rewarding by seeing that comparisons with printed guidebooks showed them to be out of date rather quickly in this fast-moving metropolis.*

FIGURE 1-7
Las Vegas Index (http://lvindex.com) offers lists of family attractions, hotels, restaurants, and shows.

Before leaving on trips to Amsterdam and Toronto, Tony found maps of these cities on the Web. He also used the Net to plan several other trips, including vacations to France and California. "We have received no poor information yet, because most entries can be rather frank and honest, " Tony says.

> We planned visits to several of the fortified hill towns (called bastides), using some of the many French tourism and report pages (e.g., *Southwest of France* at http://www.geocities.com/Paris/5334/swfrance.html). We even studied details about the local wine (*All About Wine* at http://www.aawine.com/index.html), which proved very reliable.
>
> Last year we spent a three-week family vacation in California, and real-time pictures of the beaches in San Diego (http://live.net/sandiego/) helped whet our appetite for some California sun during a cool British summer.
>
> On the journey north, we booked quiet and comfortable inns in Ventura, Monterey, and Half Moon Bay from the well-organized tourism Web pages for the whole area at *Resort Detectives* (http://www.monterey-rooms.com/). For the return journey south, we studied the Yosemite Park information (http://www.nps.gov/yose/). Getting rooms there would have been impossible if we hadn't read on the Web of the difficulty of getting rooms in the busy season.

Tony's ramblings through the Net gave him much of the information he could have found in various printed guidebooks, but with the added dimension of immediacy. He found out what shows would be running in Las Vegas during the time he planned to visit and could read other travelers' critiques of a hotel that had just opened there. For his trip to California, live images of San Diego sunshine posted on a Web site heightened his anticipation for a visit to the Golden State. He could also select inns along the Northern California coast by viewing images of the prospective accommodations from the comfort of his home computer. And thanks to timely warnings about the difficulty of securing rooms at Yosemite, Tony acted early and reserved the lodgings he needed.

PLANNING A TRIP ON SHORT NOTICE

The Net can be especially useful when you don't have much time to plan your trip, for example, if you don't have several weeks to send away for tourist brochures and sift through guidebooks. John Haney of San Diego found out his wife would be sent to Bergen, Norway, on business, and was given only a week's notice. So John turned to

City.net (*http://city.net*) and found a wealth of information on western Norway.

No doubt right now she's on a fjord cruise using the information I pulled off City.net's page on Bergen tours. Tomorrow, she's planning to take the "Norway in a Nutshell" trip that we also got from City.net.

With busy schedules, there's no way we could have done in-depth research on this trip with such short notice, and it saved us the cost of a $20 Fodor's book that has more detail than what we wanted. Earlier this year, we took a pleasure trip to Quebec. We arranged our itinerary and hotels using the information we got from the Quebec government's tourist pages. We had a great time. The Web has become an invaluable tool for this traveling couple's journeys.

John shows travelers can use the Net to get just the information they need. In his case, he didn't need an entire guidebook because his wife just had a couple of days to tour after her business trip. So he selected the information that would prove to be useful and helped his wife plan her itinerary using a quick tour suggested by a City.net site.

FINDING TOURISM OFFICES ON THE WEB

Tourism Offices Worldwide Directory
http://www.mbnet.mb.ca/lucas/travel/

Finding virtual tourism offices on the Web is easy. Several sites, including the Tourism Office Worldwide Directory (*http://www.mbnet.mb.ca/lucas/travel/*), list addresses and phones for tourism offices around the globe, and if that office is online, the directory provides a link. For a trip to Canada, for example, travelers can find a

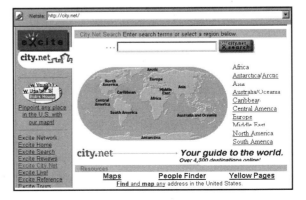

FIGURE 1-8
City.net (http://city.net) offers detailed travel information for more than 4,000 destinations.

link to the Canadian Tourism Commission (*http://info.ic.gc.ca/Tourism/*), as well as addresses and phones (including some toll-free numbers) for more than three dozen tourist agencies in Canada.

If you want tourism offices for a specific U.S. state, you can enter, for example, USA/Florida, to find the St. Petersburg visitors bureau (*http://www.stpete-clearwater.com/*). You can also find an extensive list of U.S. state and regional travel bureaus at TravelSearch (*http://travelsearch.com/tourism.htm*).

For international travel, you may have to consider visa requirements. For these, turn to The Electronic Embassy (*http://www.embassy.org*), which lists most of the embassies in Washington, D.C. Considering a trip to the Czech Republic, you find the country's embassy has a Web page with links to official Czech sites, including the Consular and Visa Authority. Another source for embassy information is The Embassy Page (*http://www.embpage.org/*). If you're wondering what you can bring into the U.S. after traveling abroad, see the U.S. Customs Service page (*http://www.customs.ustreas.gov/*).

OFFICIAL ADVISORIES

In the old days, travelers often phoned the U.S. State Department to get the latest travel advisories before traveling abroad. Today it's easy to find this information on the Net. On the official side is the U.S. State Department Travel Warnings (*http://travel.state.gov/travel_warnings.html*), with background on crime, medical treatment standards, and embassy locations. Though the advisories often suggest extreme caution, they provide context on the current political climate of the country. Minnesota's St. Olaf College handles the Travel Advisories mailing list. To subscribe to this list, send a brief message including the word "subscribe" to *travel-advisories-request@stolaf.edu*.

For broad geographic and demographic information, try the CIA World Factbook (*http://www.odci.gov/cia/publications/95fact/index.html*), which has basic geography, current environmental issues, population figures, and ethnic makeup.

FINDING TRAVEL AGENTS ON THE NET

Many people like to use the Net to research destinations, but when it comes time to book their travel, they want a professional to handle the details. The Net is an ideal place to find the right travel agent. Sure, you could just go downtown and walk into the first agency you see, but that is not the best way to pick a travel agent. You probably wouldn't pick a doctor that way.

Through the Net, you can find an agent who meets your needs. Some travelers are looking for an agent with expertise in a specific area, for example, a country, such as China, or a type of travel, such as cruising. For others, the key criterion is location—they just want to find an agent close by. Travelers who are online have added incentive to find an agent through the Net—these agents will probably be online themselves and can communicate with email, a tremendous convenience.

Travel Weekly

http://www.traveler.net/ two/twpages/twagents.html

Travel Weekly's list of travel agents.

To find an agent online, see Travel Weekly's list at (*http://www. traveler.net/two/twpages/twagents.html*) or ITN's list at (*http://www.itn. net/cgi/get?itn/members*). Another good source for finding agents is Worldwide Agency Locator (*http://agencylink.sys1.com/*), where you can search by city, country, or agency name.

ONLINE GUIDEBOOKS

Travel guidebooks have long been a primary source of information for serious travelers. Today some of the best travel sites on the Net are maintained by guidebook publishers, which is somewhat surprising considering these sites give away much of the information that these companies are trying to sell in their guidebooks. To add thorough and comprehensive information to your custom guidebook, visit these sites and select the information you need for your personal guidebook. Following are some of the best:

Lonely Planet (*http://www.lonelyplanet.com*)

For almost a generation, budget travelers have chosen Lonely Planet for journeys to remote or exotic locations such as Nepal. Today, Lonely Planet's site is an online guidepost for travelers who seek destinations off the beaten path, though often a mention in LP makes those paths much more beaten. Lonely Planet has expanded to cover mainstream destinations as well. The LP site features a clickable map—just hit the country you plan to visit to see a detailed map. Next, click on any city or hit the "INFO" icon to learn about the country's culture, environment, history, and attractions.

Selecting Vietnam, for example, you can see that budget rooms cost about $10, that it's hard to find a room during the Tet festival in late January, and that Wandering Souls Day, when food and gifts are

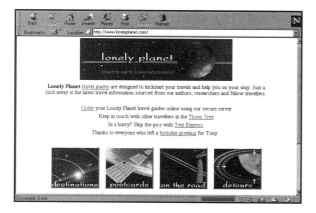

FIGURE 1-9
Lonely Planet (http://www.lonelyplanet.com) offers "down to earth travel information" and lots of it.

offered to the dead, is the second-largest festival of the year. Several beautiful photos are woven through each country's site, such as an image of monks gathered in prayer at Caodai Temple. If you want up-to-the-minute tips from LP's writers, the Web site includes Dispatches, a link in the On the Road section.

You can also read postcards that travelers send back to LP from all over the world. "These postcards are categorized by countries, and the good thing about them is that they provide up-to-date and authentic information," says Ilan Stein of Israel, who used LP guides to help plan his trip to Cyprus.

The Rough Guides (*http://www.hotwired.com/rough/*)

The online marriage of the Rough Guides series to *HotWired* has created a remarkably useful resource for travelers. Rough Guides has posted its complete guides to the U.S., Canada, and Mexico on the Web. Features such as Top 10 College Towns enliven the site, but its foundation is the comprehensive travel information it offers. If you're traveling to France or Italy and want help ordering dinner, you can print out Rough Guides' "menu decoders" from the site's Phrasebooks. Rough Guides constantly adds updates from a network of wired travelers. RG is known for its generous cultural listings, so if you're interested in the club scene and local arts, this is a must-visit site.

Will putting all this good content online will reduce book sales? Rough Guides' Richard Trillo says, "Why would anyone want sheaves of computer printouts stapled together when they can get the beautiful book? Long Live the Book!" Richard may be half right. Net travelers have lots of reasons to bring printouts with them, but these resources typically complement a good guidebook—printouts don't necessarily replace a well-written and thoroughly researched travel guide. It turns out that printed books are more than just a traveler's security blanket. With their alphabetized indexes, language glossaries, and maps, they are useful on-the-road references that travelers continue to rely on.

Fodor's (*http://www.fodors.com*)

With Fodor's "Personal Trip Planner," you can create a personal guide to dozens of cities, complete with listings customized to reflect your interests and needs. Just pick the city you'll be visiting—for example, Santa Fe, New Mexico. To test out the Trip Planner, I clicked on Santa Fe and then on Where to Stay, Eating Out, Essential Information, and Fodor's Top Picks. Within these categories, I was able to narrow my search to hotels under $100 a night, restaurants featuring southwestern or Mexican cuisine, and within Essential Information I checked Festivals and When to Go. A click on Create My Miniguide built my own custom guide to Santa Fe, complete with seasonal temperatures and a warning to reserve in advance for the peak summer season. Fodor's site also has hotel and restaurant guides, and in-depth features ranging from travel book reviews to Great American Outdoors. In the Departure Lounge, users share picks and pans.

Moon Publications (*http://www.moon.com*)

Moon has long been known for its innovative travel guides that often take the road less traveled. Moon's site includes Road Trip USA, the result of readers collaborating online with an author to create a definitive guide to some of the blue highways that crisscross the U.S. Other highlights include an interactive guide to Hawaii with a clickable map of the Big Island, and Travel Matters, a newsletter, with features from Moon's top writers and updates on the regions covered by Moon's guides.

Let's Go (*http://www.letsgo.com*)

Let's Go bills itself as the publisher of "the world's best-selling budget travel guides, written entirely by students and completely updated every year. With pen and notebook in hand and a few changes of underwear stuffed in our backpacks, we spend our summers roaming the globe in search of travel bargains." So why is one of its main areas an application for the American Express card? Well, not everything on the Web makes sense. Unlike the Rough Guides and Lonely Planet, this site does not put much of its guidebook information online. However, a monthly feature and nice list of links make this site worth visiting.

Travelers Corner (AOL keyword: Travelers Corner)

Hosted by the editors of Weissmann Travel Reports, which provide destination information to travel agents around the world, Travelers Corner is a superb resource. Frequently updated by a network of correspondents in more than 200 countries around the globe, Travelers Corner includes city profiles for the U.S. and abroad. Wondering what to do during a free evening in Detroit? Just click on City Profiles, type in *Detroit,* and up comes a list ranging from comedy clubs to folk music. You'll also find illuminating features such as Top Ten Romantic Encounters and Top Ten Tips for Smooth Traveling.

(For more information on AOL resources, see Appendix C, "Online Services.")

HARD COPY FOR THE ROAD

Despite all this online information, printed travel guides continue to have a place on the road. And of course, you can buy printed guides online. To order travel books online, point your browser to Amazon.com (*http://www.amazon.com*) which claims access to more than a million books.

Another option is to go directly to bookstores specializing in travel. Among the best places to find travel books is Book Passage (*http://www.bookpassage.com*), which features a wide selection and has a knowledgeable staff ready to answer travelers' questions. If you want to know more about a book or what's available, you can send email to Book Passage through a link on the bookstore's Web site. "The people who answer the emails are extremely familiar with the books," says store owner Elaine Petrocelli.

Other online bookstores specializing in travel include The Adventurous Traveler (*http://www.AdventurousTraveler.com/*) and The Travel Bug (*http://www.swifty.com/tbug/*). The Adventurous Traveler includes book excerpts, browsing by location or activity, and keyword searches. For a trip to the Pacific Northwest, I clicked on Browse by Location and found listings for more than 100 books about hiking, biking, camping, and more, as well as useful maps and CD-ROMs

FIGURE 1-10

Book Passage (http://www. bookpassage.com) is an independent bookstore with a rich selection of travel books you can order online.

about the region. Travel Bug specializes in guidebooks and travel accessories, from money belts to plug adapters. Each month features a new letter from a traveler describing his or her journey. For more travel bookstore listings, see the following Yahoo category: *http://www.yahoo.com/Business_and_Economy/Companies/Travel/ Publications/Books/).*

DON'T CALL IT THE BIG EASY

Even those who write guidebooks turn to the Net for current information these days. Travel guidebook writer Bruce Brumberg planned to visit New Orleans with his wife for her birthday. Seeking suggestions about what to do during their visit, he posted to the *rec.travel.usa-canada* newsgroup and quickly received about a dozen responses. The best suggestion: "Take a carriage ride in the French Quarter with Big Ray."

Next, Bruce examined America Online's travel area and found Frommer's city guides and Fodor's Worldview, where he could search for information about New Orleans.

"AOL nicely breaks the information in these guidebooks into alphabetical subsections so you can easily click through them," he says. In Fodor's section on New Orleans, Bruce clicked on Local Cuisine and found a listing for Nola's with a brief review of its "eclectic menu of reinvented New Orleans food." From Frommer's New Orleans, Bruce easily found and printed out directions for walking tours of the Garden District and French Quarter.

TIP

You can find Frommer's City Guides on AOL by using the keyword Frommers. Also see Frommer's site on the Web at *http://www.frommers.com.*

To find listings for events during his visit, Bruce turned to local newspaper sites. "You can get the local news before you go and check events calendars and restaurant reviews," Bruce advises. A single central site, The American Journalism Review's Newslink (*http://www. newslink.org*), lists more than 1,500 regional news sites throughout the world. Newslink also lists campus newspapers and alternative publications, such as metro weeklies, which typically have strong sections on entertainment and dining.

Newslink
http://www.newslink.org
Links to more than 1,500
newspaper sites.

Newslink points to N.O.net's Destination New Orleans (*http://www. neworleans.net/*), which greets visitors with the local time, and has sections on festivals, weather, gambling, and Mardi Gras. For "candid views of Bourbon Street," click on the BourboCam to see frequent snapshots of one of the world's most famous party zones. It's the next best thing to being there.

"If you know what you're doing online and where you're going, online travel research can be much more effective than perusing a bookstore or tearing through the free travel brochures you get from tourism bureaus," says Bruce. The rest of this chapter is devoted to help you, as Bruce says, know what you're doing and where you're going.

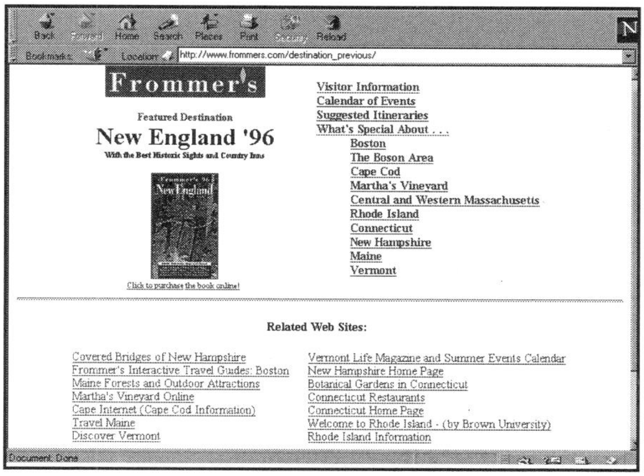

FIGURE 1-11

Frommer's site (http://www.frommers.com) covers a new featured destination each month, complete with links to sites that offer more information on the featured region.

Travel Zines Find a Home on the Web

Here is a sampling of some of the best (and some of the most irreverent) travel zines.

- The Connected Traveler
  http://www.travelmedia.com/connected
  Russell Johnson offers personal views of exotic locales such as Cambodia and Myanmar (formerly Burma), and down-home romps along U.S. backroads, including a visit to Boonville in California's Anderson Valley, where Russell discovered the century-old dialect of Boontling. And don't miss the account of his Sri Lanka trip, including a conversation with legendary sci-fi writer Arthur C. Clarke. Russell's fine photography enhances his stories. From the Sri Lanka piece: "I could see what he (Clarke) meant about his adopted country. The people are fine featured, well educated, and it doesn't take five of them to complete a simple task. You see poverty, but it doesn't grate at your conscience in scenes of maimed beggars. And once out of the capital city of Colombo, the world dissolves into a lush green dream. Banana and pineapple, teak forests, queues of brightly colored umbrellas bobbing through rice fields."

- Mungo Park
  http://mungopark.msn.com/mungo.htm
  After leading expeditions to the Galapagos and Antarctica that broadcast their findings back to the Terraquest site (*http://www.terraquest.com*), Richard Bangs moved to Microsoft and created Mungo Park. The site is named after a Scottish explorer who disappeared in Africa in the early nineteenth century, an odd choice of names considering how hard it is for most Web sites to avoid falling off the map. Richard led Mungo Park's inaugural expedition, the first whitewater rafting descent of Ethiopia's Tekeze River, with daily updates, including images and sounds. Mungo Park's plan for future expeditions is to send top authors (from the New York Times bestseller list) on adventure tours and have them share their impressions with MP readers.

AN ONLINE CONCIERGE

Travel magazines have long provided a way to plan future vacations as well as a way to dream about exotic locations. Now those pleasures extend to the online world. Some of the best travel magazines exist only online; others are based on the content of their print counterparts, but have added features such as the ability to search a database of archived articles.

Among the best is Condé Nast Traveler (*http://travel.epicurious.com/travel/g_cnt/home.html*). This magazine understands that it makes

- No S—tting in the Toilet
  http://www.magna.com.au/~nglobe/nsitt/contents.html
  For an irreverent look at the inevitable hardships of traveling on a shoestring, see the indelicately entitled site No S—tting in the Toilet, by Australian Peter Moore. The title comes from a sign Moore saw while traveling in China's Yunnan province—and he has a photo to prove it. In Moore's words, NSITT is "a celebration of everything that is perverse about travel . . . about everything going wrong and loving every minute of it." Moore doesn't hesitate to get right down to what we really want to know when we contemplate taking a trip: from sex and romance, to what to pack and the best destinations. To make it all simple, he includes a top ten list for most topics, such as the top ten bum steers offered in guidebooks.

- Monk
  http://www.neo.com/Monk/
  Authors Mike and Jim describe Monk as, "the never-ending story of two grown men who quit their jobs, sold everything they owned and hit the road with their two cats, Nurse and Nurse's Aide. For eight years they argued across America, publishing the world's only mobile magazine, traveling first in a '72 Ford Econoline van and then in a 26-foot Fleetwood Bounder motorhome, reporting on the incredible people, places and phone booths they encountered along the way, until they drove each other crazy living in such cramped quarters." If you're planning a road trip across the U.S., Monk can point you to nooks and crannies most motorists pass unnoticed.

- Split
  http://www.lainet.com/nomad/
  Split is "more a description of a traveler's feelings than a description of a specific place or city. You can feel the atmosphere of a coun-try…not the clichés you see recycled everywhere," writes one reader about this offbeat travel zine. Split also takes on political issues that affect travelers, such as the smoking ban in Paris' public places.

more sense to organize trips by theme, rather than by destination. The features on the site include stories such as "200 Sun-Soaked Hideaways" and "Find Your Perfect Golf Resort."

To get help choosing your next trip, try CNT's "Concierge," which recommends destinations based on your stated preferences, includ-ing activities, cost, climate, and what month you want to travel. I told CNT's automated Concierge that I wanted to go to southeast Asia in June and that I preferred a temperature range of 70-85 degrees. The Concierge suggested Bali, followed by list of other destinations and hotels. While I doubt many people would place their vacation in the hands of a robot, it's fun and not a bad way to begin scouting places you might want to visit. And if your vacation turns out be a bummer, Condé Nast provides an "ombudsman" service which seeks redress for travelers who feel they've been taken for a ride by a travel company.

GETTING INFORMED BEFORE YOU GO

FOREIGN LANGUAGES FOR TRAVELERS

After booking a flight and securing a hotel room, you may face more exotic needs, but few that the wired Net traveler can't fill. Are changed plans sending you to a country you hadn't planned on visiting? Need to quickly learn the basics of a foreign language? Turn to Travlang's Foreign Languages for Travelers (*http://www.travlang.com/ languages/*). Click on the language you need to learn, and select from Basic Words, Directions, or Times and Dates, among other categories. To hear how a phrase sounds, just click on the phrase to activate an audio file. You can print these translations and study them on the plane so you have some tools to communicate when you arrive. To help travelers figure out what's on the menu, Travlang has included dining terms. At press time, Travlang's site listed 33 languages, including Hungarian, Turkish, and Mandarin.

Foreign Languages for Travelers

http://www.travlang.com/ languages

Learn some terms before you go.

STAYING HEALTHY ON THE ROAD

An essential but often overlooked aspect of good trip planning is taking care of your health. This means getting the necessary inoculations before you go and getting up to speed on health conditions and disease outbreaks at your destination.

As part of her planning for a trip to eastern Asia, Mady Mac Donald, an editor from Toronto, wanted to get the latest health information for the region. Though she visited a local medical clinic before her trip, she also checked the Net, including the mailing list *travel-advisories @stolaf.edu*. She was glad she did. Mady learned an outbreak of Hepatitis E had struck northern India.

"That information was not available at the local travel clinic, and now, because of the Net, I am receiving a Hep E shot before I leave," she says.

The mother of all health sites is CDC Travel Information (*http://www. cdc.gov/travel/travel.html*), an extraordinarily comprehensive site from the Centers for Disease Control, smartly organized by region. The CDC site also lists recent outbreaks of disease, such as the summer 1996 outbreak of yellow fever in Nigeria. And if you're concerned about a specific disease, there's a list of links ranging from cholera to tuberculosis. A visit to this site does not replace going to a local clinic or physician, but it's a good place to learn about recent outbreaks and what to watch for.

Another useful source is Travel Health Online (*http://www.tripprep. com/index.html*). Say you're planning a trip to Chile and want to know which diseases pose a threat and what immunizations you need. Go to the THO site and click on Chile. You'll see you may need vaccines for Hepatitis A, rabies, and typhoid. In addition to health information, THO has country descriptions, entry requirements, and embassy and consulate locations. Of course, before you decide what shots to get, consult a physician. These sites are merely advisory and certainly do not replace the wise counsel of a qualified physician.

If you travel frequently, especially to remote areas, chances are that sooner or later you'll become ill. If you do, find a place to log on to Lonely Planet's Pills, Ills and Bellyaches (*http://www.lonelyplanet. com.au/health/health.htm*), where you'll find remedies for those nasty

FIGURE 1-12

The Centers for Disease Control (http://www.cdc.gov/travel/travel.html) lists disease outbreaks around the world and issues health recommendations by region.

road bugs. With information supplied by Australia's Traveller's Medical & Vaccination Centres, the site goes as far as specifying drug dosages for some ailments, but of course LP recommends seeking the advice of a qualified physician whenever possible. For minor ailments, such as cuts, bites, or less severe altitude sickness, this is a good site to visit. If you'll be miles from Net access, print out a few key pages and make them part of your personal guidebook. LP's health section also includes information on women's health, predeparture planning, and keeping healthy.

An excellent health guide for traveling in the developing world is Moon's Staying Healthy in Asia, Africa, and Latin America (*http://www.moon.com/staying_healthy*). This includes the full text of Moon's printed version by the same name and is organized chronologically in sections, including Before you Go, Arrival and Preventing Illness, and After you Return Home. If you want to know about a specific disease or region, use the full-text search.

FEAR OF FLYING

While most travelers worry about health conditions at their destination, what about the health consequences of certain types of travel, for example, flying? It appears clear that recirculated cabin air can lead to a number of health problems. One person who appreciates the value of staying healthy during air travel is Diana Fairechild, a former international flight attendant who flew more than 10 million miles before retiring due to illnesses she says were caused by the cabin environment. (Diana, who now lives in Maui, suffers from multiple chemical sensitivities, the breakdown of the body's ability to detoxify everyday chemicals.) To share what she's learned about avoiding illness at 39,000 feet, Diana wrote the book *Jet Smart* and created a Web page called Healthy Flying (*http://www.flyana.com/*) to help travelers reduce the risk of getting sick en route.

Healthy Flying
http://www.flyana.com/
Tips on how to beat jet lag and stay healthy in the air.

"As soon as the Net became available in Maui, I got online and searched my field of expertise, but there wasn't anything," she says. So she created Healthy Flying, with topics ranging from avoiding jet lag to overcoming fear of flying. She also discusses reasons why the cabin environment is becoming a more toxic place, for example, pesticide residues inside the plane and more recycled air rather than fresh air in the cabin. (Airlines routinely spray their cabins with pesticides, and in some countries, such as Costa Rica, New Zealand, and about 20 others, you must sit in your seat while they spray, she says.) The site offers advice to travelers, such as requesting that the pilot circulate more fresh air. Diana responds to readers—for example, the mother who asks why she should put on her own oxygen mask before taking care of her children, or the cagey traveler who wants to know what to do if he's caught sneaking into first class. Note: You can purchase *Jet Smart* through the Healthy Flying site (*http://www.flyana.com/book.html*), or send email to *diana@maui.net*.

GETTING ORIENTED

Shortly before my brother's backpacking trip to New Zealand, a friend asked him, "So you get to Auckland, and then what?" Good question. The first thing he needed to find was a good map. A good place for map viewing is the Perry Castañeda Library Map Collection (*http://www.lib.utexas.edu/Libs/PCL/Map_collection/Map_collection.html*), where you can find city and country maps from around the world and featured maps of political hot spots. In addition to standard maps, you'll find historical maps and maps of U.S. national parks and monuments.

MapQuest (*http://www.mapquest.com*) is an extraordinary site, allowing users to zoom in and highlight points of interest. Becoming a member (membership is free) lets you use the Interactive Atlas, a Java-based application. If you want to find a specific business, say, the Mark Hopkins Hotel in San Francisco, just click on the "Find" button, type in the name of the place and the city, and within seconds you'll have a street map of the area with a red star denoting the hotel's precise location. The address is posted above the map. Oh, and while you're there, why not stop at the famed Top of the Mark for a drink?

So, where are you going to go for dinner? If you know you want to try some fresh fish (and some of San Francisco's delectable sourdough bread), click on Dining and then on Seafood. Then just hit Update Selections, and your map comes back noting the locations of seafood restaurants with a silverware icon. Click on one of these icons to get the name, address, and phone number for the restaurant at that location. MapQuest can also help you find health clubs, Net cafés, banks, and bus stations throughout the U.S.

While you may want to print online maps, you'll probably want to buy some to carry along with you. Magellan Geographix (*http://magellangeo.com/*) offers both the chance to browse through maps and purchase those you need.

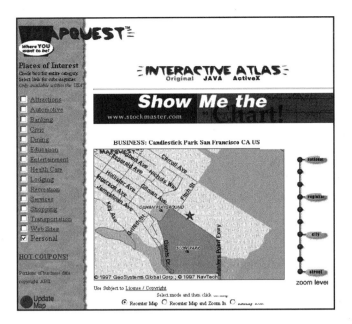

FIGURE 1-13
*MapQuest (http://www.mapquest.com)
helps you find what you need.*

Finally, if you're wondering what time it is in your destination, see Local Times Around the World (*http://www.hilink.com.au/times/*), which manages to take into account daylight savings shifts and the international dateline.

THE MONEY CHANGERS

We've all done it. After a long flight, we groggily enter a foreign airport filled with signs we don't understand. And because we haven't had the chance to change money before leaving, we're at the mercy of larcenous freelance money changers at the airport. To avoid falling prey to exorbitant exchange premiums, check World Exchange Rates (*http://www.rubicon.com/passport/currency/currency.htm*). You can see what you'll get for a dollar and what you'll pay to get German marks, Danish crowns, or Russian rubles, among dozens of other currencies.

The best way to change money, says David Koblas, who founded the first widely used currency site on the Net, is by buying the local currency with a credit card; the next best way is to use an ATM; and if neither of those options is available, try a major local bank. If at all possible, avoid changing money at rail stations and airports.

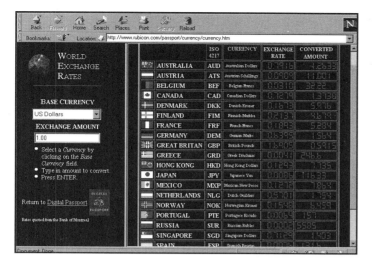

FIGURE 1-14
*World Exchange Rates
(http://www.rubicon.com/
passport/currency/currency.html)
tells you what your money is
worth in another country.*

DESTINATION INFORMATION AT ONLINE BOOKING SITES

Among the best places to find quality destination information are on-line booking sites, such as Microsoft's Expedia (*http://expedia.com*) and Travelocity (*http://www.travelocity.com*). You'll learn more about these sites' booking features in the next chapter. Although the primary focus of these sites is booking travel, they are also user-friendly and well-organized resources for destination information. The best sites are packed with destination information and have discussion areas where you can compare notes with fellow travelers or chat with experts. These sites can lead you to broad nuts-and-bolts information about a region or to very specialized tours.

Expedia
http://expedia.com
A huge booking site with lots of destination information.

FINDING A WINERY IN HAWAII

You can cut through the reams of destination information at a site like Travelocity by doing a keyword search within the site. Say you're planning a trip to Hawaii and would like to see wineries there. Enter *wineries AND Hawaii* in the search field. This yields several entries, including obscure locations like Volcano Winery, where you can "sip wine extracted from the nectar of passionfruit, guava, starfruit, Lehua blossoms or Symphony grapes on a damp, misty day while outside steaming lava oozes from a volcano."

TIP

The capitalized AND tells the search directory to look for both terms—because the term is in ALL CAPS, the search directory knows that AND is not one of the search terms but rather a command.

The ability of search directories to find even the most obscure resources makes them a joy to use. Say you need to rent a laptop in Istanbul. Out of luck? Apparently not. Typing *laptop AND Istanbul* returns a listing for the Istanbul Business Center located in the Hyatt Regency.

On one occasion, I recalled someone mentioning a train that winds through California's Napa Valley wine country. I searched for *Napa wine train* and found a listing for the Napa Valley Wine Train, "a three-hour, 36-mile roundtrip gourmet dining experience [that] takes passengers on a scenic tour of California's wine country in restored 1917 Pullman rail cars."

LOCALS AND LONG-LOST RELATIVES

Most people have found that local residents can be one of the most dependable travel resources. Locals know the area, are often eager to show visitors around, and have insider tips that travelers won't find in any guidebook.

Until the Net came along, it was difficult to connect with people in a destination before leaving home. But the Net allows people half a world away to meet, chat, and share tips. If you're planning a trip to the old country, distant relatives back on the old sod can be an invaluable resource. In the past, making connections with these needles in a worldwide haystack was a tremendous challenge. By using the Net, finding relatives and old friends is less challenging. And that's good news for travelers, because it is human connection that makes the Net such a miraculous travel tool.

If you're looking for a friend or relative, the Net offers several ways to find people. You can use Yahoo's People Search (*http://www.yahoo. com/search/people/*) or go directly to Four11 (*http://www.four11.com*), which provides the database for People Search. To find someone's email address, try the Internet Address Finder (*http://www.iaf.net*); if

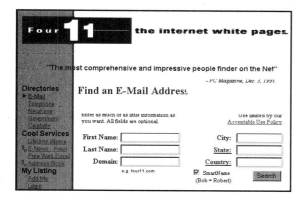

FIGURE 1-15

Four11 (http://www.four11.com) helps you find addresses, phone numbers and email addresses for people in the U.S.

that person has registered, his or her email address will be listed. Or you can try Bigfoot (*http://bigfoot.com*), a similar service. If you don't find someone through one of these services, try another.

Dave Hatunen, an engineer in his late 50s, lives with his wife just south of San Francisco. For a trip to Europe with his wife and daughter, Dave used online resources to make most of the arrangements.

> *I used Travelocity (http://www.travelocity.com) to find the cheapest non-stop flight at the time we wanted. I limited the search to only non-stops and found one on British Airways that was perfect and made the reservation online. I gave them my credit card and sure enough two days later the tickets were delivered by Federal Express.*
>
> *Next we needed to get a Eurail pass for the three of us. Through the Eurail site (http://www.eurail.com) we found a special family pass that allowed the three of us to travel together on the same pass. So we bought the pass from the site and FedEx delivered it in two days. (The site charged a $10 shipping and handling fee.)*
>
> *I also found information about the ferry from Stockholm to Helsinki—though the site was in Swedish I could figure out the schedule. So now I know when we have to be in Stockholm to make the ferry. By checking out train schedules I found that on our train trip from Stockholm to Copenhagen we'd have to change trains in Hasselholm and we'd have only 20 minutes to do it. I asked my wife if she thinks she'll be able to pack light enough for us to make it. We know we'll have to rush—that's good to know ahead of time.*

PERSONAL ACCOUNT

Dave Hatunen

hatunen@netcom.com

While researching this trip, Dave discovered relatives in Finland he didn't know he had. The news came to him through someone he "met" in a Usenet discussion group.

FIGURE 1-16
Home page for Rail Pass express, a Eurail site (http://www.eurail.com), where travelers can learn about and buy Eurail passes..

The amazing thing is that we're going to be gone three weeks, and thanks to the connections we've made on the Net, we're not going to have to stay in a hotel one night.

We have friends in London I met through a science newsgroup on the Net. The husband had seen some of my posts to this group, and when he was getting ready to visit California he sent me email to let me know he'd be coming. So I invited him to the house and we hit it off famously. Each time he came to California he would visit, and finally he brought his wife and three kids and they all stayed at our house.

Now it's our turn to spend some time with them in England. We'll be staying with them for three days on our way up to Finland and five or six days on the way back.

And when we get to Finland, we'll meet some second cousins I didn't know I had. Someone in Finland saw my last name when I posted to a newsgroup and this person knew a Harri Hatunen at the University of Oulu (Finland). So he sent email to Harri and Harri got in touch with me. We went up the family tree and figured out that we're second cousins.

So of course when they heard we were planning to visit Finland they invited us to stay with them. Harri also told me of a woman in Helsinki with the same last name who turns out to be my second cousin. She was visiting the States recently and Harri had given her our name and told her to look us up. She called and stayed with us—now we'll visit her.

We (my family in the U.S.) never knew exactly where we came from. My grandfather had Alzheimer's and even before that he didn't say much about the family history. But through these relatives we've been able to map our family tree.

What's remarkable about the connections Dave made is that he didn't have to go out of his way to make them. They were all made from the comfort of his home, using his personal computer. Dave managed to meet people across the globe who later visited him in California and reciprocated by inviting Dave's family to stay with them. Such chance encounters are common fare on the Net. Even before you leave home you can get a head start on new relationships and, at the very least, you'll get useful information you can use to plan your trip. When things really click, you end up making new friends before you step on the plane. By the time you meet face to face, you'll feel like old buddies.

By now you should have an idea of how you can get started researching travel on the Net. Beginning with search directories, mining travel indexes, and reviewing specific sites, you can collect information relevant to your trip and compile a customized guidebook. To personalize and add to the information you collect on the Web, turn to Usenet, the global network of electronic bulletin boards. The next step is to evaluate flights, hotels, and rental cars at your destination. Once again, the Net is a superb resource, whether you're just doing a little research or looking to book your flights. Let's move on to the next chapter and see how this has become possible.

Planes, Trains, and Automobiles

2

Once you know where you want to go, the next step is deciding how to get there. This chapter focuses on the Internet services that can get you just about any place—any way you want to travel. The beauty of these services is that they're open 24 hours a day, seven days a week. So if you want to sit down in your bathrobe on a Sunday morning and plan your trip to Tahiti, go right ahead. You'll find flights to compare, train schedules to examine, and even rental cars whose tires you can kick.

▶ A Quick Look at Online Booking

▶ Airlines: Finding a Better Deal on the Net

▶ Trains: Getting the Timetables Before You Go

▶ Renting a Car Online

A QUICK LOOK AT
ONLINE BOOKING

Most airline tickets are distributed through networks called Computer Reservation Systems (CRSs), such as SABRE. These systems allow travel agents to input travel dates and destinations, and then check availability and fares on hundreds of airlines. In 1985, easySABRE launched its service on the CompuServe network and the era of do-it-yourself online booking had begun. This service later became available on the Net, and by the end of 1995, easySABRE had registered more than 2 million members and was issuing 1.6 million tickets per year, according to Jupiter Communications.

The early versions of easySABRE were anything but easy to use. Travelers had to become familiar with the arcane terms and cryptic codes that travel agents had mastered. Today, however, online booking sites are genuinely easy to use. Travelers no longer have to understand destination and fare codes—they can simply enter their dates of travel, destination, even meal preference, and quickly see what's available. The automated booking agent does all the dirty work: scanning thousands of options in seconds and coming up with the flights that best suit travelers' itineraries.

We'll start with a couple of personal accounts that show how useful the Net can be when booking a flight. Next, we'll take an in-depth look at travel booking sites to demonstrate where their strengths lie and how to use these services. Then we'll evaluate individual airline sites, such as American Airlines' home on the Web. We'll explore bargains offered through the Net and whether travelers typically get the best fare by booking through online reservations systems. Finally, we'll see how to use the Net to find train schedules and take a test drive through some rent-a-car sites.

AIRLINES: FINDING
A BETTER DEAL ON
THE NET

For the recent Christmas holidays, I planned to spend a week near Cabo San Lucas, the southern tip of Mexico's Baja California. When my vacation schedule shifted, I called my travel agent and asked if I could leave a day earlier, but she said the flight was full. Given that the round-trip fare from Los Angeles to Cabo was under $400 (and thus her commission would be small), I figured she probably wasn't going to spend a lot of time checking later to find a free seat.

Although a flight shows that it's "sold out" a few weeks prior to departure, people change their plans or fail to pay for reserved seats and openings happen. So I turned to the Net. Through a Web site called Preview Travel (*http://www.reservations.com*), I was able to make daily checks to see if the Mexicana flight I wanted had any openings. Within two or three days, the flight opened up, and I called the agent and asked her to change my reservation. Remarkably, the flight I found cost even less than the discount fare I'd reserved earlier, and there was no fee to switch. So, thanks to an Internet travel resource, I was able to get on a flight that was "sold out," and fly exactly when I wanted to travel.

By March 1997, Preview Travel had more than 1 million members, selling over $1 million per week in airline tickets and vacation packages, and was rated among the top ten sites on AOL.

Though I tried other airline booking sites in the early days (circa 1995), I kept coming back to Preview, partly because it was easy to use. "We designed it with the consumer in mind," says Ken Orton, Preview's president. Preview took the "arcane commands" used by airline reservation systems and simplified them to help consumers understand how to book their own flights.

FIGURE 2-1
Preview Travel (http://www.reservations.com) lets you check flights' availability and fares.

Despite the ease of arranging reservations online, some consumers hesitate to make their own airline arrangements. Online reservations still make up only a minuscule share of total flights booked. Of the $70 billion market for air travel in the U.S., online purchases make up less than 1 percent, Orton notes. But he says his company is tracking a dramatic month-to-month numbers increase, indicating online purchases will soon make up a "big segment of the market."

Why does Orton expect the market to take off? He cites several factors. As business travelers get used to buying airline tickets online, they'll become more comfortable with online booking and will begin to arrange their leisure travel over the Net as well. Also, he says, Preview and other online sites offer more up-to-date destination information than your local travel agent. "My destination information is better," he says. Preview's site is current, easily accessible, and uses multimedia to show travelers places they can visit. On the Net, "you can find out where the hot new restaurant on the Left Bank is. We have a staff of four editorial people who are extremely well-traveled and 30 full-time travel agents providing travel consultation through email and over the phone."

A Bright Future for Online Booking

Several of the major online travel booking services are already showing substantial results. Preview Travel said it sold more than $1 million in airline bookings during the week of Dec. 2-8, 1996, through its Web site and its AOL area. And TravelWeb, which specializes in hotel booking, processed more than $1 million in hotel reservations during November 1996, just a year after opening its virtual doors.

"This demonstrates the commercial viability of electronic commerce," says Wendy Brown, head of commerce at America Online. "Companies like Preview Travel are leveraging this new medium to provide consumers with convenient and easy-to-use services, and are attracting substantial numbers of customers in the process."

In October 1996, when Microsoft introduced Expedia, many pundits forecast gloom and doom for other players in the online booking field. Although Expedia had a fast start, its competitors, such as Travelocity and ITN, continued to grow and improve. Preview Travel unveiled a new interface that made its site more user-friendly and did a booming business after replacing SABRE in mid-1996 as the main booking site on AOL.

BOOKING SITES GIVE YOU ACCESS

Preview Travel is one of several booking services on the Web. Starting in the mid-90s, several major travel Web sites ramped up to include vacation packages, car rentals, hotel room booking, and more. And rather than simply using these sites as sources of information, thousands of consumers began buying their tickets through them. Customer acceptance has grown quickly because the sites have gone beyond selling airline tickets and displaying timetables. Travelers can personalize the information by listing their priorities, from the cheapest fare to a preferred airline to on-time performance. Travelers are able to plug in a complex itinerary, tell the computer to show the three, five, or ten least expensive (or most timely) flights, and select from this list.

Helen Trillian Rose, a systems administrator who moderates an airline industry newsgroup (*misc.transport.air-industry*), has used online booking engines to plan dozens of flights.

PERSONAL ACCOUNT
Helen Trillian Rose
hrose@rocza.kei.com

> *Over the past two years I've averaged about 50,000 miles flown, and every single flight I've chosen has been because of info on the Net. The way I pick a flight is (in order): airline, type of airplane, time of departure, and whether it is non-stop or not.*

> *I recently booked a trip from Boston to London and did all of the flight research myself. I looked on numerous Web sites comparing prices and times and conveniences, and researching the amenities of various airlines.*

To research her flights, Helen used Worldspan (*http://www.worldspan. com*), easySABRE (*http://www.easysabre.com*), and the Flifo Cyber Travel Agent (*http://www.flifo.com*). About Worldspan, she says, "This is my current fave. The interface is much cleaner than just about any other plane fare pricing site out there." Helen is less enthusiastic about easySABRE. "The [easySABRE] interface is less than perfect, but if you can get past that it gives a lot of useful information." She also advises that travelers try Flifo, which "sometimes helps in finding bargain fares on routes that you otherwise wouldn't think of trying."

> *I then used the Web to check out car rental sites. I checked the available fleets, pricing, and "fine print" of Hertz, Avis, and Alamo. I ended up picking Alamo, because they had the best rate available. I rang up the airline to pay for the ticket, and rang up the car rental agency to reserve the car. Quite honestly, I don't think a travel agent should be the one getting*

the commission if I did the work. Well, I wish there was a way I could get a rebate of that commission, but for now, I'll let Delta have it.

TIP

Today there are booking sites that refund all or part of the commission if you do your own booking. See Chapter 4, "Finding the Best Deals," for details.

The airlines all have their own Web sites now. Some of them are more informative than others. When I flew Virgin Atlantic (http://www. fly.virgin.com/) last year I checked their Web site out to get an idea of what to expect on the flight.

TIP

Online booking sites don't always have all the full set of options and information available to travel agents. In an effort to make online systems more user-friendly, says travel agent Edward Hasbrouck, online agents have sacrificed choice. If you make a reservation over the Web and don't feel confident that you're getting a good deal, give your travel agent a call and see if he or she can do better. Hasbrouck is the author of *The Practical Nomad*, a handbook for planning long-term, independent, international travel, scheduled for release by Moon Publication in fall 1997.

Edward Hasbrouck

THE BEST SITES FOR BOOKING FLIGHTS

Most of the top travel booking sites have some features in common: a real-time booking agent where you can peruse the same flight data-bases as a travel agent, destination information about locations and activities throughout the world, and car rental and hotel information. And some, such as Preview and Expedia, have a staff of real-live agents who can assist you if you need some help from a human be-ing. The key sites differ in subtle but important ways. This guide should help you find what's right for you, but perhaps the best way to choose is to spend a little time at several of these sites, and see which feels most comfortable to you.

FIGURE 2-2
Expedia's "Flight Wizard" lists best-priced trips (http://expedia.com).

- Expedia
  http://expedia.com
  CRS: Worldspan

  Strengths: Easy to find schedules and fares, deep hotel directory, Fare Tracker email alerts about bargain flights to destinations you select, bonus frequent flyer miles.

  Ticketing: Credit card

- ITN
  http://www.itn.net
  CRS: Apollo

  Strengths: Low graphics mean quick loading, personal service because ticketing is through a travel agent, Java-based low-fare ticker.

  Ticketing: By travel agents

- Flifo
  http://www.flifo.com
  CRS: SABRE

  Strengths: Fare Buster feature looks for cheaper flights around the same time as the one you selected.

  Ticketing: Credit card with overnight UPS delivery

- TISS
  http://www.tiss.com
  CRS: SABRE

  Strength: Can find cheap consolidator flights.

  Ticketing: By travel agents

Airline Info FAQ
http://iecc.com/airline/
See this site for the latest information on airline booking online.

- PC Travel
  http://www.pctravel.com
  CRS: Apollo (United's reservation system)
  Strengths: Extensive destination information, discounts for members.
  Ticketing: Credit card with delivery by FedEx

- Travelocity
  http://www.travelocity.com
  CRS: SABRE
  Strengths: Deep destination information, extensive hotel and car rental access.
  Ticketing: Credit card

- Preview Travel
  http://www.reservations.com or *http://www.vacations.com*
  CRS: Apollo
  Strengths: Easy-to-use, intuitive booking engine, bonus miles for United's frequent flyer program.
  Ticketing: Credit card, second-day air delivery

AIRLINES OF THE WEB: USING AIRLINE SITES

While it often makes sense to go through major independent booking sites to get the best fare, there are other times you may want to go directly to an airline's own site. If you have a frequent flyer plan on United, you may want to go directly to the United site (*http://www.ual.com*). Or if you know Southwest has a special promotional fare, go straight to Southwest's site (*http://www.iflyswa.com*). Southwest has not joined all the major CRSs, so Southwest flights won't show up on some general booking sites.

Even when you book through a big travel site, you should also visit the airline site for the airline you select. For example, if you use Travelocity and reserve a ticket on Delta, go next to Delta's site (*http://www.delta-air.com*) to learn more about the airline.

One of the best sources for links to airline sites is Airlines of the Web (*http://www.itn.net/airlines/*), created by Marc-David Seidel while he was a graduate student at U.C. Berkeley's business school. Seidel started the page as part of his dissertation on the airline industry. The site soon grew into a valuable index for travel professionals and travelers. Airlines of the Web has links to hundreds of carriers

Flyte Trax
*http://www.
weatherconcepts.com/
FlyteTrax/*

This is one of the coolest sites on the Web— it can tell you when a flight that's in the air is due to arrive. Just type in the three-letter code for the airline, the flight number, and the airport where the plane is headed, for example: "TWA, 804, JFK. " Flyte Trax checks the progress of the flight and displays its current location and time of arrival, i.e., "TWA Flight 804 is currently over Pennsylvania and due to arrive at JFK in 19 minutes. "

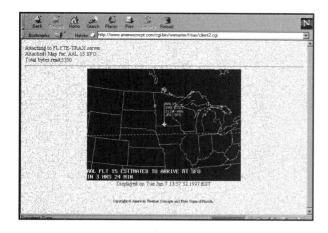

FIGURE 2-3
With Flyte Trax (http://www. weatherconcepts.com/FlyteTrax), you can find out when a flight is arriving and see where it is.

throughout the world, frequent flyer program news, toll-free numbers for airlines, and links to Usenet discussion groups on air travel. Another central site is Aviation Internet Resources (*http:// airlines-online.com/*).

"The Web is critical to the airline industry as a means of distribution. Some have realized this sooner than others," Marc-David says.

The Web is a boon to both consumers and the airlines. Consumers now have a new way to compare fares. And the airlines have discovered that the Net's immediacy gives them a wonderful outlet for last-minute bargains to fill seats that would otherwise go empty. Airlines can use their Web sites to market unsold seats on flights at bargain basement prices.

Airlines of the Web
http://www.itn.net/airlines/
Links and toll-free numbers for hundreds of airlines.

Another good resource for airline information is the Air Traveler's Handbook (*http://www.cs.cmu.edu/afs/cs/user/mkant/Public/Travel/airfare. html*), with categories on everything from charter flights to frequent flyer programs. To reach an extensive list of airline sites categorized by the Yahoo search directory, see *http://www.yahoo.com/ Business_and_Economy/Companies/Travel/Airlines/*.

LATE-BREAKING DEALS AND AUCTIONS

Several airlines use the Internet to notify people about last-minute discount flights. Each Wednesday, American Airlines (*http://www. americanair.com/*) sends out an email bulletin about its NetSAAver fares (to subscribe, see *http://www.americanair.com/aa_home/net_ saavers.htm*), which are valid on the following weekend for travel from Saturday to Monday or Tuesday. A recent bulletin listed a roundtrip fare between Chicago and Memphis for $89. Or you could fly roundtrip from Dallas to Philadelphia for $159, a substantial discount compared to the standard fare. Partners (including Avis Rent a Car and Hilton Hotels) have joined the NetSAAver program to offer discounts to these travelers.

TIP

You don't need to subscribe to American's NetSAAver list to learn about these bargains. You can simply check the NetSAAver site *(http://www.americanair.com/aa_home/ net_saavers.htm)* whenever you want to see what bargains are available. If you do subscribe and wish to unsubscribe, simply go back to the site for instructions on how to unsubscribe.

Hong Kong-based Cathay Pacific *(http://www.cathay-usa.com/)* recently used its Web site to auction enough seats to fill a Boeing 747 with passengers flying from New York or Los Angeles to Hong Kong. The bidding was silent, conducted through email and snail mail (standard postal service delivery). Cathay accepted 387 (of 14,760) bids during a summer 1996 auction, with the lowest successful bid being $775 for a roundtrip ticket. (The highest bid was $4,700 for a first class ticket. The successful bids in business class ranged from $2,000 to $2,700.) So quite a few people were able to fly from the U.S. to Hong Kong for substantially less than the going rate. The only

FIGURE 2-4
Cathay Pacific's Cybertraveler program offers special bargains to its online customers (http://www.cathay-usa.com/).

downside was that these passengers were not eligible for frequent flyer miles.

While the auctions provided some "incremental revenue" for Cathay, their primary purpose has been to "raise awareness" of Cathay's U.S. operations, says a Cathay spokeswoman, and to help the company build its database of travelers. Through auctions and other means, Cathay has signed up 120,000 "cybertravelers" and sends them email about promotions and deals.

WILL YOU REALLY GET THE BEST FARE ONLINE?

While booking tickets through the Net will clearly become common in the near future, not everyone in the industry believes that online booking services can always come up with the best fare. For example, I tried to book a hypothetical midsummer trip from Los Angeles to New York, and Travelocity showed a best fare of $372 roundtrip on Tower Air. The same search run in Travelocity's Fares section for the same days showed a roundtrip price of $278 on several carriers.

What happened here? Do computers at these online sites find the best fares, or do they pick the fares that most closely match the customer's desired travel times? Judging from a random, unscientific sample of Internet-generated fares, calls to travel agents, and calls to airport reservation lines, the answer is simple: don't accept the first fare that any of these sites cough up. Make several searches, using several different sites, including an airline's own site.

Sites like Travelocity search only for available seats, says Terry Jones of SABRE Interactive (one of Travelocity's two parent companies). So if there aren't any seats available at the budget fare for the day and time selected, no seats will show up when a user tries to book a flight. Whereas a travel agent might say, "Now let's see if there's a flight the next day or to a nearby airport," computers haven't reached that level of sophistication. Travelocity is already dealing with 52 million different fares from its more than 400 airlines, Jones says, which is why the site offers its Flight Finder, a list of current best fares between various cities. Users can check this area to see if the fares they're quoted are the lowest available.

The first versions of Net travel sites (circa 1995) couldn't match the flexibility and creativity of real live travel agents. But by late 1996, leading travel sites began using sophisticated search features to find more competitive fares. Preview Travel, for example, added "Best Fare Shopping." When a visitor to the site picks a flight preference, Preview's computers check for similar flights and display the three lowest fares that match, or closely approximate, the customer's desired itinerary.

Despite these improvements, online travel sites may not yield the best fares, particularly for complex or international routes. C. Andrew Shepp, founder of Shepp & Associates, a St. Louis-based firm specializing in international travel-industry software, consulting, and development, says the CRS systems used by major booking services

Who Should Use Online Booking Agents?

Online booking agents are not for every traveler. Some travelers might be better served using the Net simply to find interesting travel destinations and offers, and then turning to a professional to book the trip. So who should use online booking agents?

Use online booking agents if you:

- **Travel frequently.** Because it takes a little time to become adept at using these services, the occasional traveler may do better by calling a good travel agent.

- **Travel primarily in the U.S.** Booking international flights can be complicated. You may find a better deal by calling a consolidator (an agent that lists special unpublished fares). Some consolidators are also going online (more on this in Chapter 4, "Finding the Best Deals").

- **Have strong loyalties to a particular airline.** If you have a favorite airline or want to stick with a frequent flyer program, you can go directly to that airline's site or set up a preference for that airline in a booking site like Preview.

Don't rely on booking agents if you:

- **Travel to remote areas.** If you're flying to Ecuador, Pakistan, or some other less-visited destination, consult a travel agent who specializes in that area. In the previous chapter, we discussed how to use the Net to find a travel agent who specializes in a particular region or type of travel.

- **Have a complex itinerary with lots of stops.** The more complex your itinerary, the more difficult it will be for you to find the best deal through an online agent. While online sites are evolving all the time, they can't do what a human can, which is suggest alternate routes or the best times to fly.

aren't designed to find the lowest fares, and that CRS systems are dinosaurs:

> *[Old online booking systems] all have the defect of operating by mimicking the operations of travel agents; pricing of the air reservation is an afterthought because the CRS systems agencies use were designed when all prices—by law—were the same. You booked what was convenient and quoted the price later. Air pricing is an awkward and expensive add-on to the CRS companies.*

> *Well, deregulation brought a storm of discounts, and none of these online booking systems are capable of finding them. Even good travel agents can take 30 minutes of fare research before they can offer the three best-priced options.*

> *In the future online pricing might be simplified by airlines offering Net fares (that is, a lowered fare with no commission or distribution cost built in), available only to online customers. Agents, online or not, will be charging for what is currently free (their own labor and their advice).*

THE BOOK-TO-LOOK RATIO

Another big concern in the online booking world is that people will use these services to get information, but will buy tickets the old-fashioned way, from their travel agents or over the phone. "Our competition is the telephone," says Travelocity's Neal Checkoway. "We have to be better, faster, cheaper." The companies behind major travel sites are carefully scrutinizing the book-to-look ratio, though SABRE's Jones says bookings are ahead of projections.

Online travel industry leaders typically cite ATM machines as a model: for years, bank customers were uncomfortable using them, particularly to deposit money. But in time the majority of customers have become comfortable with these machines. Jones and others expect that it's only a matter of time until air travelers become similarly comfortable with buying tickets over the Net. And they're even happy to have people browse, because these lookers become comfortable by spending time online and their presence increases ad rates.

Will a significant proportion of travelers ever buy their tickets through the Net? "If it's fast, efficient, and cost effective, they'll rely on it," Checkoway says. In other words, if you build it *well*, they will come.

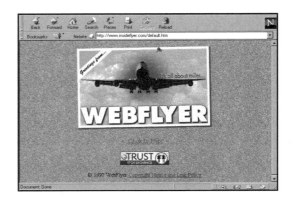

FIGURE 2-5

WebFlyer (http://www.insideflyer.com/) is a cornucopia of resources for frequent flyers.

FOR FREQUENT FLYERS

If you're a frequent flyer, see Web Flyer (*http://www.insideflyer.com/*), where you'll find features from *Inside Flyer* magazine, FAQs about frequent flyer programs, and hundreds of ways to earn miles without leaving the ground. If you want to compare frequent flyer programs or pose a question to self-described frequent flyer guru Randy Petersen, this is the place. And if you're wondering how many miles your upcoming flight will cover, see "How Far Is It?" (*http://www.indo.com/distance/*) for point-to-point distances.

For an up-to-date list of links to airlines' frequent flyer program pages, go to Airlines of the Web frequent flyer links (*http://www.itn.net/airlines/airff.html*). This site has dozens of links to frequent flyer program pages ranging from Aer Lingus to Virgin Atlantic.

MICROSOFT'S EXPEDIA

It's fashionable in techie circles to bash Microsoft. Bill's big, bad behemoth based in Redmond, Washington, has stomped on its competition and has used its marketing muscle to become a dominant player in the software industry. Will it repeat its success in the online travel business? That remains to be seen, but with Expedia (*http://expedia.com*), its first entry into this area, it is already a forceful presence.

Similar to several of its competitors, Expedia is an all-in-one site where travelers can book flights, reserve hotel rooms, and rent cars. Expedia's Travel Agent lets users tap into the same real-time reservation system that travel agents use. Several prompts, which the site calls "wizards," lead the user through the process of researching, booking, and purchasing travel products.

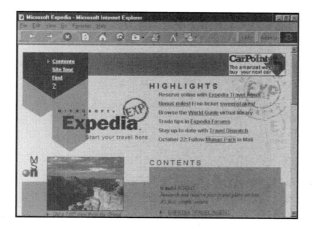

FIGURE 2-6
Expedia (http://expedia.com/), offering searches for budget fares, has quickly become one of the leading booking sites on the Web.

The Hotel Directory combines listings for more than 25,000 hotels, with pictures for many hotels and lists of amenities. There's also a mapping feature that locates hotels on a city map so travelers can see if a hotel is conveniently located.

One of Expedia's nicest features is its Fare Tracker. In this area, users select up to three airline routes (for example, Chicago to New York, Chicago to Los Angeles, and Chicago to London) and Fare Tracker sends weekly email messages with the best fares between those destinations.

And if users want to explore destinations before they travel, the site has cultural, historical, and entertainment information in the Expedia World Guide. One of the coolest features here is the Full Circle virtual tour with 360-degree panoramic views. Finally, users can experience virtual adventures by tuning into the site's online magazine *Mungo Park*. The first journey documented here was a descent down Africa's Tekeze River.

TRAVELOCITY: AN IN-DEPTH LOOK AT AN IN-DEPTH SITE

While several sites offer convenient booking features and destination information for travelers, Travelocity (*http://www.travelocity.com*) is one of the most extensive travel resources on the Net. This mega-site is a good example of the growing trend of combining booking services with travel features and discussion areas. Travelocity is produced by SABRE Interactive, which provides the booking services, and Worldview Systems Corporation, which offers abundant destination information. (Note: In August 1996, the SABRE Group, the

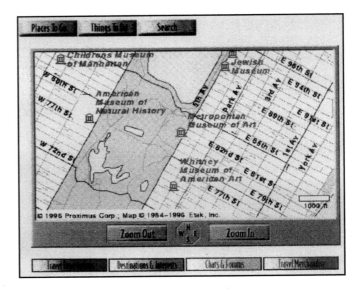

FIGURE 2-7

Travelocity's geo-enabled maps show you attractions, ranging from museums to restaurants.

Dallas-based information and technology subsidiary of AMR Corporation, acquired Worldview Systems Corporation of San Francisco.)

The Travelocity site offers reservations and tickets for more than 380 airlines, and in September 1996 added reservation and purchase capability for rooms at more than 30,000 hotels and 50 car rental companies. SABRE's FlightFinder searches for the lowest fare available between multiple cities and displays the three least expensive options. If you're wondering how a certain type of aircraft is laid out, the site has diagrams for the most popular commercial aircraft, helping passengers decide where they want to sit. The vacation section highlights package deals to popular destinations such as Mexico and Florida. And now Travelocity provides maps that highlight regional attractions, such as the one of New York City and its museums shown in Figure 2-7.

"Travelocity is a place where you can research a little, plan a little, dream a little, and then execute a booking," says Neal Checkoway, president and CEO of Worldview Systems. The site also has magazine-type feature stories and conferencing areas where users can share their experiences and chat with travel experts.

WINNING THE AIRFARE WAR

When airline ticket price wars break out, such as the Southwest blockbuster during the summer of 1996, switchboards are often jammed, and getting through to travel agents can be difficult. So when systems engineer Keith Jarett was looking for cheap tickets he turned to Travelocity after failing to get through to Southwest's phone reservation system.

> *I got three tickets from Travelocity: an Oakland to Phoenix roundtrip for me, Oakland to Los Angeles roundtrip (Disneyland) for the family, and Oakland to Seattle for my parents. For these flights, $25 per flight segment was about half the normal minimum fare, thus they were not the ultra-bargains that other routes were. This meant good availability of west coast seats on SW well into the sale period, even though other airlines such as Alaska were essentially sold out of their more limited allocations. (Alaska, United, Delta, and others matched the Southwest deal of $25 per segment on some routes.)*
>
> *I did these on Tuesday and Wednesday (the sale started Sunday) after failing in 500 or so autodial attempts by the PC to get through to Southwest's reservations number.*

Worldview's Neal Checkoway notes that Travelocity had a big "spike" in usage right after the Southwest-initiated sale. "My wife tried to get through to Southwest on the phone, but she couldn't. So she logged on to Travelocity and booked the flight in five minutes."

Preview's Ken Orton says the big sale was "a perfect example" of why online booking is better than traditional ticketing systems. "We could handle the load. Southwest triggered a fare war the likes of which we hadn't seen in 10 years." As other airlines matched Southwest's fares the outpouring of demand swamped traditional ticketing systems. "We tripled our volume. We were open 24 hours a day, seven days a week. When all the travel agents closed and the airline reservations switchboards went to skeleton crews, we were open and ready to go. That's the real magic of online and scalable systems. We have the electronic equivalent of 480 travel agents ready to handle online customers. At any given moment, we can be booking 480 people."

Is a war brewing between electronic and human agents? Orton says the war is not between online agents and storefront agents, it's

Agent using Reservisor Terminal

FIGURE 2-8
This is the way reservations were handled before the age of computers. (Copyright 1950 AMR Corp.)

between travel suppliers and all agents. Travel suppliers, including airlines, hotels, cruise lines, and tour companies, are working to "cut the agent out of the loop and save the commission." In other words, if a travel supplier sells directly to a consumer, that supplier doesn't have to pay a commission to anyone.

MASS PERSONALIZATION

Because the Net is an ideal medium for soliciting user feedback, Travelocity has encouraged users to comment on the site and is implementing some changes based on these comments. "Since we launched Travelocity (March 1996) we have received thousands of emails from visitors. One early criticism concerned our bare-bones and sometimes out-of-date hotel information," Neal Checkoway says. "In October (1996), we replaced an outside vendor with SABRE's proprietary hotel and car reservation database. Our users now have access to regularly updated hotel listings and can make reservations online. They also have access to expanded hotel listings with photos and lists of features and amenities."

Checkoway uses an intriguing, but seemingly oxymoronic, term: "mass personalization." What does this mean for the future of Travelocity? The site's goal is to offer custom information to each user, based on that person's interests. So if you key in that you're interested in whitewater rafting in Idaho and beer festivals in Germany, Travelocity will deliver information about these events or activities. Travelocity will also use emerging tools such as "collaborative filtering" to personalize Travelocity for the individual. Checkoway says, "Our plan is to create a community where users can easily talk to each other and share information about their likes and dislikes, get recommendations based on their own user-preferences for specific restaurants, hotels and other things to do while traveling, as well as obtain information directly from our travel specialists."

TRAINS: GETTING THE TIMETABLES BEFORE YOU GO

Spontaneity has its time and its place.
                    —John Cusack in "The Sure Thing"

When author/journalist Steve Pizzo began planning his vacation to Italy, he knew he didn't want to battle Italian drivers for three weeks.

Instead he decided that riding Italy's rails would be a lot more relaxing for him and his wife.

PERSONAL ACCOUNT
Steve Pizzo
pizzo@sonic.net

My wife and I enjoy touring Europe without a schedule or itinerary—and without the hassle of a car. We just purchased a first-class rail pass. But the last time we did this we had depended on local advice and broken-English instructions from train conductors which were sometimes right, sometimes wrong.

For his most recent trip, Steve searched AltaVista for Italian rail timetables. He found several useful sites, including "a great site that allowed me to choose the city I was leaving, the destination point, and the date of travel. It would return a page showing the departure and arrival times all day, ticket prices, and travel time."

Steve and his wife listed all the towns and cities they wanted to see, plugged them into IRT, and printed the schedules. "Since it was free I printed out every possible combination of departure and destination points. We packed the printouts in our luggage, and they proved invaluable on our trip."

Italian Railway Timetables
http://www.dicea.unifi.it/ ie/iefrm.htm

Check this site for schedules and fares for Italy.

As Steve's experience shows, getting schedules before you go can greatly enhance your trip. Today the Net has a variety of rail sites, ranging from the comprehensive Amtrak site to the endearing Great Little Trains of Wales (see below for URLs). And these sites offer much more than timetables: you can learn about your destinations, see route maps, and even get instructions about which subway train to take to get from point A to point B in Paris.

TRACKING TRAINS ON THE WEB

Below are a few of the most useful rail sites to help you get started down the track.

Cyberspace World Railroad
(*http://www.mcs.com/~dsdawdy/cyberoad.html*)

Worldwide timetables and information. With a carload full of features, fares, facts, and festivities, CWR is an ideal starting point for the rail enthusiast who wants to plan a train trip. While this site leans toward travel features, it also links to hundreds of useful timetable sites including the full Amtrak schedule and Canadian Railway passenger pages.

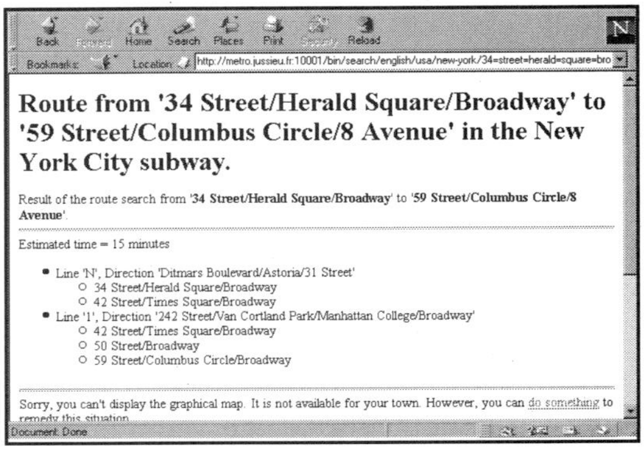

FIGURE 2-9

The Subway Navigator lets you plot your route before you go.

Subway Navigator
(*http://metro.jussieu.fr:10001/bin/cities/english*)

Information, directions, and maps for 60 metro train and subway systems in 29 countries. Say you're going to New York City—you know the subway system there is a labyrinth, but you've also heard it's the fastest way to get around the city. You could try to grab a subway map while you're there, or you can get the info you need ahead of time. Easy choice. With the Subway Navigator, just type in where you're starting from and where you're going, and it will tell you where to go. (Hey, you're going to New York. You better get used to someone—or something—telling you where to go.) For example, I told the Navigator I needed to get from Herald Square to Columbus Circle, and bang! I got a page with the estimated time of the trip (15 minutes) and the line I needed to take. The Subway Navigator lists stops along the way so I'll know when I'm getting close and can get ready to push my way out of the graffiti-covered car.

The Navigator also covers greater metro areas, so if I want to know how to get from Grand Central Station to White Plains, it tells me the trip will take about 60 minutes and lets me know which lines to take and where to transfer. Much easier than trying to ask a "friendly" New Yorker how to get there.

Rail Europe (*http://www.raileurope.com/*)

Fares and timetables for the 1,500 most-traveled routes in Europe. This site makes planning your trip easy. Just type in your departure and arrival cities and the date you're traveling, and Rail Europe will tell you the fare and schedule for that day. Rail Europe offers online booking so you can buy the ticket through the Net and pick it up from a travel agent in your local area. The site also has a special

FIGURE 2-10
Amtrak lets you plan your rail journey on the Net.

section (with fares and timetables) about the Eurostar train which links London to Paris and Brussels via the Chunnel. There's also information on the Eurail pass, car rentals, and hotel room discounts. Another excellent source is Mercurio, the European Railway Server (*http://mercurio.iet.unipi.it/*).

Amtrak (*http://www.amtrak.com*)

The official source for the U.S. rail service. You can find schedules, reservation information, promotions, and a travel planner that includes a national route map. To retrieve schedules for a certain route, you can enter your departure and destination cities and the server will display a list of options. Unfortunately, this site is a bit cumbersome, and may display trains that serve only part of your route. When I asked for a train from Oakland to Chicago, one choice displayed a train that went only as far as Sacramento. There were also links to the California Zephyr, but once I got to this link I had to search for the schedule that applied to the trip I wanted to take. Not nearly as efficient as the European rail servers. It might be easier to just call 1-800-USA-RAIL. The Promotions area is more useful, with news about discounts for seniors, students, kids, and visitors from abroad.

The Great Little Trains of Wales (*http://www1.roke.co.uk/WHR/gltw.html*)

"The Great Little Trains of Wales are narrow gauge railways built through the beautiful scenery of north and west Wales. Built in a time less hasty than our own, most originally served to carry Welsh slate from hill to harbour. Now tourists have replaced slate as the

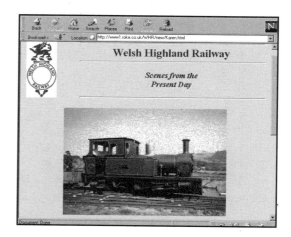

FIGURE 2-11

This engine, called Karen, powers one of the Great Little Trains of Wales (http://www1. roke.co.uk/WHR/gltw.html), classic locomotives that are still in service. Photo by A. Goodwin.

main traffic, and dedicated volunteers have joined the paid staff in the work of restoring and running these pretty little railways." So begins the introduction to this site, worth a virtual ride even if you never get to Wales. Click on the link to the Welsh Highland Railway, and see photos of the way it used to be. You'll find extensive historical information and a section-by-section description of the route. Who knows—by spending a little time here you may become inspired to explore the Welsh country side by rail.

For an extensive list of online rail sites, see the Yahoo category *http://www.yahoo.com/Business_and_Economy/Transportation/Trains_and_ Railroads/.*

RENTING A CAR ONLINE

In an early episode of the TV sitcom *Seinfeld*, Jerry arrives at the rent-a-car counter to pick up the car he has reserved. Unfortunately, it's not there waiting for him. He chides the clerk at the counter, saying she doesn't understand the concept of reservations. When she protests, "I know why we have reservations," Jerry interrupts, "I don't think you do. If you did, I'd have a car here for me. See, you know how to take the reservation, you just don't know how to *hold* the reservation."

Hertz

http://www.hertz.com

In late 1996, Hertz unveiled this new Web site featuring reservations, a fleet guide, special offers, and more.

Well, thanks to the Net, travelers can have a bit more assurance that when they get to the reservation counter, the right car will be waiting for them. On the Net, anyone interested in renting a car can peruse a company's fleet, compare prices (including special deals for Net users), and reserve a car. And if you reserve through the Net rather than over the phone, you can print out your reservation and confirmation, so if the clerk at the other end says you didn't request an economy car and offers you a Buick Le Sabre, you can stick to your guns.

The Avis site, called The Avis Galaxy (*http://www.avis.com*), has sections on rates, business travel, reservation information by location, and special offers. "Basically, we see this as a marketing site. Travelers and (car) renters are wired and we want to be where our customers are," says Thalia Cady, director of electronic marketing for Avis. "We want to be there to greet them. If they're on the Net, we'll hoist the Avis flag there. It allows us to experiment and be creative—the Net is more flexible than print. It's in line with the Avis spirit of building community. We have a chance to express ourselves. We've made a significant investment by adding 700 maps to the site—that took a fortune in time, in scanning, and getting the resolution right. We want to be good Net citizens—the Net is about free information, so you don't have to register or join a club to see the maps."

The site also includes a fleet database (click on The Worldwide Fleet) with images of the cars available at various Avis locations throughout the world. "We weren't sure people would download graphics of our fleet, but they have. It's great for people going out of the country," she says.

In the Select a Car section, you can pick a country, select the options you want, and Avis will recommend the most suitable vehicle and two alternates. To take this system for a test drive, I selected France and said I would prefer a two-door with manual transmission. I rated economy over luxury. And by the way, I told the computer, make it a convertible. The computer selected a VW Golf Cabriolet and showed a small image of the car. I could click on the thumbnail image to get the full-size image and detailed information about the Cabriolet.

The site also offers special deals specifically for Net users. For example, the application fee to join Avis' Preferred Renters club is $50, but if you apply over the Net, you could join for free (as of August 1996).

"How did we live without the Net before? I turn to it for everything," Thalia says, "including making my own vacation plans."

REMEMBER ALAMO

Gary Schwartz, an Internet services director who lives in London, used the Net to rent a car through Alamo. "Renting a car over the Net had the advantage of being a free call," he says. "I can't call 800-numbers from the UK. (Well, I can, but they're not free.) The car was more costly than I'd have liked, but it was a good lazy man's way to get the rental handled."

Some car rental Web sites are becoming good sources for local travel information. Where's the best dim sum restaurant in northern New Jersey? What road games will keep the kids occupied and quiet in the back seat? What's the best route from your home to your vacation destination—and what will the weather be like when you get there? You can find the answers to all these questions at Alamo's Freeways site (*http://www.freeways.com*).

Use the site to preview the company's fleet, reserve a car, or find Alamo's locations in more than 200 U.S. cities. Yet Freeways goes one step further by incorporating users' comments in forums ranging from favorite restaurants to scenic drives to "My Best Trip." In the Find It section are special deals, weather forecasts for major cities around the globe, an online reservation system, and locations of hotels, landmarks, theaters, and convention centers.

For the most complete list of car rental sites on the Web, check the Yahoo section at *http://www.yahoo.com/Business_and_Economy/Companies/ Automotive/Rentals/*.

Now that you've found the best way to get where you're going, you'll want to find the right hotels and good restaurants. As any seasoned traveler knows, no matter how beautiful the destination, it's hard to enjoy a trip if your hotel room also hosts roaches and your meals are giving you heartburn. So let's move on to the next chapter, where you'll find some of the best sources on the Net for good dining tips and for finding a hotel that meets your needs.

Room and Board

3

Once you get to your destination, a successful trip usually depends upon room and board. This is not to say that travelers venture to exotic locales to stare at four walls. But having a comfortable and functional hotel and finding the best places to dine are the foundations of a good trip. Whether your goal is locating a hotel that makes it easy to plug in your laptop, or finding a restaurant that excites your palate, using the Net can help you get there.

In this chapter, we'll look at ways to use the Net to take some of the uncertainties out of choosing hotel rooms and how to find the amenities you want at the price you need. We'll also consider less typical lodging options, such as home exchanges, bed and breakfasts, and hostels, and how to sort the good ones from the nightmare-inspiring. We'll demonstrate how to use Internet restaurant directories to locate restaurants and cafés and how to get dining tips from other Net users.

- ▶ Hotels on the Web
- ▶ Bed and Breakfasts: Homes Away from Home
- ▶ Home Exchanges
- ▶ Hostels: Net Tips for Affordable Lodging
- ▶ Parks and Campgrounds
- ▶ Dining on the Road

HOTELS ON THE WEB

Using Web sites and newsgroups to find the right hotel room offers travelers a solid one-two punch. It allows them to preview and evaluate hotels at their destination long before they arrive. Thousands of hotels around the world have gone online, either by putting up their own sites or by getting listed on one or more indexes. It is becoming difficult to find a town or hamlet anywhere in the world that doesn't have a nearby hotel listed on the Net.

Using the Net to choose a room has several solid advantages over using a printed guidebook. First, information on the Net tends to be more up-to-date than what is found in books, so if a hotel has a lot of empty rooms for an upcoming weekend, it can advertise a special deal on the Net. Second, a Web guide to hotels can pack much more information than a guidebook, including images of individual rooms, bathroom facilities, conference areas, and on-site restaurants. And some hotel Web sites let travelers make reservations through the Net.

Similar to airlines on the Net, hotel chains have staked their claim in cyberspace by creating their own sites, as well as by getting listed in directories that may list thousands of hotels and dozens of major chains. Web hotel directories, such as the Hotel Guide (*http://www. hotelguide.ch*), are a particularly useful tool for wired travelers. Here you can search for rooms by region, by hotel chain, or by a set of preferences tailored to your needs. You can, for example, choose a city and then search for rooms under a certain price level with the amenities (spas, conference facilities, laundry service, etc.) you want.

ANY ROOM AT THE INN?

Directories are a convenient and efficient way to find a hotel at your destination—and not just any hotel, but a place that meets the specifications you require. Following is a short list of some hotel directories on the Web. You can also use search directories to find more specialized hotel directories, such as San Francisco Reservations (*http://www.hotelres.com/*).

TravelWeb (*http://www.travelweb.com*)

Search or browse through thousands of listings of hotels around the world—also includes the "Business Traveler Resource Center" and a search engine for finding flights. The search area lets you specify city, hotel chain, and type of hotel; for example, conference center, or bed and breakfast. Next you can input your price range and select from a checklist of amenities you want, from a concierge to a fitness center. TravelWeb reported that it processed more than $1 million in bookings in November 1996, and said it was growing at a rate of 20 percent per month.

All the Hotels on the Web (*http://www.all-hotels.com/*)

An index of more than 10,000 hotel sites around the world, organized geographically. Though the name is a bit misleading (there are far more than 10,000 hotels on the Web), this is a good, deep resource. While a hotel chain site (like HiltonNet at *http://www.hilton.com*) is fine for someone who knows he'll be staying at the Hilton, typically travelers know their destination and want to browse among the hotels in that city or region.

The Hotel Guide (*http://www.hotelguide.ch*)

An international guide claiming more than 50,000 hotels in its database. The beauty of this guide is that you can use a series of preferences to focus your search. Search for all the hotels that meet your criteria or limit your search to places that have an extended description on the Web—in most cases these extended descriptions include images of the hotels and the rooms.

Hotel Anywhere (*http://www.hotelanywhere.com*)

Links to thousands of hotel sites, airlines, cruise lines, and travel agents. With a simple, mostly text-based interface, this site is easy to navigate and downloads quickly. Its real strength is its breadth. For example, a traveler seeking hotels in Australia gets recommendations for related sites that offer maps, tour information, and restaurant advice.

FINDING THE RIGHT HOTEL

PERSONAL ACCOUNT
Ami J. Claxton
claxton@epivax.epi.umn.edu

Ami J. Claxton is an experienced traveler who knows what she wants. But she's learned not to fully trust the lodging descriptions in traditional travel guidebooks. They can be dated and reflect only the reviewer's opinion. So for a week-long vacation to Rome, Ami turned to the Internet.

I heavily (and frequently) utilize the Internet for travel information. I am quite particular about hotels (location, service, amenities), so I did not want to just reserve a place that was only very briefly described in a printed guidebook.

By searching for *hotel AND Italy* in the Yahoo directory, Ami found dozens of sites with listings of Italian hotels. The most useful, she said, was Italy Hotel Reservation (*http://www.italyhotel.com/italy_frame.html*); users in North America should use the U.S. mirror site at *http://www.italyhotel.com/italy_us.html*), with listings for 6,500 Italian hotels and a search directory that lets you select parameters such as location and price. If you include your arrival and departure dates, you can check availability. IHR links to the Web pages of hotels that have their own online presence and will even send a free fax to the hotel you choose.

> *So I scoured the Web looking for hotels in Rome and found an astonishing amount of information: hundreds of Roman hotels had direct Web pages with photos, descriptions, and even email addresses. I narrowed my choices down to a few hotels and then posted on* rec.travel.europe *asking for comments and/or suggestions.*
>
> *I got about 20 emails from all over the U.S. and the world. Based on the information people provided, I made a reservation at the Hotel Julia and I feel very confident that we will love it.*
>
> *In addition, almost everyone gave me other great tips for visiting Rome, ranging from restaurant suggestions to coffee-ordering etiquette to bus information to where to visit stray cats in Rome!*
>
> *One caveat: I rarely, if ever, take advice off the Internet as gospel—I do check out the information. But most times it's quite obviously good information. For example, La Residenza got consistent rave reviews from people in very disparate locations (New Zealand, Sweden, and Louisiana!)—so I figured that it must be a pretty good hotel.*

Ami chose Hotel Julia over La Residenza because it offered a better price and was three blocks closer to the city center. After selecting the hotel, she logged on again and used email to negotiate a discount rate. Here's a copy of the email that Ami sent to Hotel Julia:

```
I would like information on your rates for 2
persons arriving this Nov 21, departing Nov 27. We
require a room with a private shower, and prefer a
queen bed if possible. Do you have any specials for
us? Here are some reasons to give us a lower price:

1) we found you on the Web

2) we will stay for 6 nights during low tourist
   season
```

3) we are staying over a weekend

4) we are very nice!

Thank you, I hope to hear from you soon!

Aware that hotels frequently offer discounts during less busy seasons, Ami used the fact that she found the hotel on the Web as a bargaining point. This shows that the novelty of a Net connection hasn't worn off—the proprietors may feel that they and Ami are part of the same community (because they're all on the Net), and thus be more inclined to offer her a discount.

> They wrote back and offered 190,000 (Lira) per night (about $125) instead of the standard rate of 220,000. I then wrote back and said I'd guarantee with a credit card that day if they offered 170,000 per night. They did, I did, end of story. I was then in contact with them periodically before we left with little questions like "Do you have hair dryers in the rooms" (answer: yes), "Do you have irons available for guests to use" (yes), etc. They were very responsive and helpful via email. I found that very useful.

Another hotel that Ami had considered didn't have email, which made her less inclined to stay there. In trying to make arrangements at this other hotel, "I had to call or fax, which was a real pain given the time zone differences and the lack of ability to fax personal international communications on my university business account." So hotel operators who may be wondering why they should get online can see that simply having an email connection can lead to booking rooms.

SEVERAL SATISFIED CUSTOMERS

Technology consultant Barry Campbell was recently invited to London to attend the wedding of a friend. He decided to book his airline tickets offline through a consolidator, and used the AltaVista search engine to come up with a list of hotels that fit his criteria. Then Barry asked for advice in the newsgroup *rec.travel.europe*.

> I was deluged with responses. "Try these folks; avoid those folks like the plague." In less than 48 hours of private email follow-up, I had my solution: the Hotel Julius Caesar (et tu, Brute?) in Queens Gardens, London W2. Spitting distance from Hyde Park. Two blocks from a tube stop. $85 a night. Several satisfied customers.

PERSONAL ACCOUNT
Barry Campbell
barry@webveranda.com

These two accounts represent a pattern repeated by many Web travelers. First they go to Yahoo, AltaVista, or some other broad-based search directory and find a listing of sites that apply to their destination. Then, based on their criteria, they select a few strong possibilities. Once they have a short list, for example, five hotels in Paris, they go to the appropriate newsgroup (*rec.travel.europe* in this case) and post a query asking about these places. Other travelers use the online conference areas of leading hotel and travel sites to get feedback about the hotels they're considering. Using the helpful comments from travelers who participate in these online discussions, they make a selection.

ADVICE FROM NEWSGROUPS

Another way to generate leads for finding a hotel is to begin your search by posting an open newsgroup query, like this traveler's post to *rec.travel.europe*, seeking:

```
A nice, moderately priced hotel (in Paris) that I
could stay at for just one night. St. Germain des
Pres would be a nice neighborhood. Has anyone had
experience with the Hotel des Grandes Ecoles? Or
others. Just a relaxing evening, a nice walk, and a
good meal before the early departure back to the
States and parental responsibilities.
```

Another traveler saw this post and responded:

```
My wife and I stayed at the Abatiale St. Germain at
the corner of Blvd. St. Germain and Rue Des
Bernardins. Small but comfortable room at 580FF per
night double. Breakfast is 45FF, but there are
plenty of places to eat nearby. Location is 1+
block from Notre Dame.
```

After seeking responses in a newsgroup, you can look for other resources, such as a hotel's Web page, that more fully describe the place and provide contact and reservation information.

As we'll see in Chapter 8, the more specific and detailed your request, the more likely you'll get a response containing helpful advice. Remember that broad, general questions ("Where should I stay on my trip to France?") are very time consuming to answer. Show that you've done some work on your own and then ask specific questions ("Can anyone recommend a hotel in Paris near the Louvre, preferably for under $100 a night?").

BED AND BREAKFASTS: HOMES AWAY FROM HOME

The low cost of Web site advertising has led large numbers of bed and breakfast inns to get online. B&Bs tend to be shoestring operations that can't afford expensive international advertising or co-marketing arrangements. And the quality of B&B lodgings can vary greatly, meaning travelers tend to gamble when they book a B&B they've never seen. So the Net serves guests as well, allowing them to preview inns before booking. There are now dozens of guides online to help travelers find B&Bs in almost any region or country. Most include photos of individual rooms and even bathroom facilities. For travelers who worry about such things, Web sites that include color photos of the rooms and inns can be a reassuring bonus.

USING B&B DIRECTORIES

Alan and Cynthia Dowdy publish Along the Way (*http://www.flinthills. com/~atway*), an online guide to bed and breakfasts in the midwestern U.S. The site lists B&Bs in 12 states and includes links to relevant regional travel sites and even recipes, such as Blueberry Stuffed French Toast from the Finnish Heritage Homestead (*http://www. flinthills.com/~atway/mn/finnish.html*) in Embarrass, Minnesota. (Yes, there is a town in Minnesota called Embarrass—and, while we're on the subject, there's also a town in Oregon called Boring and one in California called Cool, where temperatures often top 100 degrees in the summer.)

Alan and Cynthia Dowdy
Along the Way: Bed & Breakfast and Inns Directory
atway@pop.flinthills.com
http://www.flinthills.com/ ~atway

FIGURE 3-1
Iowa's Calmar Guesthouse B&B (http://www.flinthills.com/~atway/ia/calmar.html) is listed in the Along the Way guide.

The Dowdys turned to the Net recently to find a B&B in Montana for their summer vacation. They used a search directory to look for Montana bed and breakfasts and sought regional information by typing *Montana state*. Alan and Cynthia were seeking accommodations near Yellowstone, which they could find in the Montana Bed & Breakfast Association Directory (*http://www.wtp.net:80/go/montana/ directory.html*). This site has a map of the state divided into four sections. Click on the southwest section (the area nearest Yellowstone) and on the town-by-town listing for Yellowstone Riverview Lodge in Emigrant, Montana. The Dowdys were able to learn that the lodge is 20 miles from the national park. They could also see a color photo of the inn, seasonal rates, arrival and checkout times, and activities ranging from fly fishing to "fine dining at Chico Hot Springs."

Another selection was the Paradise Gateway Bed and Breakfast, 15 miles from Yellowstone. At Paradise's own site (*http://www.wtp.net/ go/paradise/*), the couple could view several images of the main lodge, a private log cabin, and nearby fishing streams.

Thin B&B marketing budgets have combined with the Net's ability to build communities of mutual interests. Paradise Gateway's site, like many other B&B sites, provides links to other B&B operations in other parts of the country. For example, Paradise offers links to B&Bs located around Glacier National Park. Linking to one another's Web sites is an inexpensive way B&Bs can reach their prime customer base. The Dowdys include links to other B&B sites in their Along the Way guide.

InnSite

http://www.insite.com

Bed and breakfast directory

To get a broad overview of the B&B world, you can stop at InnSite (*http://www.innsite.com*), where you can browse among the thousands of B&Bs or search for B&Bs by region. B&B owners who want to add their establishment to the list need only click on Add Entry and fill out the on-screen form. InnSite focuses on the U.S. and Canada, but also has listings for inns in Japan, Australia, Bulgaria, and Slovakia. InnSite's main page has links to email discussion groups on innkeeping and to the *rec.travel.bed+breakfast* newsgroup.

USING NEWSGROUPS FOR B&B ADVICE

A few weeks before heading to Montreal for a long weekend, Jayanthi Subramaniam posted to the newsgroup *rec.travel.bed+breakfast* asking for recommendations for a B&B with easy access to the Metro and to local sights. Later the same day, Diane Schmolka responded that Jayanthi could find what he wanted at Montreal Oasis Bed &

Breakfast, where she and her husband had stayed over Easter. Diane first saw the inn listed in a brochure, but went to the Net "to get a real picture of the home. I really liked what I saw, so we phoned, and the rest is history!"

"It is spacious, well appointed, reasonable, with great gourmet breakfasts," she wrote in her email message to Jayanthi. The inn is "near the Metro, has good shopping, and a great view. It's close to the Montreal Museum of Fine Arts, McGill University, etc. We liked it so much that when relatives visited from the Czech Republic, they stayed there for several nights before visiting us in Ottawa. I thoroughly recommend it. We will definitely return there several times this year. Lena tends to get booked early, so reserve as far ahead as you can." Lena Blondel, owner of Montreal Oasis, says about 15 percent of her business now comes through Internet referrals.

Tim Kloth of Naperville, Illinois, posted to *rec.travel.bed+breakfast* before heading to Indianapolis for a long weekend. "We like quiet places, not too large. We have found that when you get to around 12 rooms or larger, you start to lose the personal feeling," he wrote. One responder recommended a small place called the Camelot, but a local resident quickly warned that Camelot had gotten a *lot* smaller recently—it had just gone out of business.

The Dowdys suggested that Tim take a look at listings in Along the Way and Laura Arnold, owner of the Hoffman House in Indianapolis, jumped in and offered to provide information about her establishment. Like many posts to Usenet groups, Laura's message is courteous and doesn't attempt a hard sell.

> Just thought I would let you know that Camelot is no longer operating as a bed and breakfast, but the owner did publish a wonderful book about her experiences with her guests and yes, her camels. I can't remember the exact title of the book at the moment, but if anyone is interested I can find out with a quick phone call. There has been a healthy turn-over with B&Bs here in Indianapolis—inns closing and new inns opening. I would be happy to provide additional information.

B&B-related newsgroups represent a wonderful marketing opportunity for B&B operators. Though it is considered very bad form to overtly advertise in newsgroups, it is perfectly acceptable to cruise them and answer direct queries. Say you operate a B&B in Nevada's gold country and someone posts a query asking for B&B

America's Best Bed & Breakfasts, Country Inns, and Small Hotels
http://www.virtualcities.com/ ~virtual/ons/0onsadex.htm

Check out this site, another excellent online resource.

Yahoo's B&B Directories
http://www.yahoo.com/ Business_and_Economy/ Companies/Travel/Lodging/ Bed_and_Breakfasts/ Directories/

Yahoo's extensive list of B&B directories ranges from the Oregon Bed & Breakfast Directory (*http://www.moriah.com/ inns/*) to Gay Key West Accommodations (*http://206.55.47.90/ accommod.html*).

recommendations in your area. Go ahead and introduce yourself as an innkeeper and describe your establishment. If you do so, offer other recommendations including places to dine and sights to see in the area. And be honest about who you are.

HOME EXCHANGES

If you don't like sharing a house with others, maybe an entire house to yourself is more your style. If you are planning on an extended stay in a particular town or region, and own your own home, consider a home exchange. Over the Net, travelers can exchange pictures of their homes, discuss terms, and seal a deal in just a few days, giving new life to what had been a relatively small niche travel market. The problem had always been making complicated matches between, say, the couple living in the south of France who want to spend three months in San Francisco, and a homeowner there who wants to stay in France for same three months. The Internet helps prospective home swappers find one another and exchange information to make a deal. So home exchange sites are doing a brisk business.

Ed Bello used the International Home Exchange Network (*http:// www.homexchange.com/*) to trade his place in Maui for a house in Atlanta during the 1996 Olympic Games. Because he lived in Maui, a desirable destination, he figured he could find a place for trade in Atlanta, even during the Olympics. But he didn't want just any place— he wanted a clean, comfortable, spacious house.

While searching for information about home exchanges, Ed "just stumbled" upon the IHEN.

The International Home Exchange Network
http://www.homexchange. com/

It's free to browse listings on this site. To list your home costs $29.95 a year.

So I listed my place and began browsing through the listings for Atlanta. I saw about 10 places. Some home listings included photos. I picked four or five that looked interesting and sent email to those people asking them to respond. After hearing back from them, I narrowed it down to two.

Turns out that one of the two also requested my place in Maui. Once we got a link established we communicated three or four times through email. By the time we picked up the phone the deal was almost done. He's busy—I'm busy. Using email was efficient; I was pretty impressed. So I got to see the Olympics and he got to escape the madness.

Linda Allen of Orlando, Florida, wanted to arrange a home exchange in 1993 and asked a Net-savvy friend if there was a bulletin board

FIGURE 3-2

You can temporarily swap homes with people throughout the world through the International Home Exchange Network (http://www. homexchange.com).

system for home exchanges. When she learned that there wasn't, she founded IHEN as a BBS and took it onto the Web in 1995.

"I'd seen only five Web sites when I started designing ours," says Linda. "I considered having someone else design it, but decided to do it myself so I could make updates."

Most IHEN members used to subscribe to thick books that listed homes available for exchange, she says. To reach potential home exchangers overseas, "they'd spend over $50 in postage and would have to wait weeks for an answer." Following up on the phone would cost a lot more money, she added. With IHEN, users can browse the listings, and if they see something they like, they can send email and get a response the same day. Another advantage is that IHEN is much more current than a book that's published annually, and if you need to make a change, such as saying your home will be available in July instead of August, you can do that quickly and easily.

Carl Bauer has been using online home exchange services for three years and says the advantages of swapping online go beyond saving time and money. "Mutual screening can take place by interested parties, and a potential exchanger has a computer, knows how to write well, and can be checked if desired through directory sources." Reading between the lines, Carl is saying that most online home exchangers are professionals, and therefore he has more confidence that they'll respect his home. Access to a computer, however, doesn't guarantee that the person on the other end is reputable. So, as in other areas of Net-initiated agreements, be sure to thoroughly investigate prospective home exchangers before giving them the keys to your castle.

If you list your home on IHEN and send a photo along, IHEN will scan it and place it with your listing. You can include links to your personal home page and insert a direct email link. IHEN also lists hospitality exchange, where travelers stay with you while you're at home in exchange for your staying with them in the future. If you can't work out a home exchange, you can use IHEN to list your place as a vacation rental to earn some money rather than leave your house vacant. This can be helpful if you have pets that need feeding or a garden that needs tending. Or you can host travelers in your home for a mutually agreeable fee.

Some services, such as the Travel Exchange Club (*http://www.travex. com/travex/home.html*), don't charge to list your house, but this site has fewer listings than IHEN. As our print deadline approached, Yahoo listed more than twenty home exchange sites. To see this list, visit *http://www.yahoo.com/Business_and_Economy/Companies/Travel/ Lodging/Home_Exchange/*.

SPECIALTY HOMESTAYS

Specialty home exchange listing services are springing up on the Web. The Jewish Travel Network (*http://www.jewish-travel-net.com/*) helped a young Jewish woman from South Africa traveling through South America find kosher homes in Lima and Buenos Aires. A businessman who had to travel during Yom Kippur, the most important Jewish holiday of the year, sought a Jewish home in Lisbon to observe the holiday. Through these specialty services, travelers with common backgrounds or interests can connect through the Net and make arrangements to meet one another.

HOSTELS: NET TIPS FOR AFFORDABLE LODGING

In the old days, budget travelers got recommendations for hostels from one another, as they sat in the common rooms of their $10-a-night hostel. Or they followed—in sheep-like fashion—the gospel of Lonely Planet. Today the common room is larger; in fact, it encompasses the entire globe. Through the Net, budget travelers can evaluate different hostels by using sites that index and rate hostels, and then they can hit the sites' conference areas or hostel-related newsgroups to find good, cheap lodgings.

Johns Hopkins grad student Sandeep Gupta was planning a trip to Switzerland for a week-long conference and scheduled a few days afterwards to explore the famed Alpine countryside. In an index of European hostels (that went belly-up in late 1996), Sandeep found dozens of listings for Swiss hostels. But Sandeep says the most valuable tips came from the eight people who responded to a query he posted to the newsgroup *rec.travel.europe*.

These direct email responses were "extremely useful," he says, because they provided him with names and phone numbers for places recommended by travelers who had recently stayed at the hostels. "Like me, most were students on a limited budget," Sandeep says. For a place to stay in Interlaken "everyone recommended Balmer's" (Balmer's Herberge, *http://www.hostelwatch.com/hostels/balmers.html*). Others went beyond recommending hostels and suggested activities Sandeep could enjoy while visiting, such as parasailing near Interlaken.

Had Sandeep wanted further confirmation that Balmer's was the place to go, he could have done a bit more investigation on the Web. "Balmer's is awesome," says Hostels Europe. And a Yahoo search led to a site called Europe's Famous 5 Hostels (*http://www.hostelwatch. com/hostels/famous5.html*), where Balmer's is listed alongside such legends as Amsterdam's The Flying Pig (*http://www.hostelwatch.com/ hostels/flyingpig.html*) and Edinburgh's High Street Hostel (*http://www. hostelwatch.com/hostels/highstreet.html*).

TIP

To find hostels, see The Internet Guide to Hosteling (*http://www.hostels.com*) or American Youth Hostels (*http://www.iyhf.org*).

As seasoned budget travelers will tell you, not every hostel is sweetness and light. Unhappy travelers are using the Net to post all-points bulletins on notorious hostels. To help you avoid ending up at a hellhole, Hostels Europe (*http://www.eurotrip.com/*) has a Worst Hostels Europe link listing readers' accounts of nightmares they hope never to revisit.

"Noise, noise, and more noise. Lukewarm showers and skimpy breakfasts make this place very memorable for all the wrong reasons," writes one contributor about a hostel in Venice. Describing a hostel on the island of Crete, one traveler writes: "There were bugs in the beds, no windows, no working plumbing, and inhospitable owner/employees." He also complained that the proprietor had demanded his passport to keep during his stay. A Canadian writing about the same place said the hostel is "truly terrible. The thing about the passport is entirely accurate. When I refused to hand it over, instead of just asking me to leave, this crazy Irishman who works for George punched me in the head. I was back in Canada about two months before I got rid of the rash from the bed-bug bites."

While the hostels in Venice and Crete sound bad, none was scarier than a Budapest hostel described by a Canadian visitor. "This place is filthy, smells of stinky feet and urine, has weird guys sleeping in the halls as a result of its 'never full' policy, and is basically what would happen to your home if you let 100 freshmen live there full-time with no supervision."

HOSTEL CENTRAL

Enlighten Yourself: The Travelite FAQ

http://www.Solutions.Net/ rec-travel/general/ travelite-faq.html

If you're carrying your own bags, you may want to explore this site, featuring a load of tips about how to take what you need without weighing yourself down.

If you're planning to stay at hostels, a good place to get some familiarity with hosteling is the Internet Guide to Hosteling (*http://www. hostels.com*). In addition to listing thousands of hostels around the world, the site includes a hosteling FAQ, a conferencing area where you can ask questions or share your experiences, and reviews of budget guidebooks. In the Common Room, there are discussions of interest to budget travelers, such as "Things to Do in London that Are Free." A section called Going Places offers tips for budget travelers such as "Drive Someone Else's Car—for Free" (no, this is not a quick course in how to hot-wire a car) and "A Safer Way to Hitch-Hike," which discourages sticking out your thumb and suggests using college ride boards and hostel bulletin boards.

Another extensive hostel site is Hostelling International and American Youth Hostels (*http://www.iyhf.org*). This site lists more than 5,000 hostels in 77 countries. Find what you need by clicking on a region—California, for example—and seeing a list of links. Clicking on Point Reyes, you'll find a 44-bed hostel that costs $10-12 a night, has a room available for families, and never closes (except during the day, of course).

PARKS AND CAMPGROUNDS

The ever-increasing cost of room and board has led more and more travelers to consider camping, from pitching a tent in a national park to rolling across the U.S. in a self-contained RV. Even without financial necessity, camping is often the best way to gain a true appreciation of a place: to sleep out under the stars, fill your lungs with fresh mountain air, and warm up in the morning to a pot of cowboy coffee simmering over a campfire. It's not for everybody, but those who prefer camping or choose it as a cheap way to travel will find the Net a powerful planning tool.

Millions of people camp in U.S. national parks each year. If you're planning to be one of them, take a look at the National Park Service (*http://www.nps.gov/*) site. While the layout is a little awkward (this is a government site, after all), go to Visit Your Parks (*http://www.nps.gov/parks.html*) or find the park you plan to visit by using the search feature. The parks area has links ranging from Select by State Map to Campground Reservation Information.

National Park Service
http://www.nps.gov/

Before a recent trip to Joshua Tree National Park (in the southern California desert), I visited the NPS site and found information about campgrounds and hiking trails. While these sites are good for basic information, don't expect detailed descriptions. Campers can find more complete information at the Great Outdoor Recreation Pages (GORP) section on parks (*http://www.gorp.com/gorp/resource/US_National_Park/main.htm*). GORP's main page (*http://www.gorp.com*) is a superb resource for anyone interested in hiking information, adventure stories, or outdoor gear.

Great Outdoor Recreation Pages (GORP)
http://www.gorp.com
Park listings and camping information.

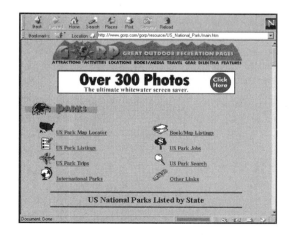

FIGURE 3-3
The Great Outdoor Recreation Pages (http://www.gorp.com) offer listings for national parks.

Campground Directory
*http://www.holipub.com/
camping/director.htm*
Private campground listings.

The GORP park area includes a locator map, parks listed by region, international parks, and related links. For private campgrounds, see the Campground Directory (*http://www.holipub.com/camping/director.htm*). This site lists more than 12,000 U.S. campgrounds, many with links to Web pages. Search by the campground's name, city, state, or zip code. Or browse the listing by clicking first on the state you plan to visit. If you have a camping-related question, post it in the Campground Directory's chat area.

One camper posted a query searching for a family campground for beginning campers in Wisconsin with electricity and hot showers. "Prefer to be near body of water. Don't need busy shopping/tourist stuff near-by. Bike trails a big plus."

Someone identifying himself only as "Ken" responded, recommending River-of-Lakes just south of Bagley, Wisconsin, "located on Mississippi River with rental boats, very clean showers, and few campers during week." Another camper, who had ventured from Ohio to camp in Wisconsin, suggested Westward Ho, "a neat place in Door County clear at the tip with a beach within walking distance and far enough from the tourists that you won't know they are around."

For a trip to the White Mountains, I clicked on New Hampshire and found a link to the New Hampshire Campground Owners Association (*http://www.tiac.net/users/oline/U_Camp_NH/*). It included information on boating, hunting, and fishing in New Hampshire, as well as a state campground directory. In the directory, clicking on White Mountains Region served up an image of a mountain-peak view and information on the area. I planned to hike up the mountain, but wondered what would happen if I petered out halfway up. Checking the site carefully I learned that I could take a cable car, gondola, or even the cog railway accessible from several points along the way.

A campground called the Cove Camping Area looked intriguing (*http://www.tiac.net/users/oline/U_Camp_NH/coveindex.html*), so I clicked on it and saw it really is by a lake, "with 1,900 feet of lake frontage" and has free hot showers. The site lists daily fees and provides a map with directions to the campground. Before the widespread use of the Net, this type of information was difficult to find—campers had to either call to request brochures, or fly blind and hope to find a decent campsite at the end of the road.

DINING ON THE ROAD

Travelers have differing opinions about what makes a good restaurant. Some people love California cuisine, with its delicate little portions presented as if the plate were a canvas and the food was the paint. Others want plenty to eat, a big burrito or a plateful of spaghetti, and they're not too concerned about presentation. So a recommendation from one person or one guidebook may not be enough information to make an informed decision. By using the tools available on the Net, however, travelers can get opinions from lots of people. They can examine online dining guides to see what a restaurant offers, seek recommendations in newsgroups where they can say what they like, and in some cases visit a restaurant's home page to get a better idea of what it offers and at what price. When they pick a restaurant, they can use mapping sites to locate it. And if they have a type of restaurant in mind, they can use sites such as MapQuest to check for all the restaurants of that type in a neighborhood.

WEB PAGE RESTAURANT GUIDES

Dining guides on the Web range from local to international. It's wise to sample more than one guide because different dining guides have different strengths. And the value of the Net here, as in other areas, is that it offers access to a world of people who can give recommendations on where to dine. Some cities even have Usenet newsgroups devoted solely to dining in a specific city. For example, *tor.eats* covers Toronto. Even if you're not traveling, these resources can be an excellent tool to find restaurants in your hometown that suit your tastes and wallet.

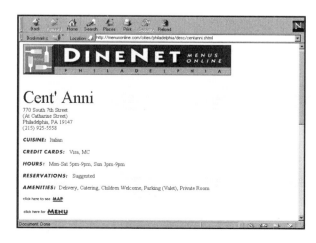

FIGURE 3-4
Philadelphia's Cent' Anni is listed on DineNet (http://menusonline.com).

DineNet

http://www.menusonline. com

Listings of U.S. restaurants.

DineNet (*http://www.menusonline.com*) covers restaurants in the U.S. To find a place for lunch in Marin County (across the Golden Gate Bridge from San Francisco), you could click on the San Francisco regional icon, then click on Marin County, where you'll find Sam's Anchor Cafe. From DineNet's page on Sam's, you'll learn the restaurant specializes in seafood, has outdoor seating by the bay, and that reservations are not needed for the weekend brunch.

If it's professional culinary opinion you want, visit the Essential Restaurant Guide, part of the Epicurious site (*http://www.epicurious. com/e_eating/e03_restguide/guide.html*), with reviews of restaurants in 10 major U.S. cities.

For another perspective, see *Bon Appetit* magazine's online reviews (*http://www.epicurious.com/b_ba/b01_index/b01index.html#rest*). A recent feature highlighted the restaurants of Portland, recommending, among others, Typhoon. "No gloppy peanut sauce or mindlessly hot seasonings here; this is Thai food the way you have always wished it would taste." *Bon Appetit* also offers recipes from the editors' favorite restaurants. Readers can voice their opinions in the Restaurant Roundtable, "a forum for praising the praiseworthy and basting the turkeys."

Another way to find specialty restaurants is through online yellow pages, such as BigBook (*http://www.bigbook.com*). On the main page, I entered *Greek restaurant Philadelphia* and within five seconds had three listings for Greek places there. I clicked on the link to the Greek Village Taverna, found its address and phone, and pinpointed it on the map provided. (You can zoom in and out with this map to get a better idea of where the restaurant is.) While BigBook doesn't

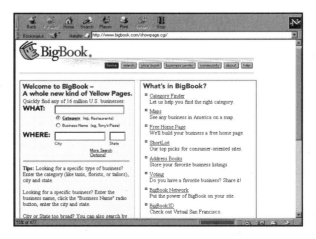

FIGURE 3-5

Big Book (http://www.bigbook.com) helps you find any of the millions on business in the U.S.

provide reviews, it's easy to use and is a good way to get an idea of what's out there. (It's also a good tool to search for hotels.)

USING LOCAL NEWSPAPERS TO FIND RESTAURANTS

One of the best sources for restaurant recommendations are local newspapers, such as the major metropolitan dailies or the alternative weeklies. To find local newspapers, try Newspapers Online (*http:// www.newspapers.com*), which has links to hundreds of newspapers in the U.S. and beyond.

To find an Italian restaurant in Los Angeles, I visited Newspapers Online and scrolled down to California, where I found links to the *Los Angeles Times* and the *L.A. Weekly*. Going to the *Weekly*, I clicked on L.A. Dining and selected Italian from the menu listing types of cuisine. I then clicked on View Restaurants and got a list of about 15 choices from throughout L.A. Each restaurant listed is linked to a review by a *Weekly* critic.

Newspapers Online
http://www.newspapers. com

Links to hundreds of newspapers on the Net.

SEARCHING FOR RESTAURANTS

As usual, you can begin your search for a restaurant directory or dining establishment from a major Web directory such as Yahoo. A Yahoo search (type in *New Orleans AND Restaurants*) for New Orleans restaurants, for example, turns up sites such as Ed Branley's New Orleans Virtual Dining Guide (*http://www.yatcom.com/neworl/dining/ resttop.html*).

Like many people in New Orleans, Ed takes dining seriously. "In New York, eating is something you do before or after the play.

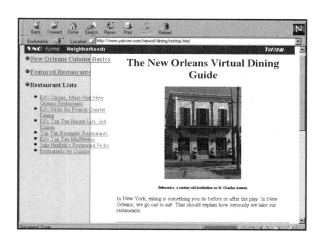

FIGURE 3-6
Delmonico, a century-old institution on St. Charles Avenue, is featured on the New Orleans Virtual Dining Guide (http://www.yatcom.com/neworl/dining/ resttop.html).

In New Orleans, we go *out* to eat. That should explain how seriously we take our restaurants." The guide includes Ed's Classic Must-Visit New Orleans Restaurants, such as Ed's Picks for the French Quarter, including Johnny's Po-Boys. A brief review follows: "Classic New Orleans Po-Boys. 'Nuff said."

TIP

Sushi lovers who want to find good sushi wherever they travel should see John Maraist's World Wide Sushi Restaurant Reference (*http://wwwipd.ira.uka.de/~maraist/Sushi/*) or the Usenet newsgroup *alt.food.sushi*.

WORD OF MOUTH

First-hand restaurant recommendations can also be ferreted out in chat rooms or conference areas in online services, such as AOL or CompuServe. Paul and Kay Henderson, proprietors of Gidleigh Park Hotel and Restaurant in Devon, England, were planning to visit Charleston, South Carolina, and wanted some suggestions for fine restaurants there. So Paul posted his questions in CompuServe forums on wine, food, and cooks, as well as in the *rec.food.restaurant* Usenet group.

> *In three days I had about 15 replies, including one invitation to dine with people, which I have accepted because they mentioned that we have mutual friends. Most of the other respondents mentioned three specific restaurants, so I have made reservations at two of them. I've already booked Magnolia's and Louis's by phone, because they were in the top five of almost everyone who replied.*

The most reliable restaurant advice usually comes through personal recommendations, and the Net has made it easy for people in one region to advise restaurant-goers throughout the world. Like many in the Internet community, Paul is as interested in sharing good advice as he is in acquiring it. A link from his home page (*http://www.gidleigh.com*) leads to "Paul and Kay's Favourite Restaurant Sites," a personal evaluation of some of the top dining establishments in New York, Paris, Sydney, Scotland, Venice, and West England.

FOR TRAVELERS WITH SPECIAL DIETS

Some travelers, such as vegetarians, have special dietary needs. In planning a trip to Paris with a vegetarian friend, Rik Ahlberg relied on the World Guide to Vegetarianism (*http://www.veg.org/veg/Guide/*). The guide has sections on Europe, the U.S., Canada, and Australia. Following the links to Paris, travelers can find a selection of more than a dozen choices, such as La Truffe, described as "a fashionable new place trying to bring the concept of upmarket dining to vegetarian food. Seasonal dishes using wild mushrooms are a specialty." The listing includes the address, phone, hours, and even the Metro (subway) line that goes to the restaurant.

World Guide to Vegetarianism
http://www.veg.org/veg/ Guide/index.html
Veggie restaurants throughout the world.

If you're an AOL member, try the Food and Drink Network (keyword: *FDN*) to see restaurant reviews or to find a dining companion (who knows, you may be traveling alone and enjoy the company). Other AOL sources for good restaurant information are Dining a la Card (keyword: *D a la Card*) and DineBase (from the AOL main page, go to travel and click on DineBase), with its searchable database of restaurants and brewpubs.

Other travelers have religious considerations. For those who require strictly kosher dining, the Net is—pardon the pun—a Godsend. For a trip to Chicago, check Kosher Eating in Chicago (*http://condor. depaul.edu/~scohn/NTJC-Fd.html*) and find listings ranging from the traditional-sounding Jerusalem Kosher Restaurant to Mi Tsu Yun (even the orthodox have to eat on Sunday night) to Bagel Country in Skokie. For broader searches, try Koshernet (*http://www.koshernet. com*) or Shamash's Kosher Restaurant Database (*shamash.nysernet.org/ kosher/krestquery.html*).

AN EXCELLENT PLACE OFF THE BEATEN TRACK

When searching for restaurants, don't overlook the Usenet newsgroups. Although some of these areas have become more crowded recently, they are still good sources of information and offer the most personal type of recommendation.

When Rob Lake and his wife were planning a 15-hour drive from their home in Cleveland Heights, Ohio, to visit their daughter at a camp in Maine, they turned to Usenet's restaurant newsgroups for advice.

PERSONAL ACCOUNT
Rob Lake
rbl@po.cwru.edu

Found an excellent place off the beaten track in Syracuse, just right for both parents and kid. Going back up to pick up the daughter a month later, we took the other two kids. We detoured to a recommended clam shack on Cape Ann north of Boston.

Rob has used newsgroups ranging from *nyc.food* to *alt.food.barbeque*. If you're not sure which newsgroups have the restaurant information you're seeking, try visiting DejaNews (*http://www.dejanews.com*), enter keywords in the Interests box and click on Find. For example, by entering the phrase *Los Angeles restaurant* I found the newsgroup *la.eats*.

GUMBO ONLINE

For a trip to New Orleans, Robert Buxbaum stuck his virtual spoon into the Gumbo Pages (*http://www.gumbopages.com*) written by New Orleans native and culinary expert Chuck Taggart. Buxbaum downloaded the restaurant recommendations page (*http://www. gumbopages.com/no-rest.html*) and then followed up by sending email to Taggart asking for some specific advice.

Welcoming people to his site, Chuck tells people just what they want to hear: "Remember that in Louisiana, alcohol, butter, cream, and big piles of fried seafood are still good for you."

This highlights another advantage of using the Net for travel: authors and experts are much more accessible. If Robert had bought a printed guide to dining in New Orleans, he probably would have had a much tougher time connecting with the author and getting responses to his questions. Another huge advantage is that online

FIGURE 3-7

Get a taste of gumbo on the Web on the Gumbo Pages (http://www.gumbopages.com).

guides can link to related sites, and the Gumbo Pages link to Web pages on Mardi Gras, a lesson in Yat speak (the local tongue), even weather at the New Orleans Weather Page.

Whatever your pleasure, from prime rib in New York to king crab in Alaska, you can probably get a virtual taste of it on the Net, as well as recommendations to make sure you don't waste your dining dollars on places that don't measure up.

Now that we've all eaten and gotten a good night's sleep, on to using the Net to find the best travel bargains.

Finding the
Best Deals

4

Travel bargains come in two forms: sale-priced trips and last-minute deals designed to sell unfilled seats or tour slots. You can find sales in the newspaper, but the Net's ability to instantly and cheaply transmit news of travel deals makes it the ideal tool for publicizing last-minute bargains. By spending just a few minutes browsing Web sites or posting to newsgroups, you can save yourself a bundle. But remember, not everything that's cheap is a bargain—be sure you're dealing with a reputable business before you buy.

▶ Deals for Cybertravelers

▶ Arthur Frommer's Outspoken Encyclopedia of Travel

▶ Budget Travel Sites

▶ Courier Flights: Travel Light, Travel Cheap

▶ Do It Yourself and Save

▶ An Online Advocate

DEALS FOR CYBERTRAVELERS

PERSONAL ACCOUNT

John Boman

jboman@netdepot.com

Experienced traveler John Boman of Woodstock, Georgia, knows airlines will do just about anything to keep their planes from flying with empty seats. So, to snag cheap tickets, he subscribes to an American Airlines' email list called NetSAAver Fares which advertises last-minute bargains. Each Wednesday, an email newsletter lets John know what cheap seats are available, on what flights, and to what destinations. The NetSAAver list includes discounted package tours as well; for example, the following was offered in late 1996 for $499: a roundtrip flight from New York to London, five nights in a "first-class" hotel, transfers from the airport to the hotel and back, and daily breakfast.

To subscribe to American's NetSAAver fares list, see the NetSAAver Web site (*http://www.americanair.com/aa_home/net_saavers.htm*). American Airlines' main page is at *http://www.americanair.com*. The NetSAAver list includes bargains on hotel rooms and rental cars from AA's partners, including Avis and Hilton.

On Travelocity (*http://www.travelocity.com*) John found a bargain flight to Halifax (capital of Nova Scotia, Canada) and used the Net to find a place to stay on nearby Cape Breton Island.

> *After I had my tickets in hand, I used my favorite search directory requesting Cape Breton and found a 120-year-old farmhouse where I could rent a room. The place was quite rustic, but it was clean and nicer than I expected. The owner's description was accurate. It would not be the right place for most people. The whole trip was cheap: $8 (U.S.) for a whole lobster meal in a restaurant!*

Cathay Pacific Cybertravelers

http://www.cathay-usa. com/

Auctions and special offers for registered members. No fee to join.

John also found a great deal at Cathay Pacific's site (*http://www.cathay-usa.com*). When he checked the site, he found an online offer for a roundtrip flight from New York to Hong Kong for under $800, a fare available only to Cathay's registered "Cybertravelers."

Another way to save on airfare is to take part in one of the growing number of online ticket auctions. Cathay recently auctioned enough seats to fill an entire Boeing 747 for passengers flying from New York or Los Angeles to Hong Kong. The bidding was silent, conducted through email and snail mail (standard postal service delivery).

Jane Nowlin, who describes herself as a "complete novice at using a computer," used the Net to discover a travel package that saved her

$130. She had first consulted her regular travel agent, but the agent didn't know about the deal that Jane found. "With Windows 95 and Netscape, even an old lady like me can learn to surf," Jane says. Through Epicurious Travel (*http://travel.epicurious.com/*), Jane found a bargain on an air/lodging package that included golf, one of her hobbies. "I printed the offer out and took it in to my agent," Jane says. "My agent had found a package which was about $65 per person more and did not include golf."

EXPEDIA'S FARE TRACKER

Microsoft's Expedia (*http://expedia.com*) offers Fare Tracker, an email notification service. You tell Fare Tracker which destinations you're interested in and it alerts you to bargains on those routes. So instead of getting a long list of bargain fares, you get a short, customized list with information only on the route that you're interested in.

Fare Tracker takes a different approach than American's NetSAAver program. Fare Tracker is designed for travelers who know where they want to go, whereas NetSAAver, by listing dozens of destinations, seems to be saying: "So, you have a free weekend coming up and want to travel somewhere cheap, why not see where you can go with us."

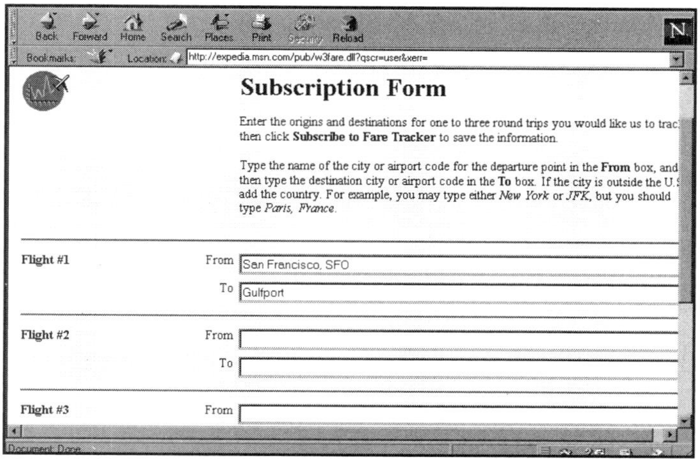

FIGURE 4-1
Expedia (http://expedia.com) can send you weekly email messages with the best deals to the places you're interested in traveling to.

LAST-MINUTE DEALS ON HOTEL ROOMS

Airlines are not the only companies using the Net to fill empty spaces. Hotels are offering eleventh-hour bargains for cybertravelers. TravelWeb (*http://www.travelweb.com*) recently began a program called Click-It! Weekends where it posts special, cut-rate weekend deals. And these are not at seedy motels; Hyatt and Sheraton are among the chains participating.

Click-It! Weekends

http://www.travelweb.com/ TravelWeb/clickit.html

Last-minute deals on fine hotel rooms.

"Click-it! Weekends captures the beauty of the Web," says Travel-Web's CEO John F. Davis III. "It's real-time and extremely flexible, enabling consumers to take advantage of last-minute deals for the coming weekend." Through this program, "hotels can take advantage of Net-based dynamic pricing and quickly respond to the ups and downs of consumer demand by posting their last-minute vacancies." In other words, if a hotel sees a period when it will have lots of empty rooms, it can cut rates on those rooms, advertise these specials on the Web, and bump up its occupancy rate. "It's a win-win situation," he says. "Travelers who can plan a trip with a couple days' notice can find new opportunities every week throughout the year by making the booking themselves in this special section of TravelWeb."

ONLINE TRAVEL AUCTIONS

Beginning in 1997, a new site on the Web hopes to redefine the online travel marketplace. The Electronic Travel Auction (*http://www. etauction.com*) calls itself "the world's first and only" independent facilitator of travel auctions designed to promote quality travel-related products and services to the traveling public at a price the market will bear.

FIGURE 4-2

Click-It! Weekends lists discount weekend rates on hotel rooms at leading chains such as Hyatt.

ETA operates three "channels"—one for travel suppliers to sell directly to consumers, one for consumers to sell or trade with other travelers, and a third for travel companies to sell to travel professionals such as travel agents. The more than 40 categories include "airline seats" and "safaris." ETA charges buyers a fee of 10 percent of their winning bid.

"ETA not only allows the distribution of perishable items at a price the market will bear, but the facility also is an excellent low-cost advertising and promotion medium for travel suppliers," says founder Mark Hawkins. "Our site is being designed to be entertaining by offering fun, friendly competition in an exciting real-time bidding environment."

Hawkins sees the site as an ideal way for travel suppliers to sell their inventory and for buyers to get extraordinary last-minute deals. Travel, like fresh produce, is "perishable," and an airline would rather sell a seat at half price than see it go empty, so ETA (and its inevitable imitators) will probably do a brisk business.

ARTHUR FROMMER'S OUTSPOKEN ENCYCLOPEDIA OF TRAVEL

Though new to the Web, Arthur Frommer is not new to online travel. He has maintained a large travel site on America Online for some time. This presented a dilemma: the best budget travel site on the Net—Arthur Frommer's Secret Bargains—was on AOL, but since AOL is a closed network, it was only available to AOL members.

In February 1997, Frommer launched his new travel Web site, Arthur Frommer's Outspoken Encyclopedia of Travel, thereby adding immeasurably to the Web's travel IQ.

Frommer's site includes the vast store of budget travel advice from his AOL site, a daily travel news section, and much more. The Outspoken Encyclopedia has "20 times the content" of Frommer's AOL area. During his years on AOL, Frommer shared his decades of travel experience with good humor and the sense of wonder that a traveler discovers on his or her first big trip.

The main focus of the Outspoken Encyclopedia is budget travel, with the daily news listings focusing on the latest travel specials. But Frommer does much more than list bargains—his writings offer insights that can help travelers become more knowledgeable, giving

Arthur Frommer's Outspoken Encyclopedia of Travel
http://www.frommer.com
or
http://www.frommers.com
Daily travel news and extensive budget travel information.

them the tools to negotiate or find a better deal. And if travelers find airfare deals they like, they can fill out a form at Frommer's site to book that fare. (The form is forwarded to a travel agent who arranges flights with the consolidators that offer these discounts.)

In the budget travel area of Frommer's Web site you'll find:

- **Airfare bargains and advice about consolidators**
  To help travelers get the cheapest flights, Frommer lists leading consolidators, cruise brokers, car rental discounters. Consolidators offer unpublished fares directly to consumers, typically for travel overseas.

- **Best package bargains, destinations, and cruises**
  How about spending a month in Spain, flights and hotel included, for under $1,000? This was one of the bargains in the Fall '96 list of specials on Frommer's site. Budget tips here included cheap trips to such exotic destinations as Bali, with its rich indigenous culture, and Costa Rica, with its abundant natural parks. In "Bargain of the Week," Frommer selects one great deal—the week I checked it was a week-long cruise for $399 aboard the deluxe Norwegian Crown. While I'd typically be wary of such a deal, Arthur Frommer's seal of approval virtually assures that it's really a bargain trip, not a scam.

- **Cheap, alternative travel**
  In a section called "Novel Travel," Frommer suggests spending some time at "intentional" communities, such as Sirius near Amherst, Massachusetts. In "America on $40 a day," Frommer traces what he calls the "Yoga Route," from California to the East Coast. "I am not a yogi," Frommer says, "and considering my feverish lifestyle, horrendous eating habits, and stubborn rationalism, that's the understatement of the year. But yogi or not, some of my happiest holidays have been spent on yoga retreats." In addition, you can discover secrets for daytrips in Glasgow, weekend bliss in Seattle, Mediterranean cruises, and much more.

TIP

Arthur Frommer hosts a monthly discussion on America Online. See his AOL site (keyword: *Arthur Frommer*) for details. If you aren't able to log on while the conference is happening, you can download the transcript from Frommer's Online Download Library in the Interactive Travel Center on AOL.

As this book went to press in February 1997, Frommer was in the process of adding to the Encyclopedia a section called "The 200 Places to Which People Go." This section will include lengthy, provocative, intensely judgmental write-ups of the 200 cities or islands accounting for 80 percent of all long-range travel, including critical discussions of 10 to 25 major hotels in each location, in all price ranges. The site is also adding a reservation engine to enable travelers to book airline tickets, hotel rooms, and car rentals.

BUDGET TRAVEL SITES

ETA and Frommer's are just a couple of the many sites for budget travelers. Following are some of the best sites on the Net for saving money on travel.

Shoestring Travel (*http://www.stratpub.com/*)

A virtual hostel where travelers trade tales to help one another save money. Shoestring also sifts the travel newsgroups to find the best suggestions for budget travel. Looking for a cheap place to stay? Click on Cheap Accommodation Listings, which lists budget hotels in New York, San Francisco, Boston, and France, as well as hostels around the world. On Shoestring's User Exchange Page, readers submit brief articles, such as "Thailand on $8 a Night," offering budget travel tips to fellow wanderers.

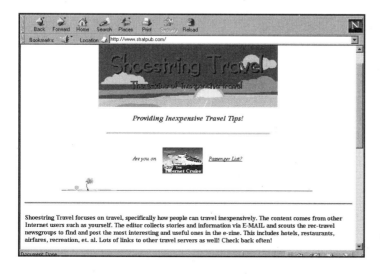

FIGURE 4-3

Shoestring is an e-zine of inexpensive travel.

American Express Travel (*http://www.americanexpress.com/travel/*)

Whether you're interested in a Mexican cruise or a tour through Spain, Amex's Vacation Specials "guarantee" that their prices are the lowest published fares. In this area you'll find escapes to sun-soaked beaches and to glittery Las Vegas (though by the time you leave you may not feel you've gotten a bargain). Last Minute Bargains offers air-fares for people who can take off on a dime (for example, Newark to London for $125, but there is a catch: you must purchase this ticket with your American Express card). Also includes a list of Amex travel offices around the world.

Budget Travel (*http://www.budgettravel.com/*)

Reams of listings for cheap flights around the world. In Travelog, travelers discuss how they survived while traveling on a tight bud-get—for example, where to find cheap guest houses on the Thai is-land of Phuket. Check BT's Message Board to get advice on where to find bargain air tickets, cheap lodging, or "the best site for backpack-ing" (*http://www.backpackers.com/*), according to at least one traveler.

Backpackers.com
http://www.backpackers.com

A leading source of information for backpackers.

1travel.com (*http://www.1travel.com/*)

A compendium of bargain airfares, cruises, and hotel rooms. With Consolidators Online, you get access to fares from more than 50 con-solidators throughout the world. Best fares on busy routes, such as Los Angeles to Tokyo, are posted. These compare favorably with sim-ilar fares in Sunday travel sections. You can use email to get quotes on any route you're interested in. This site has cruise bargains, adver-tised in a weekly email message. To receive this, fill out the form at *http://www.1travel.com/cruise.htm*. 1travel also claims discounts of 25 to 50 percent on more than 1,300 hotels in the U.S. and Canada. But when I compared 1travel's rate with the standard rate at San Fran-cisco's Clift Hotel, it was only about 15 percent lower.

Interactive Travel Guide (*http://www.developnet.com/travel/*)

This site started as "Clever Ways to Travel for Free or Little Cost," and while ITG has broadened its focus, it's still a good source for bargains, such as tips on where to change money in Europe or how to get a driveaway vehicle. Among the discounts offered are special deals for members of the American Association of Retired Persons.

Travel Deals (*http://www.travelassist.com/mag/a50.html*)

If you know where you're going, check Travel Assist's Travel Deals before you leave. This site lists dozens of deals on flights and packages, from the City Card for unlimited bus travel in Reykjavik to free cruises through Hawaii for children under 18 if they share a room with their parents.

Federal Discount Lodging Directory (*http://www.ios.com/hotels/hotels.html*)

State-by-state lists of hotels that offer discounts for federal employees. Military personnel are also eligible for these discounts.

Traveler Savings Site (*http://home.sprynet.com/sprynet/inetmktg/*)

Go to this frames-based site and click on Hot Deals, where you'll find specials such as Alamo coupon books, Radisson Hotel discounts, and last-minute deals from Continental. In the Absolutely Free section, you'll find free visitor guides and discount coupon books.

Council Travel (*http://www.ciee.org/travel.htm*)

Council Travel offers bargain tours, Eurail passes, rental cars and more. Here's a recent offering that tugged at my wallet: New York to Paris for $180 one-way, no student ID required.

COURIER FLIGHTS: TRAVEL LIGHT, TRAVEL CHEAP

If you're ready to travel on short notice and can travel light, consider becoming an air courier. Companies that need to get important documents or other valuables overseas hire individuals to carry their package to its destination. Sang Kwon, a student, wanted to visit a friend in Thailand he had met through the Net. Kwon had heard about inexpensive courier flights, but didn't know where to turn for more information, so he began his search in Yahoo's travel area.

Wouldn't you know it, there was a category for budget travel...right up my alley! After loading the budget travel site, I narrowed my search by choosing the Air Travel link and eventually landed on a site for a subscription newsletter that lists companies offering air courier services, destinations, and prices.

Initially, I thought that an air courier was something akin to Fed Ex or UPS—just for packages. And after seeing an example of some of the fares being offered, I truly thought it was a scam. So I investigated a bit more and found several articles (again, through the Net) written by Netizens and travel publications concerning air courier services.

From everything I read, air courier services seemed to be a dream come true for budget travelers like myself. And indeed, I was thoroughly satisfied with my air courier flight, especially knowing that I paid less than half of what everyone else on the plane paid for the very same flight. But the best part is that all this information was readily available and free on the Net.

On a courier flight, a traveler agrees to transport a package and gives up the baggage allowance. In exchange for this service, the courier gets to fly for a fraction of the cost of a coach ticket; in some instances, couriers fly free.

TIP

For information on courier flights, see Air Courier Travel, sponsored by the International Association of Air Travel Couriers (*http://www.courier.org*). Or try the Worldwide Courier Association (*http://www.wallstech.com/*), which answers commonly asked questions. The WCA site is probably the only budget travel site with a video clip of Robin Leach.

FIGURE 4-4

You can find amazingly low airfares on courier flights. The IAATC page (http://www.courier.org) has the latest courier fares.

DO IT YOURSELF AND SAVE

There are more ways to save money than finding cut-rate fares. Cutting the middleman out of the travel food chain is another way to save. This means doing at least some of the work that person was paid to do. But doing this work yourself allows you to save money on travel even when no special deals are available.

Think of it as getting paid a commission. A few travel agencies on the Web, such as Traveler's Net (*http://www.travelersnet.com*), will pay you up to 70 percent of its commission if you use their site to book your arrangements yourself. For example, on a $1,000 purchase that generates a $100 commission, you get to keep up to $70.

Traveler's Net, whose motto is "For people who know where they are going," maintains a mailing list called Fare Wars that sends email to subscribers to alert them when an airfare war begins. Fare Wars also includes a monthly roundup of cruise specials and package deals.

Other sites that reward travelers for booking it themselves are springing up all the time. TravelBids (*http://www.Travelbids.com/*), for example, is a site for people who know exactly what they want and feel comfortable booking it themselves. If you want the guidance of a travel agent, this site isn't for you. To save some money here, call the toll-free number of any airline or hotel and reserve your travel, but don't pay for it. Then list the trip on the TravelBids site. Travel agencies then bid on your trip— the agent that offers the lowest bid gets

Fare Wars Mailing List
Send email to:
majordomo@lists.usit.net
and write *subscribe
farewars end*–don't include
your email signature.

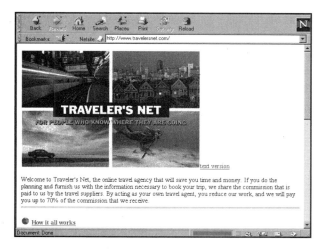

FIGURE 4-5

If you book through Traveler's Net (http://www.travelersnet.com), you earn the lion's share of the commission.

your business. So you get a discount rate and the agent gets a commission without doing much work. Because the agents don't have to spend much time arranging your travel, they refund part of the commission, adding to the savings. TravelBids promises at least a 6 percent discount.

The Savvier Traveler (*http://www.savtraveler.com/*), which specializes in cruise deals, offers consumers 10 percent off all bookings, even discounted cruises. Just like other travel suppliers, cruise lines pay a 10 percent commission for standard bookings, which the Savvy Traveler passes on to the consumer. So how does the Savvier Traveler make money? By charging a small fee for each booking, $50 for most transactions. If a couple purchases a $3,000 honeymoon cruise, they get $300 back and pay a $50 service fee, saving $250 overall. Not a bad deal.

TIP

The Net may not always be the way to get the best deals. At press time, most agents in the consolidator market remained largely off the Web. Consolidators are prohibited from publishing certain fares, so the only way to get these deals is to call a consolidator directly. The Sunday travel sections of major newspapers are good sources for finding consolidators.

AN ONLINE ADVOCATE

The Net offers hundreds of ways to purchase discount travel, but not every bargain is necessarily a good deal. On a cruise, that bargain-priced "Captain's Cabin" may be located next to the boiler room. Or that "beachfront" hotel may actually turn out to be half a mile from the shore.

When a bargain trip goes bad, the place to turn is Condé Nast Traveler (*http://travel.epicurious.com/travel/g_cnt*). Each week, the CNT's Ombudsman (click on Consumer Help) tackles a new set of disputes. Take the case of the woman whose friend was sexually assaulted at a resort in the Bahamas. Emergency personnel used her phone after the incident and the hotel billed her for the charges. When the woman complained, the hotel stonewalled her, until CNT's

Ombudsman started calling. Eventually, the resort agreed not to charge for the calls.

Whether you're looking for information that could help you resolve a grievance, trying to become a better-informed traveler, or simply enjoy learning about other tourists' woes and how to avoid repeating the same mistakes, this is a good read.

TIP

For more on how to find the best air travel deals, on or off the Net, buy a copy of *The Worldwide Guide to Cheap Airfares*, by Michael McColl. For more information on this book, see *http://www.travelxn.com/wwguide/*.

A FINAL WORD

Although most online vendors—including consolidators—are legitimate, shady operators can hide behind glossy brochures on the Net just as they can in the traditional travel world. So you should thoroughly investigate an outfit before you buy. If you're dealing with a well known travel supplier, you can probably rest easy. But if you're dealing with lesser known entities, try to check them out. See if they belong to major trade organizations, for example.

What's the gist of this chapter? On the surface it's about saving money. Beyond getting the best deal, though, there's lots of evidence that spending some time on the Net will yield a better trip. Jane Nowlin didn't just find a cheaper package deal—she found one that included golf. And John Boman didn't just find an inexpensive place to stay in Cape Breton—he found a charmingly restored old farmhouse that provided exactly what he was seeking. As John says, this farmhouse might not be right for everyone, but it was right for him. And that's the beauty of the Net: you can find a good deal that's tailored to your desires and budget, and one that ultimately (in most cases) yields a finer trip than a vacation arranged by someone else. Because no one knows what you want better than you.

Taking Care of Business

5

Business travelers demand efficiency. They don't have weeks or months to think about where they want to travel—they know where they have to go and want the arrangements to be as painless as possible. Through the Internet, business travelers can make the entire process of travel much easier. They can book their flights, find appropriate lodgings and facilities, stay in touch with the home office, and get quickly oriented in unfamiliar cities. In just the past couple of years, travel resources aimed at the business traveler have sprouted up all over the Net. The following pages show how the Net is becoming a lifeline for business travelers, as demonstrated by several accomplished business people. This chapter evaluates corporate travel booking systems and how they're changing the way business travel is booked, in much the same way that ATMs revolutionized the way people do their banking.

- ▶ Getting It Done
- ▶ Corporate Booking Systems
- ▶ Business Travel Resources
- ▶ Staying Connected
- ▶ Not Just for Business

GETTING IT DONE

A business traveler's main goal is to get where he or she has to be on time, get the job done, and get home again. The tighter they can book their arrangements, the better. And that goes for the trip planning process as well. Typically business travelers have to make arrangements on short notice. So, for the wired business traveler, the Net has become an indispensable tool.

According to a Travel Industry Association survey, 47 percent of frequent business travelers are now online. But the survey showed that the bulk of those who use the Net for travel use it for planning rather than for reservations. According to the survey, 25 percent said they expected to use the Net to make plans or reservations within the next year.

One person who has already taken that step is Thomas Lynn, president and CEO of Treasury Bank in Washington, D.C. He turned to the Net recently after his corporate travel agent retired. "I figured it was time to take matters into my own hands—using the Net to actually book your tickets is a comfort level you can reach fairly quickly," Thomas says. He now routinely uses sites such as SABRE (*http://www.easysabre.com*) to book his weekly flight from Washington to New York and also employs the Net to plan more involved trips such as family vacations. The SABRE booking engine is the foundation of Travelocity (*http://www.travelocity.com*), a leading travel reservation site on the Web, discussed in detail in Chapter 2.

"I was trying to figure out how to get my grown children down from New York, meet them at one of the Washington airports, and then have us all leave on a flight to Orlando or West Palm Beach," Thomas says. "I did all the planning on the Net and it worked. The Web sites even rate a flight's on-time performance. I feel comfortable having more information than less."

Business traveler Steve Tatarunis still uses a corporate travel agent, but he likes having a hand in his trip planning. "A lot of my trips are 10-17 days with stops in five or more countries. I like being involved in planning the where and when of my stops. I typically use Internet Travel Network (*http://www.itn.net*) to fine tune my air itinerary, then pass on the best itinerary to my corporate agent for ticketing or search for a similar itinerary with a lower fare." ITN also has a corporate booking system, discussed in the next section.

CORPORATE BOOKING SYSTEMS

According to American Express, U.S. corporations spend more than $150 billion per year for travel and entertainment, and more than a third of that figure is spent on business travel, primarily flights and hotel rooms. So it's no surprise that these companies are seeking solutions that will help them manage these budgets more effectively.

With the reduction in commissions available to travel agents, more business people will be expected to book their own travel arrangements. However, corporations aren't inclined to let their employees book just any flight. Corporate travel managers want employees to find good deals and use preferred airlines and specified hotels. An airline or hotel chain may give a company a special deal if that company books a certain amount of its travel with them. For example, Hyatt may give a business a discount if that company books more than $50,000 annually. As executives become more comfortable using the Net to book their travel, they'll be more at home with the in-house networks being used to direct them to preferred carriers and hotels.

Some employees have balked at these systems, unhappy that they constrain their choices. But in an increasingly competitive international marketplace, these systems are inevitable, and can offer added convenience for the business traveler.

Travelers can use these systems to set up a list of preferences. For example, the system can "remember" that a traveler prefers an aisle seat and must be seated in non-smoking sections on international flights. If a business person makes frequent trips to a certain destination, these corporate travel systems can make the arrangements well in advance.

The biggest player in this arena is the team of Microsoft and American Express. The companies are producing a corporate travel system slated for release in 1997. The package offers access to myriad reservation systems, destination information, negotiated discounts, and travel advice. The system, code-named "Rome," lets business travelers reserve and purchase travel from their desktop computers.

TIP

For more information on the Amex-Microsoft corporate travel alliance, see *http://www.microsoft.com/corpinfo/press/1996/jul96/amexrel.htm.*

Another player in this rapidly expanding field is American Airlines' SABRE Business Travel Solutions (*http://www.amrcorp.com/sabr_grp/ sabr_grp.htm*). SABRE's Travel Planner is a real-time booking agent that uses the layout of a daily planner. The calendar displays all planned trips at a glance. To book, simply drag the air, car, or hotel icons to the calendar and drop them on the desired date. The frequent trip feature lets users book similar trips simultaneously. The Policy Manager gives supervisors the ability to oversee company policy, vendor preferences, travel profiles, and acceptable rates. This feature uses the SABRE system to compare more than 1,000 rates, including negotiated rates, and includes features for expense reporting.

ITN'S TRAVEL MANAGER

Internet Travel Network, one of the first sites to offer real-time flight reservations, has a corporate travel system called Internet Travel Manager. Travelers can use it to record preferences for flights, rental cars, and hotels; corporate travel managers can customize the system to direct their employees to preferred airlines, hotels, and rental car companies.

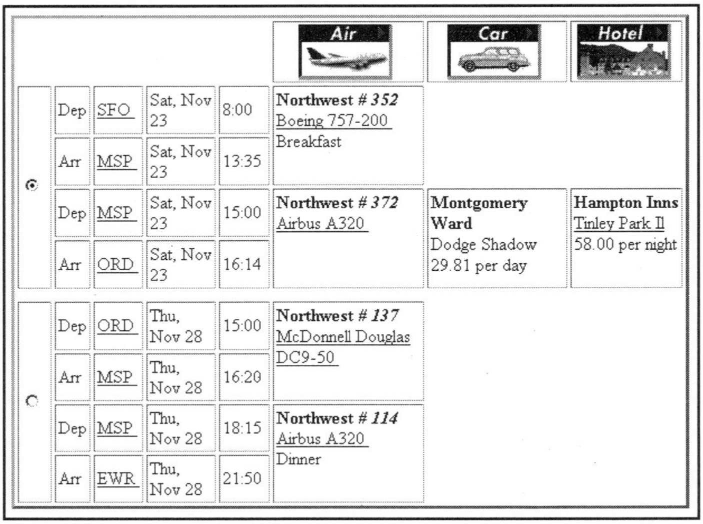

FIGURE 5-1

With ITN's Internet Travel Manager, business travelers can display a corporate profile including air, hotel, and car rental preferences (http://www.itn.net).

TIP

An intranet is an internal network, sometimes having limited access to the global Internet.

"For years companies have been trying booking systems like easySABRE to cut down on travel policy leakage," says ITN's Joe Witherspoon. "But these systems have either been too difficult to use, or too difficult to distribute. With the growth of the Internet and corporate intranets, everybody is wired. So you have ITN with this very easy to use booking system that also does things like show preferred travel suppliers over non-preferred and book the travel at the negotiated rates. Plus it allows a travel manager, someone who works for the company, not the travel agency, to monitor what is being spent, and then instantly work within that framework to bring costs down."

Companies pay ITN $15,000 to get Internet Travel Manager installed, a $500 monthly fee for support and maintenance, and $3 per booking. Companies that want advance customizations pay additional fees. For a demonstration of ITN's Internet Travel Manager, see *http://www.itn.net/xyzcorp*.

KEEPING THE LID ON CORPORATE TRAVEL EXPENSES

Rick Lifsitz, vice president of marketing for E-Travel Systems, believes that within five years up to 50 percent of all business travel will be booked using these systems. E-Travel (*http://www.etravelsystems. com*) sells software that links to leading reservation systems. Corporate travel managers can use this software to monitor travel choices and keep the lid on travel expenses. Rick sees "a clear parallel with the banking industry." In the not so distant past, most people would wait for a teller; today, most transactions are done through ATMs. The new systems are about "using tools to move market share into areas that are more favorable for a corporation," Rick says. He cites a major media company based in New York that cut a $50 million travel budget by 13 percent after it began using one primary carrier (instead of three) for the bulk of its air travel.

One of the largest electronics firms in the U.S., Dallas-based Texas Instruments, expects to save $1 million off its $200 million travel and entertainment budget in 1997 by using a managed corporate travel system. And the company expects to save 10 times that much within five years by using its system to ensure that employees use preferred airlines and hotels whenever possible, according to corporate travel manager Colleen Guhin.

Texas Instruments uses a system created specifically for the company by ITN. The system includes automated expense reporting so travel managers can monitor how employees are spending the company's travel dollars. Corporate travel managers can use these systems to calibrate the level of flexibility they wish to give employees. For example, a company could set up the system to force employees to use United Airlines for all domestic travel. Or they could set it up to *encourage* their workers to use United, for example, by listing all United flights first, and then listing flights on other carriers. This type of direction is prohibited by law in open public systems, such as the one run by Preview Travel. With an in-house system, however, a company can do what it wants.

Before using ITN's system, Texas Instruments' booking time for a single domestic trip averaged 58 minutes and sometimes exceeded three hours. In-house studies show three-quarters of TI executives would gladly use an automated system if one were available, saving time for corporate travel consultants. TI employees like the idea of improving their productivity and having some control over their travel arrangements. While they may be restricted to certain airlines or hotels, they can choose when they want to leave and where they want to stay (within the parameters) rather than giving their travel dates to a consultant and letting that person make the choices.

"From the traveler's perspective, the biggest thing was to improve their productivity and give them control over the decisions they make," Guhin told *Business Travel News*. "With the automated booking system, they are picking from a lot of options and they know that they are picking what they do for the right reasons, whereas on the phone they never have the warm feeling that they've chosen the best flight. The system puts them in control, and they can't complain to anybody else about the choices they have made."

BUSINESS TRAVEL RESOURCES

The Net is more than a useful tool for booking travel arrangements. After booking a flight, reserving a room, and renting a car (see Chapters 1-3 for general booking information), business travelers can turn to the Net to find weather forecasts, currency exchange rates, maps of their destinations, and much more. Business people can even pinpoint hotels on an online map, and find restaurants and conference facilities near their hotels. An example of these mapping services is MapQuest. If you need to meet a client for breakfast the day after you arrive, for example, you can use MapQuest (*http://www.mapquest.com*) to find a place to eat, print out a map showing how to get there, attach the map to an email message, and send it along to your client.

Business travelers often need financial services while traveling, and an American Express office may be able to help. To find one quickly, see Amex's Travel Resources section (*http://www.americanexpress.com/travel/docs/resources/*). Here business travelers can find an easy-to-search list of American Express offices in the U.S. and abroad, as well as weather forecasts and world time. For the latest passport and visa information, see Amex's Travel Tips (*http://www.americanexpress.com/travel/docs/resources/tips/*), which has information on driving overseas, electrical appliances, and travel advisory lines.

American Express

*http://www.
americanexpress.com*

Financial services for travelers and an online list of Amex offices around the world.

BIZTRAVEL.COM

Business travelers need more than Web sites to reserve flights and hotel rooms—they need information to make their trips as easy and efficient as possible. A good business travel site keeps a tight focus on the needs of the business traveler. One site that does just that is biztravel.com (*http://www.biztravel.com*), which unveiled a new look in 1997. This site is a useful blend of online tools for the business travelers (hotel booking, etc.) and magazine features to help business travelers get around.

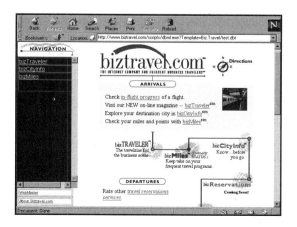

FIGURE 5-2

biztravel.com offers online tools and magazine features for business travelers (http://www.biztravel.com).

The site's online magazine, *bizTraveler*, recently featured a story on Atlanta's airport that tells business travelers about a new executive conference center equipped with work stations, secretarial support, and office amenities. Travelers who want a break from all their work can stroll down to the golf pro shops in the airport. The same article surveys the airport lounges and offers this advice: "The best airport lounge is the newly refurbished Delta Crown Room, on Concourse A. Even if you're not a member, at $25, the day pass is a bargain."

Other features tell how travelers can locate a personal trainer on the road and how to keep your laptop from being stolen. In the Executive Travel section are "The 10 Commandments of Asian Business."

The features in *bizTraveler* are complemented by biztravel.com's array of services, such as bizMiles, where you can keep track of your frequent flyer miles and learn about new programs and incentives. biztravel.com also includes up-to-date weather forecasts, links to in-depth airport information, and city profiles with information supplied by Fodor's.

To learn about Hong Kong's new airport at Chek Lap Kok, I clicked on CityInfo in the scroll bar in the left frame. Next I clicked on Hong Kong, then selected airport information which linked to a comprehensive site about the airport. Within seconds I found information about facilities and services at the new airport and located a map that clearly showed rail and bus connections to Hong Kong island.

While I may have been able to locate this same Chek Lap Kok site by using search directories, it would have been much more time-consuming. Search directories can be hit or miss. Sometimes travelers have to sort through a lot of dreck to find some valuable nuggets

FIGURE 5-3

biztravel.com links to a site about Hong Kong's new airport that shows bus routes to Hong Kong Island.

of information. But sites such as biztravel.com organize this information and make it more accessible to business travelers who don't have a lot of time to evaluate many sites to find a few good ones.

Following is a list of some other sites that help business travelers find what they need.

Business Travel Resource Center
(*http://www.travelweb.com/thisco/bustravl/bustravel.html*)

The BTRC is part of the TravelWeb site, and from here you can catch up with the news through the online versions of the *Wall Street Journal* and *Barron's*, get a package sent to you overnight through FedEx, or arrange ground transportation to your hotel through Carey International.

QTW Corporate Travel
(*http://www.quinwell.com/business.html*)

"I asked our travelers what they wanted to find on our site, and their answers were 'information, ability to email, make reservations, information, and more information!'" says QTW Webmaster and corporate travel consultant Gordon LaGrow. The site offers online reservations through SABRE, as well as sections on meeting planning, accommodations, and "hot deals." The site is packed with information about airfares, baggage allowances, and business travel services, such as preferred car rental rates.

The Business Travel Pages
(*http://www.mcb.co.uk/apmforum/travel/welcome.htm*)

Sponsored by Asia Pacific Management Forum, this site is a compendium of resources for the shrewd business traveler. You'll find a list of recommended hotels with reviews, tips for restaurants, and summaries and articles about Asian business and management. A clickable map links to regional newsgroups. For example, click on Japan and link to *soc.culture.japan* where you can post queries about the region or learn about a country's cultural practices simply by lurking in the newsgroup. To get up to speed on what's happening in your destination, see the latest news from local Asian newspapers, such as the *Bangkok Post*, *Asiaweek*, and the *Hong Kong Standard*. There's also a directory of business people in the region, with email addresses listed, who could serve as contacts.

Banks of the World
(http://www.wiso.gwdg.de/ifbg/bank_2.html)

If you're traveling to an overseas hotel and wondering where you'll be able to find an ATM that takes your bank card, check this site for links to banks organized by country. You'll also find sections on cyberbanks, investment banks, and the World Bank. And if you want to do your banking online, this is a good place to start.

Steve Kropla's Help for World Travelers
(http://www.cris.com/~kropla/index.shtml)

In some countries it's called "backsheesh," in others "a small gift." In plain English it's called bribery, which greases the wheels (and palms) of commerce in many countries around the world. Steve Kropla's site lists the top ten countries where bribery is most rampant and the countries where it is the least tolerated. Perhaps of more use to business travelers is his World Electric Guide, with tips on electrical power around the globe, International Dialing Codes with city and area codes for most regions; and the Worldwide Phone Guide, with tips for plugging in your modem from abroad (for more on this topic, see Chapter 8, "Newsgroups and Mailing Lists"). Steve also links to international weather and currency exchange sites, as well as U.S. State Department Advisories.

Association of Business Travelers
(http://www.hk.linkage.net/markets/abt/)

ABT offers a comprehensive, free online hotel reservation service, savings and discounts on hotel rooms, savings at restaurants, and even lost-luggage tracing. You'll have to join to receive these benefits, but non-members can peruse the hotel discounts, which ranged from 10-50 percent when I checked the site. ABT also provides travel insurance, clubs for associates around the globe, and discounts on restaurants.

The Executive Woman's Travel Network
(http://www.delta-air.com/womenexecs)

Sponsored by Delta Airlines, this site offers advice on "safety in a strange place" and "tips on tipping," among many others. In "Planning for Your Trip," you'll find packing hints and tips for helping the kids handle your absence, for example: "Let your children help you pack. Explain why you're going and what you'll be doing. Give them a copy of your itinerary so they always know where you are."

STAYING CONNECTED

One of the key concerns of business travelers is staying connected to the home office while on the road. Most business people today are so accustomed to being connected to a network all day that they feel like they'd just as soon leave their pants at home as leave on a trip without their laptop and modem. Spending a week without access to email or to the company computer system isn't just unthinkable, it's bad business.

At the very least, business travelers want to keep up with their email while on the road. From many countries, sending a dispatch via email will be much cheaper than a phone call. And an email message can go into much greater detail than a quick, frenzied phone call that costs $3.50 a minute. Email also knows no time zones. So a business traveler on a trip to Brussels can hit the hay knowing that when his boss gets to the office that morning his email updating her on the trip will be awaiting her. For more on staying connected while you travel, see Chapter 9, "Traveling with the Net."

TIP

A word of caution here. Foreign electrical and phone systems can damage your computer and modem. Before traveling with your laptop and plugging it into an unfamiliar system, take some time to figure out what adaptations you'll need to make rather than haphazardly trying to configure your system during your trip.

ON THE ROAD BUT NOT OUT OF TOUCH

Bill Herndon, vice president for technology for Bank of America, oversees 100 technicians, working out of seven regional sites around the U.S. This means he's on the road for about half the year and must stay in touch electronically with corporate headquarters and with the technicians he supervises. So he's equipped with a laptop, wireless modem, "follow-me" 800-number, and an email system called RadioMail that sends messages over a cellular-like network. In short, whether or not he's near a phone, the road is Bill's office, and he finds it easy to stay in touch.

"The benefit is that nothing stops (when I'm traveling)," Bill says. "When I'm away, it's the same as if I'm in town—things that need my attention keep moving." With his wireless system he even checks his email during business meetings so he can respond quickly to questions and snuff out developing problems before they become real ones.

Bill is on the leading edge of what's becoming the new business ethic. Not long ago, saying "Oh, I was on the road," was an excuse that covered many oversights. But no longer. Executives expect their co-workers to be electronically accessible and to respond quickly to questions or problems.

"I think it's rude when people don't have an email address on their (business) cards," Bill says. When he receives email, he usually responds within a few minutes, regardless of where in the U.S. he is. He expects his colleagues to do the same. And, he points out, email extends his work day, allowing him to work regardless of time zone considerations. Unlike a phone call, email is not intrusive, so if he sends a message or document in the middle of the night, the person who receives it can respond in the morning—but Bill's work is done.

Bill has become so comfortable with his electronic response system that he has done something most busy executives can't imagine doing: He's given up his physical office. Even when he was at BofA mortgage headquarters in San Francisco, he found he often used empty conference rooms instead of his office. Sometimes Bill did not use his office for days on end. "So I just bailed it," he says.

With office space becoming more expensive and cities more crowded, Bill is at the leading edge of a trend. Because he doesn't require an office and desk, BofA is saving more than $50,000 annually in office costs, he estimates. But the benefits for the company (and for Bill) don't stop there. Being able to work while on the road has dramatically boosted Bill's productivity. "My productivity is two to four times greater working electronically than it was before," he says.

Bill doesn't miss his old office. "No regrets whatsoever, *nada*," he says. "I'm at home anywhere, your office, a doctor's office, an airport, a hotel, home, a conference room. I gave up 'stuff'—that's the difference. I don't have files and I don't deal in paper."

Most business travelers won't want to go to the lengths Bill has gone. But his experience is highly instructive. Bill shows how to travel for business without missing a beat, noting that, whether you have a physical office and desk or not, there's a growing expectation in the business world that you'll be accessible and available while traveling. As the technology becomes even more affordable and easier to use, that expectation will inevitably increase.

WHERE TO PLUG IN

Wireless communications is not always an option. If you're already carrying a laptop for business and staying at a good U.S. hotel, chances are you'll be looking for places to plug it into a phone line so you can log in to your employer's or home Net account.

Tips for Taking Your Laptop on the Road

Following are a few questions to consider before traveling with your laptop.

- Does your hotel have extra electrical outlets where you can plug in your computer? If you are traveling abroad, are you prepared to deal with the electrical system of the country you're visiting? See the TeleAdapt site (*http://www.teleadapt.com*) to help get these questions answered.

- Does your hotel room have a dataport in the room where you can plug in your computer? Also, are there two lines in the room, one for your computer and the other for the telephone? Ask the hotel before you make a reservation.

- Does your hotel have a business center where you can get access to a printer or obtain other computer services?

- Does your Internet service provider offer an 800-number or local dial-up number so you can log into your home account without paying long-distance toll charges?

- Did you remember to change your dial-up configuration to include the new telephone number you'll use to log in from the road? Remember you typically need to dial "9" or "8" to access an outside line from your hotel room.

A final note: Remember to charge your batteries and/or bring extra batteries. They'll likely run down faster than you anticipate.

Most U.S. hotels will have a data port where you can plug in your computer. But beware that a hotel may charge for local calls. Many Internet service providers have access through local telephone numbers across the country. Others have a nationwide 800-number you can call for access. If you're traveling abroad, logging on can be a bit more dicey, as electrical and phone systems vary by country. One business traveler says:

> Another caution: ask the front desk if the phone system is digital or analog. Even technologically sophisticated travelers have fried their modems by connecting to digital systems. This problem doesn't affect all modems. Some just won't work over a digital line, but won't self-destruct. Many new card modems are being equipped with a sensor that prevents this from happening, but if you don't own one of these, you better ask before you plug in.

The imperative to remain wired while on the road grows stronger each day. Richard Peck, vice president for business development for computer book publisher O'Reilly & Associates, can't imagine traveling without a Net connection.

> The Internet, when traveling, is like oxygen: you wouldn't want to travel where you couldn't get it!

> Obviously, I stay in touch by email. The one trip I made without a laptop I felt totally unable to remain part of the discussions my colleagues were having about several important topics. At the same time, I couldn't relay to them the success I was having during the trip.

> Similarly, since I've come to depend on the Web as my all-purpose "reference library," I didn't have access to the resources from which I would otherwise get business leverage (e.g., knowledge of competitors' most recent product offerings or marketing tactics, statistical and strategic perspective to assist in making decisions, etc.).

> The Web has also been useful as a place to pick up a file or presentation that I forgot to bring, or that has been updated since I last was in the office. For example, while in Europe, I pulled the most recent PowerPoint presentation for one of our software products off our internal Web sites.

> And there have been trips when one of our book designers would put up new book cover designs on their Web site(s). Via the Internet, I could review and comment, whereas otherwise they would have had to either wait, catch me with FedEx (expensive), or proceed with only part of our team's input.

Richard sees his connection to the Net as an umbilical cord, a way to stay connected with the greater body of colleagues and information he relies upon to take care of daily business tasks. He uses the connection to update his co-workers on his progress while traveling and to get late-breaking reports from the mothership. And to him the Web is a lightweight reference library, a source of volumes of current information, often saving him from the ordeal of lugging around heavy reports on his business trips.

STAYING IN TOUCH

Richard's colleague, Ron Tomich, is O'Reilly's regional director for the Asia Pacific region. He uses the Net mainly for email while he's on the road, to keep him in touch with clients and with his co-workers back home. He has become so effective at managing his communications electronically while traveling that some colleagues don't realize he's away. And even if they did, it wouldn't matter because Ron remains as accessible when he's on the road as he is while working in the office.

> *I couldn't easily be effective without it (the Net) at this point—I'm able to attend conferences on remote Asian islands and still maintain a virtual presence for all the other Asian accounts I handle. They often never know I'm away. And I always take satisfaction by being able to close a deal in China, fix a problem in Thailand, fill an order in Australia, and woo a customer in Singapore, all in the course of a couple of hours while sitting on my bed with a laptop and jetlag in Malaysia.*

> *Nearly all the medium to large hotels in Asia offer international direct dialing—I usually input my international Sprint card number into the remote access software, and (as long as a Sprint operator doesn't interfere—if a live voice interrupts all is lost) dial into my office, download my mail from the server, and terminate in about a minute. Keeps the charges down.*

> *Occasionally I use the Web as well, but it depends on the kind of speed I'm getting out of my dial-up connection. In some locales I only average 9600, but sometimes out of the blue I'll get a full 28.8K connection and then fire up the browser.*

NOT JUST FOR BUSINESS

Book editor Melissa Koch says Net access came in handy during a recent business trip to Chicago. Melissa uses the Net to access an array of Net resources without carrying around a ton of paper. She says she is able to find the address of her hotel, download a schedule for conferences, and stay connected with the office back home. And when she has time for a little sightseeing, she says, she can find information on sites like City.net (*http://city.net*), which help travelers get oriented in a new destination.

I arrived in Chicago on Saturday afternoon. By Sunday morning, I was back online catching up on my email. On Sunday evening I realized that I didn't have the address for the hotel where the conference was being held. I was staying with my aunt so I first checked her phone book. Unfortunately, her phone book was a year old and the Intercontinental Hotel was a new hotel. At this point, I might have used directory assistance, but since I needed to get online to download the conference schedule anyway, I decided to try a search.

I went to Yahoo (http://www.yahoo.com) and searched for Intercontinental Hotel. One of the search results was the Intercontinental Hotels and Resorts (http://www.interconti.com/interconti/). This site also had a search directory that allowed me to type in Chicago and select Hotel Information. It then displayed the address, phone and fax numbers, and a brief description of the hotel.

I also downloaded the schedule for the EdNet conference. I had the URL with me so I didn't need to search for it or guess. I may make it a practice to store conference URLs in my bookmarks; it certainly reduces the amount of paper I need to carry.

At the conference on Monday, I met with a potential business partner to go over some details of the project. In talking with her, I realized that she had not seen a copy of the full proposal. Later that same evening, I was able to send her the proposal and provide a follow-up on our discussion.

On Tuesday evening, a friend and I met for dinner. During our conversation, we realized that some information I had on my hard drive would be useful to her for a class she was teaching. I had the information with me on my computer, but I didn't have access to a printer. Instead, I sent the information to her via email the next morning, allowing her to prepare for her class the following evening.

Throughout the week, I could keep up with projects at work even though I was spending 10-hour days at the conference. Sometimes when I am on business in a new city and have a little bit more time, I'll check CityNet (http://www.citynet.com) or do a search on that city to see what interesting places or events I can discover.

COMING SOON TO A HOTEL NEAR YOU

After a hard day on the road, a business traveler is apt to settle into his or her room and turn on the TV, and maybe pay a few dollars extra to watch the latest feature film. As this book was going to press in early 1997, hotels were discussing upgrading their in-house cable systems to include Internet access through the TV. Though Net TV did not have a great reception in the home market, it may find its place in hotels and motels.

Typically pay-per-view offers access to current movies. But with some modifications, these systems can offer access to the Net. So instead of having to figure out how to plug in a laptop, the business travelers could pay a fee of about $5 an hour (plus phone charges) and access the Net through the TV in the hotel room.

Travelers could use these connections to scan the Web or catch up on their email. More sophisticated users would probably still take their laptops along, because the features available through the television are limited.

Hotels can benefit from this by freeing up their crowded phone lines. Hyatt's Chris Elam told the *New York Times* that guests' phone calls used to average just seven minutes, but with more business travelers carrying laptops, calls often run as long as three hours, overwhelming phone systems.

BEYOND THE BASICS

The aim of this chapter has been to serve as a handy guide for business travelers, a set of resources and personal accounts designed to show business travelers how to efficiently use the Net. But this chapter doesn't cover it all—it's designed to work in concert with the first three chapters on finding destination information, booking flights, renting cars, selecting hotels, and choosing restaurants, all through the Net. By this point, you may have the information you need, but certainly every business traveler needs a vacation, so read on to see how to use the Net to create the best vacation possible.

The Ultimate Vacation 6

Many travelers work most of the year just to have a couple of weeks to do what they please. So they don't want to fritter away their hard-earned vacation time on trips that don't meet expectations. By learning to use the Net's varied travel resources, vacationers can make better trip decisions, reducing the likelihood of a wasted vacation. The Net is ideal for finding information about specific types of vacations, whether it's a cruise or a safari. It's also superb for travelers who have special needs, such as seniors or people with physical challenges, who can preview much of their intended itinerary and scope out appropriately equipped accommodations. The following pages discuss a few travel niches and show how to find information on any particular interest, even if it's not specifically listed here.

▶ Cruising the Net

▶ Package Tours Online

▶ Family Travel: Taking the Kids

▶ The Great American Road Trip

▶ Travel Opportunities for Seniors

▶ Disabled Travelers

▶ Alternative Lifestyles, Alternative Travel

CRUISING THE NET

The vacation cruise ship business has exploded in recent years. Most major cruise lines have set up Web pages and several travel agencies have set up Web sites specializing in snagging the online cruiser. Royal Caribbean Cruise Lines (*http://www.royalcaribbean.com/*) has added mega-liners to its fleet, meaning they will have more cabins to fill. RCCL and its competitors have discovered that the Web is a wonderful way to fill empty cabins before pulling away from the dock. The Net offers these cruise lines an immediate way to post last-minute deals to fill cabins that would otherwise sail empty. So if you're looking for a good deal on a cruise, a good place to start is RCCL's site, one of the cruise sites listed in Appendix A, or in Yahoo's cruise line directory (*http://www.yahoo.com/Business_and_Economy/ Companies/Travel/Cruises/Cruise_Lines*).

Going directly to the sites of the various cruise lines is also the best way to comparison shop and narrow down your choices. Most of these sites let you view deck layouts on their ships, showing photos of rooms and suites.

With Royal Caribbean's Cruise-o-matic feature, you can select where and when you want to travel, and examine your options. I took Cruise-o-matic for a spin, telling it that I wanted a week-long summer cruise in Alaska that would include wildlife viewing. With a click, I found I could take the *Legend of the Seas* sailing out of Vancouver on a seven-night journey past the Hubbard Glacier and Misty Fjords with stops in Haines, Skagway, and Juneau. In other parts of the site, the company listed special deals and an online contest that allowed me to enter to win a free cruise.

BOOKING YOUR CRUISE ONLINE

Internet Cruise Travel Network
http://www.cruisetravel. com/
Compare and book cruises.

Many sites have the tools to let you go beyond researching trips to booking them over the Net. Internet Cruise Travel Network (*http://www.cruisetravel.com*), created by a Florida travel agency, serves up a full menu of cruise line offerings, their sailing itineraries, and ship and cabin layouts. ICTN agents will take your reservation online and handle your reservation and billing. This agency has deals such as free cruises for those who bring enough friends to fill 15 cabins, and offers coupons for onboard drinks or merchandise.

To explore cruises from a variety of companies, see The Cruise Web (*http://www.cruiseweb.com*), which organizes listings by cruise line and destination. This site has a section for bargain cruises, and a button labeled Hot Rates that promises up to 50 percent discounts for those who book through the Cruise Web.

The Cruise Web

http://www.cruiseweb.com

Listings organized by cruise line and destination.

Another useful site is Cruisin (*http://www.asource.com/cruisin*), founded by former Air Force captain Robert Longley and his wife Chrys, an accredited cruise counselor with eleven years in the cruise business. The Cruisin site is a testament to the feasibility of an online storefront—Cruisin has no sidewalk storefront and does all its business through its Web site. "This keeps our overhead low and allows us to pass on the best deals," says Robert.

For an unconventional cruise experience, see Freighter World Cruises (*http://www.gus.net/travel/fwc/fwc.html*), which provides links to more than a dozen freight lines whose ships also offer limited passenger accommodations. Some of these cruises are a relative bargain, such as passage from Montreal to England or France for $1,100 on Mediterranean Great Lakes Line. The site is maintained by a travel agency in Pasadena, which says it's the world's largest agency for booking freighter cruises. This type of cruise is not for everyone. But for those who are flexible and don't mind if the cruise gets behind its schedule, freighters can be an exciting way to see destinations off the beaten path.

TO THE SEA IN TALL SHIPS

Newsgroups and conference areas have been used extensively by cruise-goers, as well as by people considering taking a cruise for the first time. The following account shows how younger people, who are seeking alternatives to formal cruises, are using the newsgroups to find the right cruise.

Ethan Solomita, a 25-year-old software engineer for Silicon Graphics, wanted to spend his vacation on a cruise ship, but didn't want to play shuffleboard and dress up for dinner every night. Following is an excerpt from a message entitled "Choosing a cruise when you're weird," which Ethan posted to the *rec.travel.cruises* newsgroup.

PERSONAL ACCOUNT
Ethan Solomita
ethan@engr.sgi.com

```
I am not comfortable if I'm dressed up. I can do a
suit and tie for a couple of dinners if I must, but
I'd feel really uncomfortable in a suit for a whole
evening.
```

I don't want a touristy cruise. I have images of
the boat docking at yet another Caribbean island,
with yet another set of locals selling goods to the
tourists. I don't enjoy shopping. I can't just sit
on a beach for hours. Hiking, snorkeling, and
ancient ruins all sound great. Driving in a bus to
a "Mayan ruin" surrounded by tourists and people
selling T-shirts is less than I'd hope for.

During the next few days, several people wrote back to Ethan, assuring him that no one is too young to cruise, that many cruises don't expect people to dress formally for dinner every night, and that he should look for long port visits, giving him time to explore.

"You might try cruising out of San Juan, and get there a couple of days early. That way, you could independently (we sense that's your style) take in Old San Juan, some nightlife, then take your cruise," wrote Michael Wright, a businessman and veteran cruiser from Nashville. Michael suggested that Windjammer's sailing ship cruises might be what Ethan is looking for. Notice the phrase in parentheses: Michael's use of "we" shows the sense of community in the newsgroup—members of the group are ready and willing to help one another find the most suitable cruise, and many post cruise reviews to help each other find worthwhile trips and avoid bad deals.

Windjammer Barefoot Cruises

http://wheat.symgrp.com/ symgrp/windjammer/

Casual cruises on sailing ships.

Michael also suggested that Ethan post to the newsgroup, letting members of the group know what cruise he selected and inviting others booked on the same cruise to get in touch with him before the trip. Since Ethan said he's not into the big party scene, another cruiser recommended he avoid Carnival cruises and eschew traveling during spring break.

FIGURE **6-1**
You don't need a tux on a Windjammer cruise.

Clicking over to Windjammer Barefoot Cruises (*http://wheat. symgrp.com/symgrp/windjammer/*), Ethan found this brief message, encapsulating the company's spirit: "Informality rules! T-shirts and shorts are all you'll need to pack, so trash the tuxes and ballgowns. Stow your gear in your air conditioned cabin. From dorms to honeymoon suites, all feature modern amenities. Who said anything about roughing it?"

The site also had detailed information about Windjammer's fleet, departure dates, special singles cruises, and an informative FAQ. Ethan could see images of the Windjammer sailing ships and ask follow-up questions through an email address or toll-free number on the site. Since Ethan was on a limited budget, he could consider six-day cruises in the British Virgin Islands or French West Indies, which start at $650.

Neil Newson, Windjammer's Internet services manager, says the company is attracting a new breed of traveler through the Web: people who are younger than the average cruiser and have some disposable income to spend on their vacations. Until they set up a Web site, Windjammer's fame was spread largely by word of mouth. They attracted travelers like Ethan—wanting to cruise, but in the old-world sense—not on a floating motel. The Windjammer site reaches the Internet community which is filled with people with high-tech lives and low-tech fantasies. Windjammer also uses the Net to publicize special deals, such as a recent offer of 10 percent off, sent through its email list.

For a list of some of the best cruise links, see Dr. Memory's Cruises, Charters & Boating (*http://www.access.digex.net/~drmemory/cruises. html*). And since the best cruise leads often come via word of mouth, be sure to visit the Web site Cruise Review Library (*http://www. pagesz.net/~jbdavis/rtc*), which organizes the thousands of posts to the *rec.travel.cruises* newsgroup, and lets you access cruise reviews and shore excursion guides.

Cruise Review Library
http://www.pagesz.net/ ~jbdavis/rtc
Reviews and personal evaluations of dozens of cruise lines and hundreds of cruises.

PACKAGE TOURS ONLINE

Not all travelers want to do it all themselves. If you work 50 weeks a year and just crave an easy getaway of sun and surf, package tours offer a nice way to escape. SunTrips (*http://www.suntrip.com*) offers air-hotel packages to prime vacation spots in Hawaii and Mexico.

For a truly all-in-one vacation, hop over to Club Med (*http://www. clubmed.com*), which lists all-inclusive tours for singles, families, and couples. At Club Med's site, you can take a virtual journey among its "villages" in the Americas, Asia, and Africa. By spending just a few minutes at Club Med's home on the Web, you can learn what to expect from a Club Med vacation, including activities, cost, programs for kids, sports schools, and whether you have to pay for drinks.

There are hundreds of other tour operators on the Net—Yahoo has a fairly comprehensive list and organizes these groups by category, for example, Adventure, City Walks, and Seniors. To see this list, go to *http://www.yahoo.com/Business_and_Economy/Companies/Travel/ Tour_Operators/*.

FAMILY TRAVEL: TAKING THE KIDS

Traveling with youngsters poses a new set of challenges: balancing the practical aspects of a trip with things that will keep the kids engaged and entertained. Using the Net to plan a family vacation allows the entire family to get involved in the process. While the parents may focus on the schedules, routes, and reservations, the kids can search for points of interest to them while learning more about the area they will be visiting.

By using the Net, families can make trip planning a more collaborative process. Kids can start their journey of discovery by searching the Net for destinations that entice the entire family. When travelers decide where they want to go, they can turn the kids loose to find attractions, historical sites, and museums at the destination.

A good way to start planning a trip is for the whole family to surf the Net together. Who knows—your kids may teach you a thing or two about how to find cool travel information. And by being included in the planning process, they'll probably enjoy and appreciate the trip more while traveling.

Brad Bollinger, business editor for *The Press Democrat*, a daily newspaper in Santa Rosa, California, turned to the Net with his family to plan a family trip to the Grand Canyon.

In our family, everyone uses the Net. I use it to help plan our family backpacking trips. I planned a six-day trip through the Grand Canyon and even downloaded a map, which I printed in color. This map became one of our prized possessions. It was the best map we had of the area—even better than the one in the book I was using.

To find the information, I used AltaVista (http://www.altavista.digital. com/) and searched with the words Grand Canyon. I was looking for various itineraries that backpackers typically use. For example, if you want to go for a four-day backpacking trip, national parks will frequently produce a guide or booklet that gives you the different options or itineraries, including campsite and trail characteristics.

We also found weather information—specifically median temps for late May when we planned to travel. A day or two before our trip, I checked the actual weather in the Canyon through AOL's weather source (keyword: weather). With a little effort, I quickly located an excellent source for information on the Canyon (http://www.kaibab.org/).

I found the National Park Service home page (http://www.nps.gov/grca) less useful, though it's good for basic information.

Using the Net, I could get good information when I wanted it, which was usually late at night when I had time. The National Park Service isn't open then. And have you ever tried to telephone a backcountry office? The words themselves seem like an oxymoron.

I have subsequently used the Net for other backpacking trips, one most recently to Yosemite (http://www.halfdome.com).

AltaVista

http://www.altavista.digital. com/

This search engine yields a diverse range of sites.

As Brad discovered, the Web can serve up a wealth of useful resources for family travelers. One of the best places to start is Parent Soup (*http://www.parentsoup.com*), a general resource for parents. Click on Library/Search and scroll down to the travel section where you'll find tips on family touring, museums, and budget travel. Par-

FIGURE 6-2

Bob Ribokas' Grand Canyon site (http://www.kaibab.org) is a superb resource.

ent Soup lists over a dozen good museums for children, including the Exploratorium, a magnificent science and discovery center at the San Francisco Palace of Fine Arts (*http://www.exploratorium.edu*). Visit it first online and then see the real museum during your trip. The online exhibits will whet your child's appetite for the real thing.

A good place to start planning a family trip is KidSmart Family Vacations (*http://www.travel.carlson.com/kidsmart.html*), a site sponsored by tour giant Carlson Wagonlit Travel (*http://www.travel.carlson.com/*). KidSmart lists family trips by category (adventure, educational, theme park) and by destination (California, Hawaii, Florida, Las Vegas). Also valuable is Travel Tips, which offers advice for traveling with kids.

In the ever more competitive hotel business, hotels are trying to lure families with special programs for children. If you're staying at a Hilton, for example, visit Hilton's site (*http://www.hilton.com*) before you leave to see what's available for kids. The Hilton Vacation Station (*http://www.hilton.com/^8393346789720/programs/families.html*) offers an online gameroom for kids, complete with lists of supervised activities at various Hilton hotels and games that kids can print out to make the trip more enjoyable.

Another kid-friendly hotel chain is Westin Hotels & Resorts. Their Family Travel section (*http://www.westin.com/world/famtrvl.html*) lists cultural and ecological programs designed especially for kids. You can also use this site to learn about Westin's child-friendly rooms and safety tips to childproof your room.

If you love traveling the high seas and want to find a cruise that has special activities for kids, see Family Cruises' Big Red Boat (*http://www.familycruises.com/big_red.html*), which has lots of activities to keep the kids busy so you can relax.

America Online members can tap into AOL's Family Travel Network (keyword: *family travel*). The Travel Library here is full of information, deals, vacation packages, and more. Parents and kids post details about their experiences, so you can benefit from stories of hits and misses from the recently returned travelers. Taking the Kids has tips for traveling families, including advice about how to survive traveling with teens.

Disney.com

http://www.disney.com

Disney's main site on the Web.

DISNEYLAND ONLINE

If you're headed to Southern California or Florida, the kids are going to demand a stop at one of Disney's theme parks. So before you leave, check into Disney's travel site (*http://www.disney.com/News/docs/ travel.html*). The site links to park maps, hours, show schedules, ticket information, and special events. Disney also includes links to directions, local weather, and traffic reports, and lets you know about hotels and campgrounds.

Says Tony, the Oxford professor who shared his story in Chapter 1:

> *We used L.A. Web sites to get details needed to pre-book early morning preference visits to Disneyland and special parades* (http://www.disney. com/Disneyland/funedu/magic), *which we do not normally find out about and cannot be found in guidebooks.*

ONE FAMILY LIVES ITS DREAM

Many folks dream of selling their house, quitting their job, packing up the kids, and hitting the road for a year or two. David Cohen, his wife, and their three children did just that, embarking on a year-long, round-the-world odyssey. But, thanks to the Net, they didn't have to sever all ties to their life back home. The Cohens packed a portable computer which enables them to communicate with their friends and family. David's 10-year-old daughter Kara uses the laptop to send trip reports to her classmates at Park School in Mill Valley, California, and to "chat" with her friends and classmates.

David Cohen and family

Through his email address, I got in touch with David in Mykonos, Greece. I asked how the family was faring and how staying connected has helped. He responded a day later:

```
Email is very useful to us, and we log in wherever
we can. My mother is handling a lot of our business
while we are gone. I gave her an old Powerbook, and
we communicate with her most conveniently through
AOL. In fact, many of our friends have gotten email
just to communicate with us while we're gone, so
now almost everyone I know (at least in the San
Francisco Bay Area) can be reached via email. We
get 5 to 10 messages a day.

I also wrote an article for the San Francisco
Chronicle about selling the house, quitting the
job, and hitting the road for a year with the 3
kids. I put our email address at the bottom and was
surprised to get nearly 50 responses. Most were
from people who had done, planned to do, or wished
they could someday do the same thing. A lot of
```

encouragement. Several people invited us to drop in
when we were in India or South Africa, for example.

The email relationship between Kara and her class
is very positive. The kids in the class are
learning a lot about the world, and Kara loves
getting the email and keeping in contact. (Her best
friend Caitlin started crying in class when they
got Kara's first email.) It is also a good writing
discipline for her, and has taught her how to use
the computer and the Net pretty painlessly. It is
not magical to her at all. She has been around
computers since she can remember, and thinks it is
all as normal as the TV or the telephone or
traveling around the world.

Later in the trip, Kara was on AOL at the same time as her friend and
classmate Christine Ogawa. Kara and Christine used AOL's Buddy
feature to see that they were online at the same time and began a chat
session, whereby they could "talk" to one another by typing messages
back and forth.

A trip around the world may not be your cup of tea, but even if your
family journey is just for a month or so, letting the kids stay in touch
with friends back home is great idea. Email lets them share the excitement of the trip with their peers during a time when they are
cooped up with stuffy grown-ups, and can help keep homesickness
at bay.

TIP

David Cohen is writing a book entitled *Are We There Yet?
How We Quit Work, Sold Our House and Traveled Around the
World with Our Three Children for a Year*. It is scheduled to be
published by Simon & Schuster in early 1998. Cohen is the
former director of the Day in the Life series of photography
books.

THE GREAT AMERICAN
ROAD TRIP

The great American road trip is as much a part of the American
dream as apple pie and fireworks on the Fourth of July. For decades,

Americans (and countless visitors to North America) have been piling into their cars seeking adventure on the highways and byways of the U.S. Now there's a new way to plan a road trip. As more people offer their tips for the road, more road-trippers are turning to the Net for maps, advice, or ideas about where to go.

Perhaps the classic American road trip is a journey along Route 66, the blue highways between Chicago and Los Angeles. While there's no longer a highway marked Route 66, the Net has several guides that can lead you along this fabled route. See the Route 66 Collection (*http://www.kaiwan.com/~wem/*) for a traveler's guide and maps.

Before a recent rendezvous with a bunch of other VW bus trippers in California's Mammoth Mountain area, Scott Allred checked the Net for directions, weather, and camping information. He found directions from his Las Vegas home to Mammoth at MapQuest (*http://www.mapquest.com*), weather at the Weather Channel (*http://www.weather.com*), and regional information at the Eastern Sierra Web Page (*http://206.86.249.2:80/sierraweb/*) where he found hot springs locations, mountain biking routes, and campsites.

Scott adds to the Net's road-trip database by filing regular reports to his own Web site, sharing what he learns with others on the Net. On Adventures in a VW and Other Interesting Things (*http://coyote.accessnv.com/wayback/*), you can follow Scott's excursions in his trusty '71 "Westy" to the Grand Canyon, southern Utah, and Death Valley. Sites like Scott's are a mixture of good old-fashioned "show-n-tell" peppered with hot tips for those following in their wake.

Ride-sharing for people on a tight budget is a time-tested mode of travel. In the past, getting a ride to the right place was hit or miss, at

AAA Online
http://www.aaa.com/
The American Automobile Association maintains its Web site at this location.

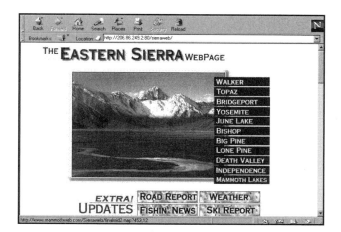

FIGURE 6-3
The Eastern Sierra Web Page (http://206.86.249.2:80/sierraweb/) is a gateway to recreation opportunities in this mountain region.

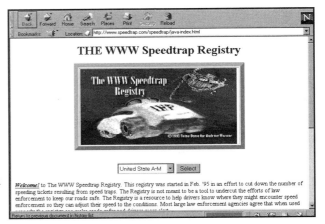

FIGURE 6-4

The WWW Speedtrap Registry (http://www.
speedtrap.com/speedtrap/) lets you know
where cops are pointing their radar guns.

best. But the Net has proven the perfect medium for those looking
for rides or riders. For those traveling in England, Freewheelers
(*http://www.freewheelers.co.uk/freewheelers/*) helps people going to the
same places get in touch and share rides.

And if you're the type who doesn't always abide by speed laws, it may
behoove you to have a look at the WWW Speedtrap Registry
(*http://www.speedtrap.com/speedtrap/*), which organizes traps by state,
based on tips from readers. What started as a small site now has listings that go beyond the U.S. to Canada, Mexico, Germany (didn't
know they had a speed limit there), and even Israel. So before you
start careening through the streets of Jerusalem, check the Speedtrap
Registry.

TRAVEL OPPORTUNITIES FOR SENIORS

Seniors are taking to the Net, with their presence strong and growing
at sites such as SeniorNet (*http://www.seniornet.org*) and services such
as America Online. According to a 1996 survey conducted by Fred-
erick/Schneiders for SeniorNet, one third of U.S. adults over 55 own
a computer, and of that number, 28 percent regularly go online.

Among the favorite online destinations for seniors are travel sites.
Seniors typically have the time, money, and inclination to travel, and
make up a big segment of the travel market. They enjoy many of the
trips already discussed, such as cruises, but can also use the Net to
find information about trips designed especially for seniors.

One of the most popular travel options for seniors is Elderhostel (*http://www.elderhostel.org*), "for people who know they're never too old to learn." At the Elderhostel site, travelers can examine a catalog of courses that appeal to older travelers, such as a week-long course on San Francisco's literary heritage, or an astronomy course in New Hampshire. Elderhostel offers "adventures of mind, body, and spirit," and travelers can use the site to help them find a course that matches their interests.

Elderhostel has put its catalog online so users can search the site by season, state, or interest. To see what the catalog would come up with, I searched for the keyword *myth* and it delivered several options in various regions, such as "The Power of Myth: Exploring the Work of Joseph Campbell," held at the Shenoa Retreat and Learning Center in Philo, California. After reading the course description, I clicked on Display Site Description to learn that Shenoa is located a couple of hours north of San Francisco near the Mendocino coast. The Elderhostel site also has information for people with disabilities, and includes news about intergenerational programs and scholarships.

Another site aimed at seniors is Toronto-based ElderTreks (*http://www.eldertreks.com/*), which specializes in adventures for people over 50. Travelers can use the site to learn about ElderTreks' philosophy and tours. A link leads to information about ElderTreks' tour leaders, which can help seniors feel more comfortable about the trip they are considering. ElderTreks uses the Net well to give a description of each trip, for example, a 16-day tour of Turkey. The description includes text, images, a map, a detailed itinerary, cost, and departure dates. If travelers still have questions about any tour, they can click the Contact Us link to send email to ElderTreks and get a quick response to their queries.

When seniors retire, they gain an advantage in making their travel plans—namely, they acquire flexibility. Because they can travel just about anytime, they can take advantage of last-minute deals. As discussed in Chapter 4, travelers can find these deals through Web sites and via email newsletters, such as American Airlines' NetSAAver Fares (see *http://www2.amrcorp.com/cgi-bin/aans* to subscribe to this weekly newsletter).

Other airlines have special deals for seniors, including TWA, which offers its Senior Travel Pak (*http://www.twa.com/TWA/Airlines/vacation/toursp.htm*). Through this offer, seniors can fly in the continental U.S. at rates far below even standard discounts.

For seniors hunting for bargain tours, On-Call Vacations (*http://www.on-call.com/*) is an example of a site where seniors who can travel on a dime can get good deals on cruises, hotel rooms, and resort vacations. The tours are available to seniors ages 55 or over who belong to United Airlines' Silver Wings Plus. One example of a recent bargain was a 16-day cruise tour of the Greek Isles and Israel for $1999, including airfare and two-day stays at hotels in Athens and Istanbul. The tour company even threw in 20,000 bonus frequent flyer miles. For a more comprehensive listing of senior travel sites, see Appendix A.

DISABLED TRAVELERS

Earlier in this book, we discussed how the Net, at its core, is about people helping one another. For travelers with special needs, this type of communication is even more essential. Fortunately, several excellent sites serve the disabled, and some have trip reports from travelers evaluating the accessibility of travel destinations around the world.

On Global Access (*http://www.geocities.com/Paris/1502/*), disabled travelers offer reports on what hotels are accessible. Each month this site features a new destination and explains how disabled travelers manage to get around there, what is accessible and what is not, and other useful tips. The November 1996 issue, for example, featured a story on visiting the ancient Inca ruins of Machu Picchu in Peru's highlands. "The greatest strength of Global Access lies in its ability to provide disabled travelers with a place to network and share ideas and experiences," says Richard Stricker, who maintains the site. For general advice, see Trip Tips & Resources, which has recommendations on choosing an airline, packing, and finding an attendant to travel with you.

Access-Able Travel Source
http://www.access-able.com/
Helping disabled travelers help themselves.

Created by Carol Randall, who has multiple sclerosis, and her husband Bill, Access-Able Travel Source (*http://www.access-able.com/*) is another not-to-be-missed site for disabled travelers. Here's the message from Access-Able's welcome page:

```
We have always liked to travel, and, like many of
you, don't get to do it enough. Carol has MS and
uses a wheelchair or scooter. This has given us
some first-hand experience with unpleasant surprises
and access problems. That's why we started Access-
Able Travel Source. We are not travel agents, just
```

travelers. We think we have come up with a way to help fellow travelers help themselves.

We have spent the last year researching not only accessible accommodations, but have included information to make a vacation fun and exciting. We found scuba diving for persons with all types of disabilities. There are accessible safaris, sailing, raft trips, and even a place where you can learn to drive a race car. We've included information like hands-on attractions for persons who are blind and seashore areas that have beach wheelchairs.

Access-Able Travel Source is dedicated to aiding travelers with disabilities. All too often these travelers experience unwanted surprises or difficulties with access. These problems discourage many people from traveling. Armed with access information these problems can be eliminated.

Access-Able lists accessible tours and has a search engine that lets you type in a destination and search for a type of trip. A search for travel adventures in California yielded six listings, including one for deep sea fishing in San Diego. Access-Able also has a superb list of links for specific regions or cities, such as the Atlanta Accessibility Guide (*http://www.shepherd.org/disres/guide/toc.html*).

For more links, see Disability Travel Services (*http://www.dts.org*), where you can find online newsletters, travel guides, travel agents that specialize in serving special needs populations, and travel assistance services. You can also use the Net to find a travel agency that specializes in special needs travel, such as AccessAbility Travel in Cambridge, Massachusetts (*http://www.disabled-travel.com/*).

Disability Travel Services
http://www.dts.org
Travel guides and travel agents for the disabled.

If you're looking for adventure, use a search directory to find an outdoor organization in your area, for example, Environmental Traveling Companions (*http://www.hooked.net/users/stuarth/ETC/*), a San Francisco-based group offering whitewater rafting and sea kayak trips for disabled people. For a more leisurely excursion, try Getaway Cruises (*http://www.cruiseaway.com/*), which lists "escorted cruises" for the disabled.

Finally, if you have specific questions about travel for the disabled, the best sources can be newsgroups and email lists.

For special needs travel, try these three newsgroups: *bit.listserv.dsshe-l*, *misc.handicap*, and *bit.listserv.l-hcap*. You can also post to general newsgroups, such as *rec.travel.cruises,* and mention you have special needs. An excellent email list for disabled travelers is Travable. To subscribe, send email to *LISTSERV@SJUVM.STJOHNS.EDU*, and in the body of the message, type: `subscribe travable Bob Dole`— don't include your signature. (Of course, if your name is not Bob Dole, substitute your name.) Chapter 8 explains how to use newsgroups and mailing lists.

ALTERNATIVE LIFESTYLES, ALTERNATIVE TRAVEL

Because the Net is so effective for sorting through its own clutter, it's particularly useful for people who want to travel with and among those who share their lifestyle. Lesbian and gay travelers can use the Net to find a homestay abroad or a resort in Key West that caters to a gay clientele. Here, even more than in other areas of specialized travel, checking the appropriate newsgroup or chat area can reap enormous benefits.

TIP

Newsgroups where you'll find information on gay travel include *bit.listserv.gaynet*, *ba.motss*, and *alt.homosexual*.

John Davis, a marketing manager in Seattle, used the keywords *home exchange* to find Mi Casa Su Casa (*http://www.well.com/user/ homeswap/*), an international home exchange network for gay and lesbian travelers. John and his partner stayed with two gay couples while traveling in France and will return the favor by hosting these couples when they visit Seattle. "They went out of their way to make us feel at home, accompanied us to see some of the local sights, and made us dinners on a couple of occasions," John says. You may also find a homestay (or offer one) through QTCompanion (*http://www.bures.com/qtc/*).

Several tour companies specializing in gay travel have already set up shop on the Net. You can find them easily by doing a keyword search under gay travel in Yahoo or another search directory. One that will

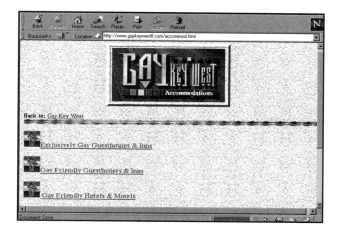

FIGURE 6-5
Gay Key West (http://www.gaykeywestfl. com) highlights gay-friendly hotels and inns.

pop up is Alyson Adventures (*http://www.channel1.com/alyson/*), specializing in bicycling, hiking, skiing, and diving tours for lesbians and gay men. "Imagine, holding hands without a second thought," begins the online brochure from Olivia Cruises and Resorts (*http:// www.oliviatravel.com/*), offering trips—exclusively for women—to Canada, the Caribbean, Tahiti, and other destinations.

Q-Net (*http://www.q-net.com*) is a comprehensive site for gay and lesbian travelers, offering links providing information about where to go, what to do, and where to stay. Also see *The Guide* magazine's gay travel section (*http://www.guidemag.com*), with country-by-country listings of hotels, bars, and attractions.

Regional guides to popular gay or lesbian destinations include Gay Key West (*http://www.gaykeywestfl.com/accommod.html*), which lists exclusively gay guesthouses and inns, as well as gay-friendly accommodations. Some hotel listings link to more information, such as rates, nearby attractions, and images of the hotel. If glitter, gambling, and fabulous faux Sphinxes are your scene, take a look at Gay Las Vegas (*http://coyote.accessnv.com/kmess/gayvegas/*), an extensive list of things to do on and off the strip.

Heading to London? Check Lesbian and Gay London (*http://www. users.dircon.co.uk/~zzyzx/tourist/glguide/glguide.htm*), which includes "finding the perfect local pub," gay and lesbian friendly hotels and restaurants, and links to other sites for travelers to London. For more gay and lesbian travel links, see travel agent John Clifford's site (*http://www.geocities.com/WestHollywood/1993/*).

FIND IT ONLINE

It's hard to overemphasize how useful the Net is for finding information about special travel areas. Travelers can use the multitude of
search directories to find just what they need and explore their options (see Appendix B, "Basic Internet Training" for more on using
search directories). As we'll show in more detail in Chapter 10, tour
companies and travel agents are exploiting these niches to reach travelers around the world. Travelers seeking a particular type of trip—
from helicopter skiing to walking tours—can find specialists on the
Net and have online discussions with them. Now, without further de-
lay, let's move on to adventure travel, and see how the Net can be the
first step on a journey of 10,000 miles.

Adventure Travel

7

Perhaps the most extraordinary feature of the Internet is that it allows the adventurous traveler to find the proverbial needle in the haystack—the offbeat, unusual, or exotic journey. Some use the Net to learn about excursions led by professional guides, such as trips to remote rivers or group ascents of Himalayan peaks. On the Net, travelers can read first-hand accounts written by adventurers who have just been to a particular place. Or they can visit newsgroups, where they can ask fellow travelers about their recent journeys. Connecting with other adventurous travelers through the Net can be especially valuable for destinations that aren't covered in detail by guidebooks. And, as tour company managers say, the Net has given them a way to convey more information to window-shopping travelers. Through the Net, travel companies can go beyond showing a couple of pictures—they can include the sound of a barking seal or a short video of an expedition.

▶ Into the Great Wide Open

▶ Adventure Tour Companies Online

▶ Dispatches from Fellow Travelers

▶ Around the World in 80 Clicks

▶ Staying Healthy During an Adventure

▶ Newsgroups as Virtual Guidebooks

▶ Finding the Answers Online

▶ Working and Studying Abroad

INTO THE GREAT
WIDE OPEN

Before the advent of the Internet, anyone wanting to research or arrange an exotic journey had only two choices: depend on hearsay advice, or hire an expensive specialty travel service. But now travelers can learn about journeys to places where only a handful of people travel each year. Want to drift down the Amazon in a native dug-out canoe, for example? Well, Mad Dog Expeditions (*http://www.mad-dog.net/amazon/itineraryf.html*) can arrange it for you.

In recent years, ecotourism and adventure travel have seen growing popularity. But, by their very nature, many of these trips lack the kind of travel industry infrastructure and literary documentation of traditional travel.

Some adventure tours are, well, works in progress. They change with the season, the countries, regional politics, and the people organizing them. All these variables—which can make these trips unattractive to the mainstream travel industry—make the Internet the perfect medium for both trip organizers and their clients. New itineraries and trip offerings can be posted on the Net as they occur. Travel advisories and transportation changes can be updated hourly, if need be.

The Internet really shines as a travel resource when travelers head off the beaten path without the guidance of a tour company. Susan Bott and Jim Klima (Jet City JimBo, as he's known on the Net) embarked on just this sort of around-the-world adventure in 1996, and Jim says the Net was essential for their pre-trip planning and for getting updates during their trip.

> *It's the only way to get timely and biased as well as unbiased information. For example, we checked Lonely Planet's Web site for postcards from readers. Travel agents are of little use to budget backpackers like me.*

> *The literature gets outdated rather quickly. Since I travel unreserved and prefer the unpredictable, my need for reliable information is paramount. There's no substitute for communicating with someone who's just been there. Even now I get queries from people all over the world planning trips like the one I am on.*

To read detailed accounts of JimBo and Sue's journey, see JimBo's "Klimagrams" at a site called Travel @ the Speed of Light (*http://vanbc.wimsey.com/~ayoung/travel.shtml*). For dozens of other tales from intrepid travelers, see Cyber Adventures (*http://cyber-adventures. com/*).

Before leaving I prowled every travel-related discussion group I could find to locate people who had actually done an overland trip. Since few Americans travel this way, using the Net gave me access to Europeans and Australians who had first-hand experience. I received very good feedback, both negative and positive, about overlanding in general and specific [trucking] companies in particular. It also gave me a splendid opportunity to query these people about what equipment and precautions I should take.

Another great source of concern before we left was getting permission to enter the Central Asian countries, Uzbekistan in particular. Everything there is in a state of flux since the collapse of the USSR, and corruption is quite rampant. So once again reading travelogues posted by others who had been there really helped.

I joined (Usenet discussion) groups related to Russia and monitored them for relevant information. As I gathered useful electronic contacts, I emailed travel agents in Moscow, B&B proprietors in Uzbekistan, and even a penpal in Tashkent. Eventually, after using every search tool I could find on the Web, I stumbled across travel agencies in Seattle and Australia that could provide visa assistance.

One Net resource that was quite useful was the Travel-L listserv which gave my posted queries international exposure. For example, I was worried about bandit hijackings of buses to Lamu, Kenya. Online State Department information was not timely enough, so I posted a query on Travel-L.

Cyber Adventures
http://cyber-adventures. com/
Wired adventurers share their stories.

FIGURE 7-1
JimBo and Sue travel at the speed of light. See Travel @ the Speed of Light (http://vanbc. wimsey.com/~ayoung/ travel.shtml) for detailed dispatches about their trip around the world.

A quick reply put me in touch with a man whose son goes there every year and was very knowledgeable about current conditions. Aside from being informative and up-to-date, this allowed me to cross-check and verify or chuck other information which I had accumulated—a necessity when you are doing independent travel.

We wanted to enter Kashgar, China, from a remote pass called Torgut in Kyrgyzstan to avoid going the long way around via Kazakhstan with its reputedly ugly border crossing. The Lonely Planet Guide for Central Asia was not in publication yet, so information was scarce. But through Travel-L, I was able to establish contact with people who had attempted this border crossing within the last year or two.

Another note: I wanted a solar charging system for my laptop since electrical connections where I was going in Africa were nonexistent. I posted queries in several computer discussion groups as well as on the manufacturer's home page and was eventually directed to a company called KISS, Keep It Simple Stupid, in Montana. I contacted them by email, submitted a list of technical questions, and subsequently purchased one of their solar panels.

Through the Net, Jim found others who had gone before him, people who had been there recently and could let him know what the conditions were. These folks could give Jim much better information than a year-old guidebook. And for some regions, such as the former Soviet republics bordering western China, no printed guidebook could have helped Jim find what he was looking for. So he searched the Web for travelers' accounts and connected with others in online discussion areas and through Internet mailing lists.

Jim found reliable information from travelers who had just been to the places he planned to visit. Then, while he traveled and after he returned, he served as a resource for other travelers. Through newsgroups he learned what it would be like to travel overland and found a trucking company that led trips over the route he was interested in. And through the Net he was able to connect with knowledgeable people in the regions he planned to visit, such as travel agents in Moscow. To get reliable news about border crossings, he posted a query to the Travel-L mailing list, where he could hear from more than one person, cross-checking and confirming his information.

2 CHICKS, 2 BIKES, 1 CAUSE

You don't have to be traveling to the remotest corners of the world for the Net to be useful. Two former advertising executives, Porter Gale and Donna Murphy, embarked on an across-the-U.S. bicycle trip in 1996 as part of a program to raise awareness about breast health. Before leaving they created a Web site they dubbed 2 Chicks, 2 Bikes, 1 Cause (*http://www.2chicks.org*). They were also able to use this connection to set up events and publicize their fund-raising ride. Porter says the Web was extremely valuable for their trek planning.

> *We put together about 15 events across the country. To save time and money, we ended up coordinating all the events via email (when possible). We also talked with lots of bikers and breast cancer survivors (using AOL chat) to find out what their opinions were about our trek and if there was any advice they could give us. Also, a group of physicians in Astabula, Ohio, saw our site and offered to do two events for us in Pennsylvania, so we rerouted. They treated us like queens. We received a lot of press (newspaper, TV, newsletters) in their area, raised several thousand dollars, and they took us sailing, gave us lodging, and even took us to the Cleveland Orchestra at Bloom Field.*

As they traveled, Porter and Donna received support and advice through email. Thanks to email tips from those following their progress, they made several changes to their planned course, adding stops at Zion National Park, Estes Park in Colorado, and Erie, Pennsylvania.

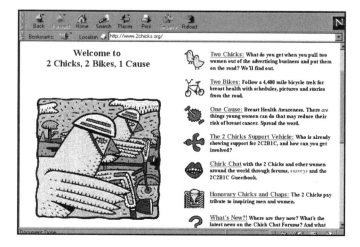

FIGURE 7-2
The two "chicks" rode more than 4,000 miles while logging updates on their Web site (http://www.2chicks.org/).

FROM RUSSIA WITH LOVE

The Russian Chronicles (*http://www.f8.com/FP/Russia/index.html*) represents another intersection between adventure travel and the Net. For this "experiment in interactive photojournalism," freelance writer Lisa Dickey and photojournalist Gary Matoso spent several months on a 5,000-mile journey, traveling through remote regions in Russia, documenting the outlook and opinion of contemporary Russians. Lisa says:

> *Email was obviously our lifeline, not only in the sense that it was the means of uploading our information to San Francisco, but also as a source of contact with our families and friends, feedback from readers of the Web site, and just generally getting news of what else was up in the world besides our monomaniacal drive to cross the trans-Siberian.*

ADVENTURE TOUR COMPANIES ONLINE

Until the proliferation of the Net, adventure tour companies could not provide very detailed information about their trips and destinations. Travelers had to choose a trip by looking at a couple of color photos and a few paragraphs of text. The limitations were equally frustrating to tour operators who always wished they had a better, more affordable way to communicate with their clients.

Mountain Travel Sobek, which offers packaged adventure tours such as mountain climbing trips in the Austian Alps and whitewater rafting trips in southern Africa, was one of the first big tour companies to recognize the potential of going online. On its site (*http://www. mtsobek.com/*), MTS goes far beyond the unchangeable information in its catalog to post trip updates, letters from the field, search capabilities, and more.

In the introduction of this book, Richard Bangs, former head of MTS, discusses how the Net enables adventure tour companies to put much more information online. Before the emergence of the Net, Richard felt that adventure tour companies couldn't fully convey what they had to offer.

> *We'd always been frustrated with the lack of a suitable communications tool. To have a two-week trek through the Himalayas and try to convey that with one photo wasn't good enough. The question was how could we bring the experience closer. As soon as the Net started to show its hand, we knew*

this is the tool we wanted, and not just because the Net can deliver more text and images. On the Net we can deliver sound—the trumpet of an elephant, groan of a shifting glacier, or the gamelan of Indonesia—and distribute this globally. It's not just that you can provide infinitely more material; you can provide emotional material.

Rather than choosing a trip based on a picture or two and a little text, travelers today can get detailed itineraries complete with tour dates, trip highlights, and up-to-date additions. Bangs notes that a catalog is static—it's already somewhat out of date when it's published. But companies can update a Web site anytime, for example, to add a new trip. And Web sites can include features such as recent postcards from travelers or guides that give an up-to-date view of conditions in a particular region.

Furthermore, Web sites are interactive. So if a traveler reads through the material, he or she can then click on the email link and send a quick message, which can be easier and more convenient than making a phone call.

Adventure company Web sites are among the most innovative on the Web. MTS, for example, includes a world map. Just click on the map and select a region you're interested in. To test this out, I clicked on South America and then on Chile and found that MTS offers five trips in this country, from an action-packed whitewater rafting trip on the Futaleufu River to a hiking tour of Patagonia. Another way to pick a trip would be by date. So if you have a vacation in March, you could see what MTS has available during that month. Or select by budget: in the Adventure section, click on Pricing to see a list of trips under $1,500, for example. There's also an Activities section where you can search for the type of adventure you want.

The Climbing Archive
http://www.dtek.chalmers. se/Climbing

Looking for a climbing partner? This site is loaded with information about the best walls to scale, climbing gyms, and knot tying, but perhaps its most useful link is an extensive list of climbers you can contact if you're looking for a partner.

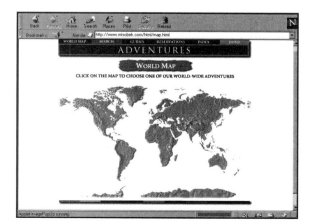

FIGURE 7-3

Mountain Travel Sobek (http://www. mtsobek.com) uses a world map on its site to help travelers find adventure tours in the regions they want to visit.

MTS uses the Web to publish its in-house newsletter, with updates of political and environmental news from around the world. And through the Web, the company offers discounts on trips that aren't filling up before the departure date.

DISPATCHES FROM FELLOW TRAVELERS

In the past couple of years, a wealth of new resources have come to life on the Web, from mega-sites like Outside Online (*http://outside.starwave.com/*) to tightly focused sites such as the Himalayan Explorers Club (*http://www.abwam.com/himexp/*).

For those interested in active travel options, *Outside Online* is a good place to start. The site lets you plan your own trips, or—if you're an armchair adventurer—you can follow another traveler's journey from the safety and comfort of your own home. A column called The Virtual Adventurer answers readers' questions, such as "Where can I swim with Aussie whale sharks?" and "Where can a kid discover rafting?" Going Places has a guide and insider tips for the 369 national parks in the U.S.; Global Voyagers has the latest dispatches from expeditions around the world, such as a mid-1996 ascent of the Himalayan peak K2.

If you're interested in dispatches from other adventure travelers, see Lonely Planet's Thorn Tree (*http://www.lonelyplanet.com/feedback/thorn.htm*), which operates a computer bulletin board organized by region, as well as special sections for women travelers and gays/lesbians. If you have a trip in mind and want to find someone to

Himalayan Explorers Club
http://www.abwam.com/himexp/

A must-visit site for anyone planning a trip to the Himalayas.

FIGURE 7-4
Outside Online (http://outside.starwave.com) helps you plan your adventure and find like-minded travelers.

share your adventure with, link up with other travelers at Travelling Companions. (*http://www.lonelyplanet.com/feedback/comp.htm*).

Often the best travel advice comes from like-minded travelers. To glean some of this wisdom from the Net, see The Doc's Favorite Travel Stories (*http://www.access.digex.net/~drmemory/sow.html*) and Cyber Adventures (*http://www.cyber-adventures.com*), two sites where "technomads" relay their tales as their trips unfold from points around the globe.

If you'd like to share your travel adventure with the world, you can create your own Web site or submit your story to Cyber Adventures or any of the other sites that post travelers' accounts of their journeys. Major guidebook sites, such as Lonely Planet and Moon Publications, include "postcards," or accounts of travelers' journeys from the front lines. Those who create their own Web sites usually do this after returning. To post dispatches from remote areas, it's much easier to submit to an existing site rather than trying to maintain your own.

Jim Klima, who discussed his adventures earlier in this chapter, says documenting his trip on the Web greatly enriched his travels.

> *To do a long journey without keeping a daily diary of what happened or a journal to measure the effect of your travels would be a monumental waste. On a long trip, say a couple months up to a year, you will reach saturation, especially if you keep moving, and will need either a written or photographic record to recall all you've experienced. The written form can be better than images on film when your camera fails (like mine did in Central Asia) or when you are not permitted to photograph freely (e.g., Muslim women in Pakistan or corrupt officials in Zaire). The Spousal Unit and I once did a Caribbean cruise on which I misloaded the camera, resulting in zero pictures. However, I wrote a long, romantic account of the trip that reduces her to mush even a decade later.*

> *Documenting my trip online has allowed me to share it with a large group of family, friends, and former co-workers, as well as travel junkies from all over the world. The former now understand (in shocking detail) where the Unit and I went. We do not have to tell our story over and over again. It would have been even better if we had been able to upload trip photos enroute using a digital camera. That would have negated the need for endless slide shows.*

> *Both people we knew and strangers on the Net said it was exciting to follow our progress despite the erratic updates caused by problems locating Net access. We also found ourselves corresponding electronically with individuals (a fair number of mad Australians) who either had done a trip*

like ours or wanted to do one. In all my Net travels I never found an account of an overland truck tour, let alone one written from a gut-level, what-can-go-wrong perspective. If I had not posted my adventure on the Net, I would never have been able to locate the crazy Aussies for commiserating about the joys and pitfalls of overland travel in Africa.

Doing the Web thing gave me impetus for searching out adventures to document what I might otherwise have skipped or not even found. For example, I would have never been able to persuade the Unit to visit war zones (Kashmir) or bizarre places (India's Temple of Rats) without this flimsy excuse.

Another benefit of pumping my material back to the world was more mundane: good backup. When I travel I suffer from diary-loss paranoia. Posting materials to the Net relieved me of some of the worry. This proved advantageous when the hard drive on my laptop crashed. I also had problems with diskettes going south and had to retrieve postings from the Web to see what I had written.

AROUND THE WORLD IN 80 CLICKS

Round-the-World Travel Guide

http://www.solutions.net/ rec-travel/rtw/html/faq.html

Essential advice for the ultimate adventure.

It's the ultimate earth-bound travel adventure— a trip around the world. When you're ready to make that step, visit the Round-the-World Travel Guide (*http://www.solutions.net/rec-travel/rtw/html/faq. html*). Compiled by Marc Brosius of Florida, the RTW guide considers topics ranging from whether to travel east or west to how long you can afford to be away. There are also discussions and tips on how and where to find work while traveling, how to stay in touch through email and faxes, and how to find a reliable traveling companion. Marc posted the guide in 1995, just before leaving on an around-the-world trip he expects will last two and a half years.

In September 1993, I was staring at the world map on the wall, contemplating all the places Karin and I planned on visiting in the next 20 years of short excursions. Suddenly, I realized we could make a continuous path out of the trips. I immediately justified it by saying that the separate trips would not leave enough time to see much, and would be more expensive. So I organized this guide as a starting point for further discussion, and as my small contribution to fellow travelers.

Marc and Karin used Net cafés to stay in touch with friends and with one another, as they embarked on different routes.

We find Internet cafés just about everywhere. They cost anywhere from $1 to $10 an hour. Free at the Singapore and Auckland, New Zealand, libraries. Kuala Lumpur, Malaysia, has a few—Poet had ridiculously cheap prices. Bangkok has a few, but the best is the Haagen Dazs diagonally across from the World Trade Center in the Maneeya Center, where you get free access in return for buying. Karin and I even did a talk session when she was in Seoul, Korea, at the Netscafé, and I was in Bangkok.

The Around-the-World Airfare Builder
http://www.highadv.com

This excellent site offers dozens of possible RTW routes and fares, with some under $1,500, and shows you how much you can save by using a discount broker. You can also build your own RTW itinerary and see what the fare will be.

Like many of the best travel sites on the Web, the RTW Guide includes contributions from readers. For example, fellow traveler Russell Gilbert warns prospective round-the-world travelers that long-term traveling is, in its own way, like a job.

Your new job will be to learn new currency, new local transportation, new languages, new places to sleep, new types of people, and new types of food. Every day, instead of driving to work, you will do these things. But the moments in between make it all worth it. So many people told us we were crazy for leaving our jobs when the economy was so bad. Don't listen to them! Go! You'll never regret it, even if you have a hard time finding a job when you get back. The trip was the best thing I've ever done in my life.

For this kind of travel, Marc suggests buying your air tickets through a consolidator. For an extensive guide to these agencies, refer to round-the-world specialist Edward Hasbrouck's Consolidators and Bucket Shops FAQ (*http://www.solutions.net/rec-travel/air-travel/consolidators.html*).

The Web is not the only online source for adventure or ecotravel. Some of the best information comes through mailing lists, such as Green Travel (*green-travel@igc.apc.org*). For more information, request an "info" file by sending email to *majordomo@igc.org*.

Here's a sample of a recent message posted to this list (the writer enclosed her email address for people who wanted further information):

```
Our small group of eight people recently returned
from three weeks of grassroots travel in Senegal.
We found the following five medical items most
useful: 1) a small plastic bottle of rubbing
alcohol (we brought this with us) for cleaning
abrasions and sterilizing the thermometer, 2)
paragoric for nausea and malaise (bought in Senegal
for $2 at pharmacies), 3) flagyl for amoebic
dysentery (bought in Senegal for $4 at pharmacies),
```

4) eye wash to cleanse the eyes of dust, and 5)
surgical masks (found in the U.S. at drugstores)
against the dust and fumes of the road and cities.
Even our Senegalese friends have taken to wearing
them. We really got to live the culture and to know
the Senegalese as we traveled to different parts of
the country experiencing village life.

FREE EMAIL

If you're on the road and don't want to spend a lot of time and money trying to dial into your home account, set up a freemail account through a Web-based email service. The two leading services are Hotmail (*http://www.hotmail.com*) and NetAddress (*http://www. netaddress.usa.net*). These services are supported by advertising that accompanies mail messages. For more information on setting up a freemail account, see Chapter 9, "Traveling with the Net."

STAYING HEALTHY DURING AN ADVENTURE

Few calamities can sink an adventure as quickly as a serious health problem. Even the most adventurous travelers—those who can handle camping out in subfreezing weather or braving a 12-hour bus ride over a dirt road, can be forced to call an abrupt end to a trip if someone becomes severely ill. So before you go, take advantage of the health information resources on the Net.

The Centers for Disease Control (*http://www.cdc.gov/travel/travel.html*) keeps tabs on the world's worst bugs, and lists travel advisories at the CDC Travel Information Web site when an outbreak occurs. The CDC site is extraordinarily comprehensive and smartly organized by region, making it easy for travelers to check the area they are visiting.

For a trip to Mexico and Central America, for example, click on this region and learn how to protect yourself from dangerous water and how to limit your risk of contracting malaria. For specific information on Costa Rica, click on the Costa Rica link at the bottom of the Central America section. The CDC site records recent outbreaks of disease, such as the summer 1996 outbreak of yellow fever in Nigeria. And if you're concerned about a specific disease, there's a list of links ranging from cholera to tuberculosis. If you're traveling to a fairly exotic destination you should check this site a few weeks before you leave so you will have time to get shots if necessary.

There are some routine precautions you should take regardless of specific disease outbreaks. For example, if you're planning a trip to a place where immunizations may be needed, see Travel Health Online (*www.tripprep.com/*). In addition to health information, THO has country descriptions, entry requirements, and embassy and consulate locations with contacts. You should not, however, blindly follow the advice on medical sites—these sites are merely guides and you should value the judgment of a trained medical professional over advice that comes through the Net.

Adventurers on their way to the developing world should not overlook Moon Publications' Staying Healthy in Asia, Africa, and Latin America (*http://www.moon.com/staying_healthy/*). This site includes the full text of Moon's book by the same name and has a feature that lets travelers search for a specific disease or region.

Finally, before you go, be sure to check World Travel Watch (*http://www.ora.com/ttales/editorial/wtw*), by veteran travel reporters Larry Habegger and James O'Reilly, editors of the Travelers' Tales series of books. Each month, WTW delivers a global roundup of events that affect conditions for travelers. Whether it's a cholera outbreak in Mongolia or a flood in Costa Rica, WTW lets you know what to watch for and when to reconsider a trip to a certain region or province.

NEWSGROUPS AS VIRTUAL GUIDEBOOKS

In 1993, before the phenomenal growth of the World Wide Web, writer Allen Noren found Usenet newsgroups most valuable in researching a three-month motorcycle trip around the Baltic Sea. "I research all my trips before departing, but this one had a twist," Allen says. "I planned and researched it almost exclusively over the Internet. I made it a challenge to myself to see just how much I could accomplish digitally."

While Allen could have easily found information about Germany and the Scandinavian countries in print guidebooks, learning about the newly liberated Baltic states of Estonia, Latvia, and Lithuania was another matter.

Those countries had just broken free from 40 years of repressive Soviet control. Not a single guidebook existed. Accounts of independent travelers having navigated through these countries were as rare as a youth hostel in Siberia. I called their U.S. embassies, and the common refrain was, "You want tour information? Ha! We don't have even telephones in Estonia, and you want tour information?"

Within days of getting online, I was able to find current political and cultural information on Usenet soc.culture newsgroups (such as soc.culture.russia and soc.culture.baltics). Russians warned me of bandits on the road to St. Petersburg, and how to avoid corrupt police. An Estonian gave me the name of a man who could help me obtain a travel permit for the island of Saaremaa, an area that had been closed even to Estonians since World War II.

A Latvian student gave me directions to a beach where I could find amber, and the address of his uncle who sold black market gasoline. A Lithuanian astronomer invited me to his observatory. Within two weeks I had been invited for dinners and weekends. I was even offered a job, and I hadn't even left home.

In the rec.travel.europe newsgroup I met a Dutch businessman who had recently driven part of the same route I would be taking, and when I wanted more information from him, he invited me to a private chat room on IRC (Internet Relay Chat), where we communicated for half an hour uninterrupted. He also rode a motorcycle, and was able to provide me with a valuable perspective of the region.

I created IRC discussion groups on Finland and each of the three Baltic States, and before long I was deluged with good information. On more than one occasion I used IRC as a place to meet people I'd exchanged email with and wanted to have lengthier discussions with.

Did I find answers to all my questions on the Internet? No, and that's not the point. For me, traveling is about a constantly unfolding set of questions that only grow more complex the further one goes. What the Net did was enable me to create an informed context, one that allowed me to become a better traveler.

IRC (Internet Relay Chat)
IRC is a multi-user chat system, where people convene on "channels" (a virtual place, usually with a topic of conversation) to talk in groups or privately. IRC was created in 1988 by Jarkko Oikarinen. Since starting in Finland, it has been used in more than 50 countries. IRC gained international fame during the Persian Gulf War, when updates from around the world came across an IRC channel.

Allen's story illustrates how useful newsgroups can be, particularly for the roads less traveled. Among the statements most often repeated by travelers planning their trips online is "Use the newsgroups—they're fabulous sources of information." And keep in mind: in 1993 there were fewer than a third the number of newsgroups there are today.

TIP

Some of the best newsgroups for adventure travel are *rec.climbing*, *rec.backcountry*, *alt.rec.camping*, *rec.bicycles.off-road*, and *rec.skiing.nordic*. For more on using newsgroups, see Chapter 8, "Newsgroups and Mailing Lists."

FINDING THE ANSWERS ONLINE

Though printed travel guides have extensive information and are by no means obsolete, online sources can represent a more current resource. Web sites are becoming increasingly interactive, allowing you to conduct searches, ask questions, get answers, and make reservations, feats printed guides can't match.

For those traveling to exotic locations, no printed guide can include the latest U.S. State Department travel warnings (*http://travel.state. gov/travel_warnings.html*). If it's a Caribbean bareboat sailing vacation you have planned, current hurricane forecasts can be more than a passing interest.

So why refer to a guidebook to find average temperatures for July in Capetown when you can find all that information *plus* current forecasts online? And why spend weeks waiting for a brochure from a foreign country's tourist bureau when you can access it in seconds through the bureau's Web site? When you find information online that you want to take with you, just print it out and pack it up.

LEARNING ABOUT A LONELY ISLAND

PERSONAL ACCOUNT

Dan Fost
danfost@well.com

Journalists are comfortable doing their own research, so it was natural for Dan Fost, a reporter with the *Marin Independent Journal* in Novato, California, to turn to the Net when he was researching a trip to Vanuatu, a small South Pacific island nation located between Fiji and Australia.

> *We had a little information—a Lonely Planet guidebook; a few chapters in Paul Theroux's travelogue,* The Happy Isles of Oceania; *an account of a woman's time on a remote and primitive island,* Journey to the End of the World. *Every little bit, however, piqued our curiosity, and we wanted more.*

Vanuatu: A Canadian's Perspective
http://www.silk.net/ personal/scombs/ vanuatu.html

That's where the Internet came in. Armed with Netscape and all those search directories, we freely punched in Vanuatu *and got responses much more manageable than if we had punched in, say,* France. *Very few news accounts materialized. A weather site told of a cyclone that had passed Vanuatu.*

One site, found through an AltaVista search, was particularly interesting. A Canadian guy named Stan Combs had put photos and extensive text online about his two-year stint on Malekula in a Peace Corps-type capacity.

Stan tells of tropical diseases, poverty, geology, geography, and weather. He writes of the "real Vanuatu." This fascinating site was also useful in explaining to friends and family where our travels were taking us. We'd just email the URL around and they, too, were treated to a glimpse of this place that, until we announced our plans, they'd never heard of.

I should note, however, the crowning irony I find in my use of the Web. I barely read Combs' material online. But I printed the whole thing out, brought it with me, and—while sitting on a porch by a palm tree under a thatched roof on the Vanuatu island of Espiritu Santo—found it compelling reading.

FIGURE 7-5
Vanuatu: A Canadian's Perspective (http://www.silk.net/personal/ scombs/vanuatu.html) shows an image of a bird that signifies the social rank of its owner.

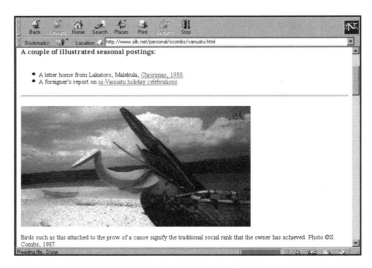

WORKING AND STUDYING ABROAD

It's a common dream of many college students to leave the familiar confines of their home country and live abroad. Many actually live the dream. Others wait until later in life to take the plunge. But when they do, the Net provides a bridge to help them make the transition to a new life and new culture.

If you are a student thinking about studying overseas or a parent with a child looking for overseas study opportunities, stop by studyabroad.com (*http://www.studyabroad.com*). The site has hundreds of overseas study listings and links. Whether your pleasure is a semester at sea or studying Spanish in Guatemala, studyabroad.com is a good starting point.

Another good place to learn about international education and volunteer opportunities is the Council on International Educational Exchange (*http://www.ciee.org/*), which includes the Departure Zone, where travelers share their stories and photos. The Departure Zone lets you pose your travel questions to CIEE's experts. CIEE's Travel Planner (*http://www.ciee.org/zone/planner/basics.htm*) covers student travel basics, from Money Matters to Health and Safety.

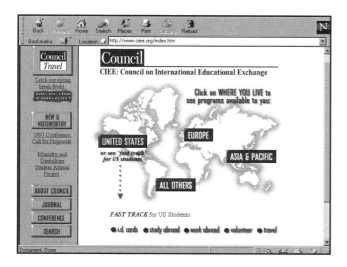

FIGURE 7-6

CIEE (http://www.ciee.org/) helps students and other adventurers get around the world.

SABBATICAL SUGGESTIONS

For those planning a sabbatical, Sensational Sabbatical Suggestions (*http://omni.cc.purdue.edu/~alltson/sabbat.html*) has tips on everything from renting your home to income tax issues. The authors, Allison and Alastair Morrison, created the site to help others avoid the mistakes they made on their sabbatical.

PERSONAL ACCOUNT
Allison Morrison
alltson@vm.cc.purdue.edu

"I wrote [Sabbatical Suggestions] to cleanse my soul after we made so many terrible mistakes," Allison says. "We lost $6,000 on a car purchase and could not even take it as a tax deduction. I learned the best way to do it now to save on taxes. Now we stay in cheap university housing and rent cars."

Here's a sample of the advice offered by Sabbatical Suggestions:

```
Furnished housing is ideal for a family. Renting
furniture is extremely expensive. If you can't find
a furnished place, consider a long-term lease at a
hotel or holiday apartment. Alternatively, stay in
a holiday apartment for a couple of weeks and
collect furnishings at garage sales, auctions, and
used furniture stores. Hopefully, you'll be living
in a city where these options are available. This
link to Global Travel Apartments' Comfort Zone
(http://www.globaltrvlapt.com/) may be a starting
point to consider.
```

LEARNING VACATIONS AND FAMILY HOMESTAYS

The demand for vacations that offer more than a tan has jumped in recent years. The trend began when several research universities began offering a limited number of slots on field research trips to novice researchers. These trips ranged from archeological digs in the Holy Land to specimen-gathering trips in the Amazon. The vacationers paid a hefty fee to go along, thereby helping finance the research. For their money, they got to work beside professional researchers, similar to armchair jocks who pay thousands of dollars to spend a week at a training camp with professional athletes.

For those who want to do more than lie on a beach during their vacations, Learning Vacations (*http://www.learningvacations.com/*) is a site where travelers can choose trips ranging from sailing schools to safaris. Or join a field research team through Earthwatch (*http://gaia.earthwatch.org/*) where, for example, travelers can sign up for a trip to Nanning City, China, in an effort to help preserve the habitat of the white-headed langur, a highly endangered primate.

Others may be interested in a birding tour in Costa Rica's forests, or an excursion to Nepal to see the Dumje Festival, a four-day celebration with chanting, dancing, and exotic costumes. To explore these and dozens of other travel alternatives, see EarthWise Journeys (*http://www.teleport.com/~earthwyz/*). Another source for learning vacations is World Neighbors' Journeys of the Heart (*http://www.halcyon.com/fkroger/heart.html*).

If you're in the hospitality business and would like to spend some time working in another country, see Hospitality Net's Virtual Job Exchange (*http://www.hospitalitynet.nl/job/*), where you can find temporary or long-term restaurant and lodging jobs throughout the world.

JUST GETTING STARTED

As we said at the start, this chapter is not a comprehensive list—it's meant merely to get you started. As they do when embarking upon any adventure, travelers start at some known points of embarkation and move on to the new and unknown. By starting at the sites listed in this chapter, you can get a sense of the potential to enrich your travels by connecting with others who have blazed similar trails. Speaking of connecting with others, let's now move on to Chapter 8, where you'll see how to reach people anywhere in the world through newsgroups and mailing lists.

Earthwatch
http://gaia.earthwatch.org/
Join field researchers when you travel.

Newsgroups and Mailing Lists

8

Internet newsgroups represent the marriage of the old with the new—the Net and the tradition of veteran travelers sharing their experiences and advice with tales of their travel adventures. Travelers' tales have come to the bubbling interactive world of online travel newsgroups in a big way and represent a tremendous resource for travelers researching journeys of their own. In the following pages, fellow travelers illustrate how you can use travel newsgroups to make contacts around the world and get the information you need. This chapter shows you how to automate your search through the forest of newsgroups to find just the subject you're seeking. And it discusses mailing lists (also called listservs) where you can participate in email discussions.

▶ The Virtues of Newsgroups

▶ The Ultimate Newsgroup Search Tool

▶ America Online, CompuServe, and Other Services

▶ Finding Listservs

THE VIRTUES OF NEWSGROUPS

Imagine, for just a moment, that you could get in touch with people anywhere in the world, communicate with them for free, and find a way to connect with others who could answer your specific travel questions. Thanks to the Internet, this form of communication has become part of our daily existence, as thousands of travelers every day are connecting with people from New Brunswick to New South Wales. Through these connections, travelers are learning where to stay, what to bring, where to eat, and much, much more.

Throughout the research for this book, one traveler after another has extolled the virtues of newsgroups. What's so wonderful about them? Simply that you can get honest advice, straight from other travelers. While the Web has loads of valuable information, commercial Web sites are often skewed by their sponsors' point of view. With newsgroups, just about everyone is simply sharing their own opinions and experience, so the information is less shaded by, shall we say, commercial considerations.

Unlike guidebooks, which are limited by their size and lack of timeliness, people you meet on the Net can answer specific questions. A traveler headed to Munich who wants recommendations for bars during Oktoberfest could post to newsgroups ranging from *rec.travel.europe* to *rec.crafts.brewing*, and people will respond with tips and advice. If you're going someplace where the guidebook information is thin, tap the newsgroups and find other travelers—or local residents—who know the area and will give you the lowdown.

ADVICE FROM PEOPLE WHO HAVE BEEN THERE

Ami Claxton, who used *rec.travel.europe* to research her trip to Italy (see Chapter 4), has this to say about the value of newsgroups:

> *The Usenet community is a fabulous source of travel information. The best part of Usenet is that it is up to the minute. Very often, people who wrote had just returned from Rome within the past month, so that the information is timely and relevant. It's also much cheaper than buying a guidebook and/or making many international phone calls (to people who don't necessarily speak English). Another bonus is that these are just regular people (most times) who are trying to help you enjoy your experience— they have no financial stake in where you stay or visit. If you go to travel*

*agents, you're just never sure if they are directing you to a certain place
because it really meets your specifications or because they have a nice little
deal worked out for commissions!*

Note in the above example that Ami doesn't just turn to the newsgroups when she has a question—she also scans them often and if
she spies a topic she's knowledgeable about, she responds to the person who posted the query.

If you're new to all this and still shy, remember that you can learn
from newsgroups by simply "lurking" in them. Lurking is the practice of reading posts without posting a message yourself. It's typically
good netiquette (Net etiquette) to lurk for a while to get a sense of a
newsgroup before posting to it. It's also wise to read the Frequently
Asked Questions (FAQ) summary which often answers the most
common questions posted to a group. Someone else may have already asked the question you had in mind, and the answer will appear alongside the question. These linked series of posts and
responses are called threads. You can start at the beginning of a
thread and follow it to its culmination.

A VAST ELECTRONIC BULLETIN BOARD

Usenet is nothing more complicated than an electronic bulletin
board. It is comprised of more than 16,000 different newsgroups,
each a forum for a specific topic. There are no gatekeepers or censors
on Usenet—just about anyone with a Net connection can post a message or create a newsgroup. But there has developed an informal list
of dos and don'ts. For example, it's considered rude to create another
newsgroup on a theme for which one already exists.

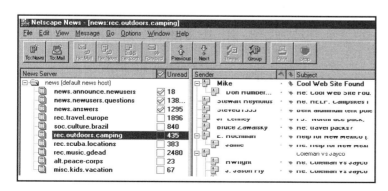

FIGURE 8-1

*Netscape's newsreader is a
window to Usenet newsgroups.
Copyright Netscape
Communications Corp.*

These discussion areas range from the mainstream, such as *rec.travel.marketplace*, to the fringes, such as *alt.bitterness*. A few hundred newsgroups contain adult material that some might find objectionable. But their names are a pretty clear tip-off, such as *alt.tasteless.jokes* and *alt.sex.erotica*, so the chance of accidentally stumbling into one is fairly slim. But this is a good time to point out that the Internet in general, and newsgroups in particular, is not the kind of neighborhood in which you would want to leave a young child unsupervised. There are some filtering programs such as Net Nanny that will block many adult sites, but no program can catch them all. So, as with television, it's a good idea to supervise a child's Net surfing.

With that one caveat, Usenet groups are an incredible resource. Every day thousands of users post queries to newsgroups, such as the post below from Alan Chen of Singapore to *rec.travel.asia* asking for information about a destination he planned to visit:

> Hi, I'm going to Hong Kong for the first time early
> next month. I will stay for 6 days. I am just
> wondering how to optimize my time over there. I
> plan to spend 2 days shopping for the summer sales.
> Any recommended place, good price for branded
> clothes, both men's & ladies'?
>
> Is Ocean Park worth a visit? Any other good places
> for Dim Sum or famous Hong Kong dishes, like
> roasted duck?
>
> Any recommended sightseeing places? I heard Stanley
> Market is nice, with a bus ride over the hills &
> you can get a good landscape view from there. In
> fact, I plan to visit Macao for a day, do I have
> enough time?
>
> Any suggestion will be appreciated. Thanks in
> advance. —Alan

A woman named Michelle responded:

> Hi Alan,
>
> For shopping, try the shopping complex at Shatin
> (can't remember what it's called, but it's HUGE
> with heaps of stores selling both branded and non-
> branded stuff). For really branded stuff (Chanel?
> Louis Vuitton?), try the shops at Causeway
> Bay/Central (HK Island), and at Harbour City (Tsim

Tsa Tsui, Kowloon). That will take up your 2 days
<grin>.

Yep, been to Ocean Park twice, and enjoyed myself
each time! Definitely worth a visit! (Personally, I
find the cable car rides a bit too scary for me!)
Victoria Peak is awesome... you can get a bird's
eye view of HK! You can get to Victoria Peak via
bus or tram (I think the tram leaves from Central).
One day in Macao is more than enough (half day will
be just nice)! Don't forget the casino(s) — you
might be lucky! And try those almond biscuits while
you're there. Oh, and watch out for those behind
the wheels!

Stanley Market is okay, a bit overrated, I think.
And it's quite far away, on the other side of HK
Island??! If you're travelling to HK Island, try
taking the ferry across from Tsim Tsa Tsui — you'll
love the view!

Can't remember which restaurants I've been to —
there're so many of them! But I've always enjoyed
the skewered fish balls that are sold at the side of
the road (rare to find these days!).

Have fun in HK. You'll love it!- -Michelle

LURK, THEN LEAP

When you're done lurking and ready to jump into a newsgroup, how
do you know where to begin your online conversation? Among the
most popular for travel newsgroups are those in the *rec.travel* category, such as *rec.travel.air*, *rec.travel.europe*, and *rec.travel.usa-canada*.
Also useful are the *soc.culture* newsgroups. Say you're planning a trip
to Brazil and want to learn more about Brazilian culture. If you use
Netscape, you click the Window button and scroll down to Netscape
News to open your news reader. Once there, open *soc.culture.brazil*
and spend some time lurking in this group.

Most major newsgroups have FAQs, a set of answers to Frequently
Asked Questions. For those new to the group, this is a good first
stop. FAQs are set up by newsgroup moderators so people don't have
to waste time answering the same questions whenever a new member
joins. For example: "What does this group do?" "Can I post pictures
in this group?" If your question is not answered in the FAQ and it

seems that the group is the appropriate place to post your question, then go ahead, don't be shy. Post it.

TIP

Troels Arvin
tarvin@mdb.ku.dk
*http://www.mdb.ku.dk/
tarvin/copenhagen/*
**Budget Hotels
in Copenhagen**

When you post, be sure to craft a short but descriptive "Subject" line. As frequent traveler Troels Arvin of Denmark says:

The flow in the travel newsgroups is quite high. When I look through the headers of newsgroups, I don't want to spend too much time doing it. So I only take a closer look at messages which immediately look interesting from their specific subject headers. For example, if you want to receive answers to a question about accommodations in Copenhagen, don't post a question with a subject line that reads: "A question about travelling" or "Help." Instead, use "Question about Copenhagen" or even better: "Copenhagen accommodations??"

You may ask potential responders to send email directly to you (rather than just posting the response in the newsgroup), but be forewarned that some people resent this unless you have a good reason. Since the whole premise of using newsgroups is to share information, some feel it's selfish when someone just mines the group for what they need without contributing to the discussion. So, unless there is some pressing privacy-related reason to do so, don't ask for a personal email response. If you are afraid you'll miss the response because you don't check the group regularly, then ask the person to post a response and "cc" a copy to your email box as well. Then all your bases are covered. Most people will gladly oblige if you ask politely.

THE ULTIMATE NEWSGROUP SEARCH TOOL

DejaNews
http://www.dejanews.com
Find the right newsgroup
with this search tool.

While the *rec.travel* and *soc.culture* newsgroups are logical starting points for cybertravelers, there may be other newsgroups that pertain to particular destinations or types of travel. In the past, finding such obscure groups meant sorting through thousands of newsgroups. But, thankfully, in 1995 DejaNews (*http://www.dejanews.com*) launched a newsgroup search directory to help people sort through

FIGURE 8-2
DejaNews (http://www.dejanews.com) lets you search for newsgroups and individual posts, and even lets you see other users' posting histories.

the thousands of groups and millions of posts. DejaNews archives and indexes these posts and has an extraordinarily fast and accurate search directory to help you find the right newsgroup for your search. You can even use DejaNews to post articles directly to desired newsgroups without having to call them up in your newsreader.

DEJANEWS ALL OVER AGAIN

Until DejaNews came along, newsgroup users posted to their favorite groups without having to worry too much about where their post might show up six months later. In fact, the chances of finding a random post among the millions of other posts was like finding the proverbial needle in the haystack. But today anyone can type an email address into DejaNews, and it will find any post authored from this address. In other words, you can have DejaNews find all posts written by *shapiro@songline.com* and you'll get a list of newsgroups that I've posted to. Then you can click on any post from this list to see what I've written in each post. This has led to embarrassing revelations for some people: "Busy executive looking for clothing-optional vacation." Not that this person has anything to be ashamed of—he just might not want his boss to know he'd been hanging out with a bunch of naked people during his week off.

TWO WAYS TO SEARCH

DejaNews' main page offers you two ways to conduct your search. You can enter keywords and see where they show up in any newsgroup, or enter the keywords in the lower box to find the most appropriate newsgroups. For a camping trip in Maine, one user entered *camping Maine* in the lower box to find which newsgroups would be the right forums for her questions. DejaNews searched for a few seconds and returned the following list:

```
All the newsgroups in the following list contain
*camping Maine* in some article. The confidence
rating indicates how sure we are that people talk
about your query in the newsgroup. Clicking on the
newsgroup name will show you all of the articles
within the group which match your query.

Confidence     Newsgroup
99%            rec.outdoors.camping
87%            rec.backcountry
85%            rec.boats.paddle
82%            rec.travel.usa-canada
48%            rec.outdoors.national-parks
46%            rec.travel.marketplace
31%            rec.outdoors.rv-travel
23%            alt.rec.camping
15%            .misc.kids.vacation
14%            alt.personals
14%            alt.personals.ads
14%            rec.guns
12%            rec.music.phish
12%            rec.sport.disc
10%            rec.outdoors.marketplace
```

From this screen you can select the groups you feel will be useful, for example, *rec.outdoors.camping*, and eliminate those that don't apply, such as the groups about personals, guns, and the alternative rock group Phish.

Now here's the beautiful part: from this page just click on a newsgroup, and the DejaNews search engine will select posts in this newsgroup that contain the search terms. So when you click on *rec.outdoors.camping*, you'll get only the posts in this group that mention "camping" and "Maine."

For an early fall camping trip to Maine, a woman named Connie from North Carolina posted this message:

```
We are going to Maine Oct 3-8. Plan to visit Acadia
and Baxter state parks. We would like to camp but
don't know the best places in these areas. I'm also
wondering if we are going to freeze our butts off.
(I know this is relative to what you're used to.)
```

```
Does anyone have any thoughts on these things?
Thanks, Connie
```

Within a few days she received about a half dozen responses, including the following from a couple in western New York.

```
Hi—we were just at Acadia, and found a private
campground which was great. Don't know how much
comfort you need, or if you have a trailer or just
tenting, but try White Birches Campground:

Seal Cove Road, PO Box 421

Southwest Harbor ME 04679

Phone 207-244-3797

Props. are Ann & Pete Murphy

We enjoyed our stay, and you are right in the
middle of everything on Mt. Desert Island. You can
try the National Park, but they may be full.
```

Usenet offers the best chance of getting specific answers to any questions you may have. Unlike the Web, which is mostly a one-way medium, Usenet opens a window to a network of correspondents around the world, including residents in the place you're visiting.

HONEST PICKS, BRUTAL PANS

Nothing can ruin a trip faster than traveling thousands of miles only to land in a lousy location. A lot of Usenet postings read like product label warnings. Connie's husband Bill says:

The hints are usually what places to avoid, who has good food, what to see that the tour books don't cover but are worth the trip. Example: Part of our trip included a side excursion to Baxter State Park to see Mt. Katahdin. However, after getting mail from people we found out it might be pretty cold up there then. In addition, we wouldn't be able to fish. We had one post from someone who had just returned saying 'Avoid this hotel on Moosehead Lake. It's a dump!' We had considered staying there as the name was nice, the view great, and the price cheap. After reading the review, we tossed that place as an option.

Troels Arvin of Denmark says the best advice often comes from other travelers who may know more than people who live in the area you intend to visit.

When people asked about tourism and accommodations in my hometown, I was actually not very capable of answering them: of course, I have never been a tourist in my hometown. So providing useful information to foreign travelers actually takes some effort—even for people living right in the middle of the destination. Consequently, to a great extent, one should look for responses from other travelers when one asks a question about a certain destination; the locals may not be very well-informed on issues of practical interest to the traveler.

A Sampling of Travel-Related Newsgroups

Note: If there's no description, the subject of the group is clear from its title.

Rec.travel sites

rec.travel.europe	
rec.travel.usa-canada	
rec.travel.asia	
rec.travel.latin-america	
rec.travel.caribbean	
rec.travel.africa	
rec.travel.australia+nz	
rec.travel.air	Airline and airport information
rec.travel.cruises	Cruise reports and reviews
rec.travel.marketplace	Buy/sell tickets, travel bargains
rec.travel.misc	Miscellaneous travel topics

Other *rec* newsgroups

rec.backcountry	Hiking and backpacking
rec.outdoors.camping	Camping in campgrounds
rec.outdoors.rv-travel	Travel in campers or RVs
rec.outdoors.national-parks	National parks (all nations, not just U.S.)
rec.scuba.locations	Dive sites and destinations
rec.outdoors.fishing	Where to fish
rec.bicycles.off-road	For mountain biking
rec.climbing	For rock climbing
rec.boats.paddle	Rafting, canoeing, and kayaking
rec.skiing.alpine	Downhill skiing
rec.skiing.nordic	Cross-country skiing
rec.skiing.snowboard	Hitting the slopes without skis
rec.food.restaurants	
rec.food.drink	

The following response (from a woman in Australia) to a post about White House tours is a classic example of Troels' point:

```
>My son and I would like to tour the White House on
>Saturday, September 21st. Realistically, what time
>should we be in line in the morning?
```

```
It's too bad you didn't let us know sooner. You can
get advanced tickets from your local state
representative's office.
```

> An arrow or "carrot" to the left of a phrase shows that it was part of a previous message.

soc.culture newsgroups

Note: With about 150 *soc.culture* newsgroups (from *soc.culture.afghanistan* to *soc.culture.zimbabwe*), there's almost certainly a *soc.culture* newsgroup that applies to your destination. The *soc.culture* groups are among the most useful Usenet groups for getting a sense of place and an idea of the way people think. For travelers who seek to be more sensitive and respectful of the local culture, these groups are excellent sources of advice, whether you have a question or want to learn by lurking. Following are some of the most popular *soc.culture* newsgroups:

soc.culture.african	*soc.culture.hongkong*
soc.culture.argentina	*soc.culture.indian*
soc.culture.british	*soc.culture.italian*
soc.culture.brazil	*soc.culture.japan*
soc.culture.canada	*soc.culture.jewish*
soc.culture.china	*soc.culture.pakistan*
soc.culture.europe	*soc.culture.singapore*
soc.culture.german	*soc.culture.usa*
soc.culture.french	*soc.culture.vietnamese*

Other useful newsgroups:

bit.listserv.travel-l	General travel topics
alt.rec.camping	Where and when to camp
uk.rec.youth-hostel	British hostels
alt.travel.road-trip	Choice routes, sights, and places to stay
alt.peace-corps	Insider views of the corps
misc.transport.air-industry	For travel pros
misc.kids.vacation	Ideas for family vacations

```
Just a side note: When my mom and I visited the
White House we saw the regular tour that is
provided by having the tickets from the State
Representative. But as we were walking away, around
the perimeter of the White House, I struck up a
conversation with one of the guards. Long story
short, he took my mother and me on a tour of the
EAST wing. We saw the press room, which is where
they make the state of the union address from,
etc., and which sits over an indoor pool. And we
saw the Oval Office.

I don't know how rare that was, but, boy, was it
great. You never know, give it a shot.

Janelle in Melbourne

*********************

From the Land of
Kangaroos & Koalas

*********************
```

Planning to relocate from San Francisco to London, avid bicyclist Gary Schwartz (who comments on renting a car over the Net in Chapter 2) posted some questions to a newsgroup about bicycling. Gary asked about bicycle headlight laws in England and began conversing with several cyclists in the group.

Rob answered with good information; I wrote back, and we agreed to get together to ride when I moved to London. We did, and we've remained good friends since, riding together occasionally, and socializing "off-road." Emma and I have had dinner at their place, and should be having him and his wife over to our place sometime.

Note how a personal connection through a newsgroup led to a real-world friendship. That's one of the greatest benefits of the newsgroups: meeting and getting to know people in a virtual space often leads to a genuine (offline) friendship.

AMERICA ONLINE, COMPUSERVE, AND OTHER SERVICES

While there's a newsgroup for just about every topic you can imagine, Usenet is not the only place where you can get advice directly from the hearts and minds of other travelers. If you're a member of an online service such as AOL or CompuServe, don't overlook chat rooms and forums, which can be good sources of information for travel planning.

To get to the most popular AOL travel boards, use the keyword *traveler* which brings up the Independent Traveler. From here you'll find links to travel boards, the Traveler's Resource Center, the Travel Café, FAQs, and Rick Steves' Europe Through the Back Door.

Before a recent trip to Rome, Pamela Terry used AOL's Europe travel board to ask for tips on where to dine. Here's her story:

> *The other two times I'd been to Rome I always ordered the wrong thing at restaurants. The first time I thought I ordered pasta with salmon and got lox on toast. The second time I was there I thought I ordered spaghetti with meat sauce and I got spaghetti with half cooked bacon and a heavy cream sauce. Major stomach problems a half-hour after that one!*

> *Then a guy on AOL told me about Abrizzi's in Rome—he even told me the square to look for and to order the Abrizzi cannelloni. I found the place and the cannelloni was great. It broke my Rome food curse.*

INSTANT CHAT

In AOL's Travel Café, you'll find a list of weekly chat programs, such as "Ask a Travel Guide" where you can pose questions to the experts, or "Shoestring Travel" where you can discuss the best travel deals on the planet. Other Travel Café topics range from Disney Chat Hour to Solo Travel. These forums typically occur at 9 p.m. or 10 p.m. Eastern time, though you can drop into the cafe anytime and find a few fellow travelers willing to share advice.

Unlike newsgroups, where you post and may hear back a few hours or a few days later, chat groups are immediate. So if there's an AOL travel expert and 30 members in an AOL chat auditorium, you can get your question answered just minutes after it's posted. Some people just tune into these forums to "listen," while others have specific questions on their minds and post those queries by writing them into the chat group.

Others get the information they need through listservs, also known as mailing lists. On a mailing list, once you subscribe, you receive—directly in your email box—all messages posted to the list.

FINDING LISTSERVS

Liszt

http://www.liszt.com

Find listservs that apply to subjects of interests with Liszt's search engine.

To find mailing lists for whatever subject you're interested in, see Liszt (*http://www.liszt.com*). Just enter the topic and Liszt will give you listservs related to that topic. For example, a search for the term "diving" produced the following:

```
Your search on (diving) produced 7 matches:

HYPBAR-L
  HyperBaric & Diving Medicine List

ne-diving
  New England Diving provides local contacts for New
  England divers.

plongee
  Bilingual Diving / Plongee Bilingue

scuba
  "UCD Scuba Diving Program news"

SCUBA-TR
  Turkish Skin/SCUBA Diving List

skydive
  UseNet News "rec.skydiving"

wga-scuba-diving
  The Wharton Scuba Diving Club
```

The name of each list is color-coded. If a list appears in green, complete information is available; if it appears in blue, Liszt has not requested information for this listserv. Clicking on the name of the

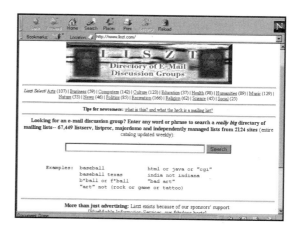

FIGURE 8-3

Liszt has a catalog of more than 40 listservs related to travel.

group gives you more information about the group and in most cases tells you how to join it.

LISTSERVS AS ONLINE COMMUNITIES

Before leaving for a vacation in Puerto Rico, Jane Nowlin of New Hampshire found a fellow list member there who answered her questions about "hurricane damage, which areas were fully restored and which were hardest hit." Though power was still out in Puerto Rico, the hotel owner there sent his messages using "a battery for power since he did not have power for a few days after the hurricane."

Mailing lists can be especially helpful for trips to far-flung destinations. Before a trip to Malaysia and southern Africa, Lollie Roberts of San Jose posted a notice to the Travel-L list.

> *I started out by sending a message directly to Travel-L telling people my plans and asking for suggestions and names of travel agents who could help me. I received lots of comments and the names of several travel agents from other members of the group. In addition, I made contact with a person from Kuala Lumpur, one of the stops on my trip. I corresponded with him via email and learned that he would be coming to San Jose where I am currently living. We met for dinner while he was here, and he gave me lots of tips on what to see and do in KL. People also sent me addresses for Web pages that would have information, including a page about Zimbabwe, another place I was planning to go. From these Web pages I learned background information about the countries I would visit as well as specific information about things to see and do.*

TIP

To subscribe to the Travel-L listserv, send email to *listserv@vm.ege.edu.tr* and type `subscribe travel-l` and your name in the body of the message. Don't write anything else in the message and don't include your signature.

Michael van Verk of the Netherlands researched a trip to Borneo through the Travel-L list.

> *When I travelled to Borneo last year, the Travel-L list was the only source for vital, first-hand information. Without the information people on Travel-L gave me, I probably never would have gone there. For my last trip to Egypt,*

Michael's Lodge
http://www.mediaport.org/~michaelv/
Michael van Verk shares travel stories from people who participate in the Travel-L listserv.

the list provided me with the date for the Coptic Easter, something you won't find easily through conventional channels. And people who had been there recently could give me information on security.

THE INSIDE SCOOP ON NORWAY'S OLD FJORD FARMS

Ginger Brusca of Los Angeles wanted to learn more about Norway's *storfjords*, "fjord farms" built high on steep fjords because of the lack of arable land below. Ginger says, "They were on such steep slopes that people would tie their young children to a house or a tree so they wouldn't plummet down into the fjords."

After seeing a documentary about these farms, Ginger wanted to learn more, so she posted a message on the Travel-L list.

One young Norwegian woman gave me a few clues, including the tourist authority in the area she thought these farms were chiefly located. The tourist authority eventually sent me literature—all in Norwegian! Another Norwegian woman, Berit, and I started corresponding about these fjord farms and she helped me translate (via email, of course) some of the passages.

We eventually figured out that there is an organization called the Storfjordens Venner (friends of the Storfjords) that does work on preserving them and has an annual meeting. By this time, Berit was interested in them, too. And we had gotten to be friends. So, the upshot is that I have joined the Storfjordens Venner (probably the only American in the organization) and will attend their annual meeting next June with Berit! She will drive up from her home south of Oslo and meet me; we will do a little hiking and then drive to her town where I will meet her husband and family (before going off to visit my relatives in Sweden). This would not have happened without the Internet, of that I am sure.

Travelers interested in leisure travel should try the Travel-Ease mailing list. You can subscribe to this listserv by sending email to *list-serv@kajor.com* and writing in the body of the message (not in the subject line) `Subscribe Travel-Ease Abe Lincoln`. If your name isn't Abe Lincoln, then substitute your name.

While many posts in this group are about luxury travel, some are more down to earth. Here's an example from Cindy Roberts:

```
I've traveled alone a lot in Mexico, both by bus
and in a VW camper bus. Sure, the men are always
making comments and whistling, but I feel safer
than when I travel alone in the U.S. I think
```

verbally appreciating women is part of the Mexican
male's psyche; attacking them is not.

Cindy, a longtime user of listservs, describes how these lists have
helped her plan her travels:

PERSONAL ACCOUNT
Cindy Roberts
cr31@umail.umd.edu

*Two years ago we went on a camping trip to South Dakota. Of course I had
maps and books and everything that had camping information. At that
time I subscribed to Travel-L so I asked if anyone had any personal
experience with campsites in that area. Someone wrote back to tell us that
one particular site was almost treeless with campers crowded together, but
that the site further down the road was very nice. This is the kind of
personal information that you just can't get from a book.*

*I never go on any major trips without first asking Net travelers for their
ideas. But I always do some reading first, so I can ask more specific
questions than "What should we do in Hawaii?" The answers to these types
of questions are too broad. It would be better to have done a little research
first and then ask what else is interesting in a certain town, or for a hotel or
camping reference, or any good hikes that someone has taken.*

Cindy makes a key point here: do your homework. Those who frequent newsgroups almost always respond to thoughtful, carefully
crafted questions. But they're not amused by overly broad questions
that suggest you'd rather have someone else do your research. And
with the vast amount of information online, travelers don't have to go
to the library to do their research. As we've seen, anyone with a Net
connection can log onto the Net at any hour and use search directories to uncover a treasure trove of valuable information. When you're
prepared to ask intelligent, specific questions, post to newsgroups
and listservs. But don't hesitate to lurk (monitor newsgroups or lists)
as a way of getting up to speed. You can often get your questions answered by simply following interesting threads or discussions.

Cindy goes on to discuss how over time she began to recognize "like-
minded travelers" in her discussion list.

*I was on the Travel-L list for quite a while and so was able to recognize
some of the participants. Thus I knew that some people traveled in the
same style I do, while others like to travel differently. On that basis I was
more interested in the responses from like-minded travelers. For a trip to
southern Arizona I was wondering if summer was too hot for camping in
the area I planned to go. When I posed this question I received several good
responses. Also, I save hotel recommendations and other specific information even if I'm not planning to go that place, because you never know.*

The down side of all these travel lists is that they take up a lot of time. I eventually unsubscribed to Travel-L because there were too many non-travel postings: things like Canadian nationalism, the merits of one group of people over another, censoring people for their opinion on a place, etc.

TIP

For those who want to know what goes on behind the scenes at airlines, travel agent Edward Hasbrouck recommends the airline list. It's an open list, although only subscribers may post, "but it originated with airline employees and most of the subscribers are either airline employees, airline news junkies, or other travel professionals," Edward says. To subscribe to the airline list, send an email message to *listserv@cunyvm.cuny.edu* and in the subject line type `subscribe airline yourname`.

Other Useful Listservs	■ Green Travel: Send a message with `Subscribe green travel yourname` to *majordomo@igc.apc.org* ■ Eurotrav: Send message with `Subscribe eurotrav yourname` to *listserv@ptearn.cc.fc.ul.pt* ■ Cruisers, by RCCL (for experienced cruise ship enthusiasts): Send message with `Subscribe CRUISERS yourname` to *listproc@rccl.com* ■ Travel_Agents (for travel professionals only):Send email to moderator Joseph Goodman at *goodmanj@voicenet.com*

YOU GET WHAT YOU GIVE

Like other Internet tools, newsgroups and listservs are a remarkable resource, opening new channels of communication and offering direct links with other travelers around the globe. But remember, for the system to work, it's important to give as well as receive. So don't just hit the newsgroups when you need a question answered. If you have the answers to someone else's question, go ahead and respond. As in most arenas, the more you give the more you get. You could end up with new friends across the ocean who open their homes to you or volunteer to show you around their homeland.

So now we've covered just about all the bases; all that's left is to take off and go. But just because you're hitting the road doesn't mean you have to unplug your virtual travel guide. The Net can be as valuable and indispensible on the road—in some ways even more so—than it is while you're planning your trip. The next chapter shows you how to stay wired wherever you travel.

Traveling with the Net   9

Throughout this book, we've focused on how to use the Net to prepare for a trip. Yet one of the great joys of having a Net connection is using it *while* traveling. By staying connected, travelers can share impressions with friends and family, stay on top of developments at work, and find destination information wherever they are. A traveler may arrive in Budapest on a Sunday evening, the tourist office will be closed and finding good information in English may be difficult. But through a Net connection a traveler can find Web sites that will lead to the right hotel, a good place to eat, and ideas for what to do. Some travelers bring their laptops when they travel; others find an Internet café equipped with the right computer equipment and connections. This chapter offers tips for traveling with a laptop, as well as cautions and advice about where to plug it in.

- ▶ Traveling Wired
- ▶ Options for Wired Travelers
- ▶ Computing Across America
- ▶ Staying in Touch Around the Globe
- ▶ Miles from Nowhere, Minutes from Contact

TRAVELING WIRED

Whether travel is for business or pleasure, increasing numbers of travelers prefer to stay connected while on the road. From some countries, sending a dispatch via email may be much cheaper than making a phone call and much more reliable than using the local mail. And an email message can go into much more detail than a quick, frenzied phone call that costs a small fortune. Email also knows no time zones. So a traveler can send news at any time, without worrying about calling in the middle of the night and disturbing the person at the other end of the line.

Beyond communication, the Net is a phenomenal resource for travelers. Jim Klima, who discussed his adventures in Chapter 7, says access to the Net bailed him out when he was on the road.

Jim and his wife, Sue, began their journey as an overland trip across Europe and Africa, and then did some "independent, Lonely Planet-style" travel in central and southern Asia. Their account shows how using the Net while traveling helped make a grueling trip a little less difficult. Jim and Sue brought their laptop along, using it for Net access during the first part of their journey. But after the laptop "lost a battle with a Nigerian sewer," Jim began using cybercafés to check email and adjust their itinerary.

We used email to ask Lonely Planet about release dates for new editions of the guidebooks for Pakistan and Central Asia and who the local distributors were in Nairobi and Islamabad. We got both in Nairobi, which really saved our butts. Going into those areas blind would have been much more difficult.

When we were ready to come home, we used email to let friends and family know of our return plans, which evolved as our illnesses did. Telephoning from India was not practical (too many time zones) and expensive. Faxes were not so good because most people we know don't have fax machines in their homes. Little long distance telephone and fax shops are becoming quite common in the third world. Luckily we found one in the budget backpacker neighborhood in Delhi that also sent email for 60 rupees (just under two dollars) a page. They had some crude Sprint software, but business was booming.

FREE EMAIL WHEREVER YOU GO

Among the most appealing tools for travelers who move around a lot and want to stay connected are services like Hotmail (*http://www. hotmail.com*) or USA.NET's NetAddress (*http://www.netaddress.usa. net*). With Hotmail, for example, you can read your email through a Web browser, meaning that you don't have to log in to your home account. You can read your mail from any place you can get a Web connection: a library, airport, Internet café, or a friend's computer.

TIP

While these free email services are convenient, some travelers have reported that they can be unreliable, with mail simply vanishing into thin air, without even an error message to let you know your mail was not received. Some form of backup communication is advised.

Hotmail's service is free—it is supported by advertising that appears above the messages you receive. And if you're traveling for an extended period, you can either cancel your home account or keep it and have your ISP forward your email to your Hotmail address. (However, your ISP may charge a fee to forward messages to the new address.)

ONLINE ON THE ROAD

In addition to staying in touch, using the Net while traveling gives you access to all the resources you've used while planning your trip.

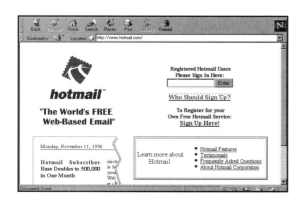

FIGURE 9-1

Hotmail (http://www.hotmail.com) offers free email services through the Web, making it easier for travelers to stay in touch while on the road.

Need to find out how far you are from the nearest hostel? Visit the Internet Guide to Hostelling (*http://www.hostels.com*). Or say you have a free day in New York and you're wondering what exhibition is at the Metropolitan Museum of Art. Just tap into the museum's site at *http://www.metmuseum.org/*.

Travelers whose main interest is plugging in a laptop while abroad should explore the several excellent sites on the Net that offer help. One of the best is TeleAdapt (*http://www.teleadapt.com/*), which offers detailed technical instruction about how to hook up in dozens of countries. And if you're stumped, you can call or send email to one of TeleAdapt's offices (in the U.S., England, or Australia).

TeleAdapt

http://www.teleadapt.com

Tips and tools for plugging in around the world.

TIP

A word of caution here. Foreign electrical and phone systems can damage your computer and modem. Before traveling with your laptop and plugging it into an unfamiliar system, take some time to figure out what adaptations you'll need to make, rather than haphazardly trying to configure your system during your trip.

OPTIONS FOR WIRED TRAVELERS

Today, travelers can choose among an ever-widening range of connection options. For vacationers hwo want to travel light, stopping at an Internet café may be the best choice. For others, such as business travelers, carrying a laptop may be the way to go.

By late 1996, a few dozen Kinko's (*http://www.kinkos.com*) outlets were wired to offer Net access, and the company was considering widening the program if successful. At most of these outlets, Net access is included in the $12 per hour rate to rent a PC. In other words, renting a PC at Kinko's is $12 whether or not you use the Net. (Note: Prices may vary.)

If you're not a member of an online service or international ISP, you may want to consider a service such as GeoAccess (*http://www. geoaccess.com/*). Through this innovative company, you can dial a local access telephone number in most countries and then pay just

$3 per hour for Net access (plus a 25-cent connection surcharge). The registration fee is $25.

INTERNET CAFÉS

The number of Internet cafés is growing, making it easier to find a place to log on while traveling. These coffee shops offer Net access on their own computers by the hour. At the Internet C@fe in Honolulu (*http://www.aloha-cafe.com/*), anyone can rent a computer with full Internet access for $6 an hour. The café has a high-speed (T1) connection to the Net, enabling users to quickly download Web pages. So travelers who need maps or directions can stop into a Net café, find what they need online, and print it out.

Net cafés typically cater to travelers and locals who don't have Net access themselves and want to do some Web browsing or email retrieval over a cup of coffee. Michael Feeney, proprietor of the Internet C@fe, says there is no typical user.

"We have young, old, deaf, even homeless. We also have a lot of tourists. They are all email junkies," he says. "And the Europeans love us because we save them a bundle in telephone costs. Even business travelers have been using our facilities because we are cheaper than Kinko's."

While there are several online guides to cybercafés, the fact that a café is listed does not necessarily mean that it exists. The café business is unstable—it seems that for every new café that's born, an "old" (six months or older) one dies. So if you're compiling a list of cafés in your destination, send an email message to the café before you leave to see if it's still in business.

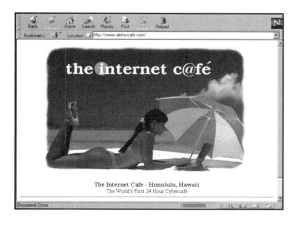

FIGURE 9-2
The Internet C@fe's Web site (http://www. aloha-cafe.com) may inspire you to visit the islands.

Another good source of information on Internet cafés is Yahoo, under the category Society and Culture: Cyberculture: Internet Cafés (*http://www.yahoo.com/Society_and_Culture/Cyberculture/Internet_Cafes/*). This is possibly the most up-to-date list of Net cafés and links to their Web sites.

For a specific question such as "Can anyone recommend a Net café in Paris?" you can pose a query in the Usenet newsgroup *alt.cybercafes*. Or you could try a Yahoo search for the keyword *Ireland* and find a couple of good prospects, such as Cyberia Café (*http://www. cyberia.ie/*). This café offers a rapid-fire Web connection for browsing as well as email services. Cyberia's staff is on hand to train new users.

While some Net cafés are content to offer services, Cyber Java (*http://www.cyberjava.com/*) in the beach paradise of Venice, California (near Los Angeles) is on a mission. The café even has a manifesto:

> The profound gains for society offered by the Internet
> may be unevenly distributed if the large population without
> knowledge or access to computers are left out of cyberspace.
> Promises of a "global village" and "digital democracy" may be
> unfulfilled if computers remain the exclusive tool of the
> specially educated or affluent. Cyber Java's mission is to bring
> Internet education and connectivity to coffee drinkers
> everywhere!

WHERE TO PLUG IN

Most modern U.S. hotel rooms have data ports where travelers can plug in their laptops. At most places, a traveler can remotely log in to his or her employers' or home Net account. If your Internet provider has a wide network of places to hook up, look for the local dialup number to save on toll charges. But beware—many hotels charge for local calls.

Most Internet service providers have access through local telephone numbers across the country. Others have a nationwide toll-free number you can call for access. If you're traveling abroad, logging on can be a bit more dicey, as electrical and phone systems vary by country.

Another caution: ask the front desk if the phone system is digital or analog. Even technologically sophisticated travelers have fried their modems by connecting to digital systems. This problem doesn't affect all modems. Some just won't work over a digital line, but won't self-destruct. Many new card modems are being equipped with a sensor that prevents it from damage, but if you don't own one of these, check with the hotel before you plug in.

International traveler Greg Smith reports there's a nearly fail-safe way to tap into a phone system from almost any country.

> *Hooking up is pretty simple, really, assuming you can use a screwdriver to open the jack —which is the case 99 percent of the time, although I've run into a few hotel rooms where the wire just goes into a hole in the wall or something.*
>
> *My laptop, of course, has an RJ-11 receptacle (like U.S. phones) in back. I have a phone cord with an RJ-11 jack on one end, which goes into the computer. The other end has an alligator (crocodile) clip attached to the RED and GREEN wires (i.e., one clip on each wire). The yellow and black wires are NOT used for anything (they carry a second line in two-line installations).*
>
> *The somewhat more difficult thing is deciding which two of the contacts to clip your clips to. I use a combination of past experience, visual inspection of the jack (sometimes it's evident that only two contacts have any wire connected to them—so these are obviously the two you need), and trial and error to get it to work—but it usually doesn't take me more than a few minutes.*
>
> *The design of some jacks makes connecting a bit difficult, and in these cases I do sometimes just carry a jack for the country I'm in—in most countries these are easily found at hardware or electrical stores. German jacks, for instance, don't have any protruding contacts that you can easily clip on to, so I just stick a German phone jack in with the back plate off and the screws (that normally would hold down the wire) exposed and clip on to those.*
>
> *One word of caution: some foreign phone lines, particularly those on PBX (digital) systems, have much higher voltage than U.S. systems—it is possible to fry your modem. This has never happened to me after connecting in several dozen countries, but it did happen to a friend in Moscow.*

COMPUTING ACROSS AMERICA

A handful of travelers have figured out how to combine travel and the Internet to make a living. In the mid-1980s, freelance writer and technophile Steve Roberts created the Winnebiko, a recumbent bicycle equipped with a computer, and began traveling across the U.S. For more information on Steve's travels, or to see what he's up to today, see Nomadic Research Labs (*http://www.microship.com*).

PERSONAL ACCOUNT
Steve Roberts
wordy@microship.com
http://www.microship.com

Way back in 1983, I was doing what most struggling young freelancers do: taking on a succession of projects, destroying old passions by turning them into businesses, and trying to make enough money to stay afloat. My lifestyle had become suburban, and as I clattered around my boring acre in an itchy haze of midwestern pollen and lawnmower smoke, I wondered what had gone wrong. "Freelancing" was an illusion; I was chained to my desk and deep in debt like everyone else. Stuck.

Where had all my passions gone? One afternoon I listed them: writing, adventure, computer design, ham radio, bicycling, romance, learning, networking, publishing. . . each of these things had at one time or another kept me up all night in a delicious frenzy of fun and giddy intellectual growth. Yet my reality had become one of performing decreasingly interesting tasks for the sole purpose of paying bills, supporting a lifestyle I didn't like in a house I didn't like in a city I didn't like. I had forgotten how to play. Could it still be possible to construct a lifestyle entirely of passions, or was losing the spark a sadly inevitable part of growing up?

Combining the passions in my list and abandoning all "rational thought," the obvious solution was to simply equip a recumbent bicycle with ham radio and computer gear, establish a virtual home in the nascent online networks, and travel full-time while writing and consulting for a living.

Was such a mad idea really possible? Amazingly, it was. Six months later, to the obvious dismay of parents and girlfriend, I hit the road—having liquidated the three-bedroom ranch in suburbia and most of its contents. The bike was a custom recumbent dubbed the Winnebiko, the computer a little Radio Shack Model 100 laptop, the data communication link CompuServe, the power source a small 5-watt solar panel.

FIGURE 9-3
Steve Roberts pedals across the U.S. on a recumbent bicycle equipped with computers.

Immediately it became obvious that I had hit upon something significant. In 1983, the concept of decoupling from a fixed home without becoming a bum in the process was alien to most people, especially with the trappings of high technology allowing an active freelance lifestyle. Daily email from pay phones became routine, and soon the magazine assignments started pouring in—then a book contract (to write) Computing Across America. *I was interviewed in almost every town I passed through, appeared numerous times on national television, and amassed a loyal following of fellow online denizens who offered support facilities all over the country.*

For 10,000 miles I wandered solo, high on the energy of beginnings and change, never really seeking publicity but becoming amazingly well known. But it wasn't me so much as the Winnebiko. . . a machine that eloquently symbolized the daring notion that people could indeed be free, follow their dreams, and break the chains that had always bound them to their desks. In small towns and big cities all across America, I saw the same faraway look, the same dawning of understanding. "Mah gawd, man, you mean to tell me you're runnin' a business from that thang? Reckon I could do somethin' like that? Always did wanna see the world. . ."

STAYING IN TOUCH AROUND THE GLOBE

Most travelers won't go to the lengths that Steve Roberts has: giving up a home to pursue a mobile freelance lifestyle. But you don't need to go to those extremes to stay in touch with a worldwide audience. Jim and Sue Klima, who discussed their adventures earlier, created a worldwide network of friends and advisors by posting accounts of their travels online. For those traveling in remote areas, such as Nigeria or Pakistan, Jim has some tips. Even those who are traveling where there is more access can benefit from Jim's tips.

- Find a stable individual at home to act as your electronic broker who can consolidate your incoming email into a single message and disseminate your outgoing email. You might want to have a backup for this person as well. Some third world countries treat email like facsimiles—they charge by the page or the message and do not permit multiple recipients.

- Don't assume you will be able to attach a file to your email. Once again, there is a lot of clunky software in use out there. And make sure your ISP supports incoming binary files. Using CompuServe proved particularly aggravating because the buffer would overflow with junk email and I would miss legitimate messages. It was better to open a personal account at a local ISP when you are on the road in a faraway place.

- Pick your Internet service provider carefully—make sure you have FTP capability for moving binary files. You might want to test your ISP on a non-AT&T system.

- If you are going to bring a computer, consider the following in the context of your destinations. Power source: I carried extra batteries, a variety of plug adapters, an auto cigarette lighter plug, and a solar panel. Don't believe any manufacturer's specs and advertising about laptop battery life. If your style is upscale enough to afford hotel rooms with electrical outlets, use them. If you don't bring a machine, hunt down small businesses that offer computer classes such as word processing. I rented time on boat anchor 386s for a dollar or two per hour.

- If you are going to carry fancy equipment, remember that the third world can be very hard on delicate electronics. You won't be able to get computers fixed anywhere. A laptop may identify you as a journalist—not an attractive occupation to list on customs declarations in some countries. The weight and bulk of the machine and its accessories are substantial. When various local people realize what you are carrying, you will be more vulnerable to theft, appropriation by corrupt officials (for example, in Zaire or Kazakhstan), or excessive "import fees."

- To locate an Internet service provider, ask around in the computer stores, even if the store is a tiny one-room affair (as in Zanzibar or Uzbekistan). Also scan billboards on the way in from the airport. Or approach institutions of higher education. Academic connections take time to establish. I did much better at this game if I hung around town for a week or two. Cybercafés are a coming thing, but don't be surprised if there are only two terminals and a SLIP connection at 9600 baud (as I found in Nairobi). After you have located an ISP, you may have to buy a temporary personal account or hornswaggle your way onto the system. Impressive business cards will help you grovel (mine were from IBM). If you can demonstrate your presence on a Web site, they are more likely to believe your line about being an "international Internet correspondent." I had business cards for that, too. If you have your own machine, you can prepare everything (including email) offline and sneakernet your way through the ISP's system.

Otherwise, you must use the ISP's own equipment—a proposition of many perturbations and fees. Get used to paying for services by the hour or the page.

TIP

Sneakernet refers to the archaic practice of moving files from one computer to another by hand-carrying a diskette containing the files, typically by a bithead (software engineer) clad in baseball cap and sneakers, between the machines.

- Allow for emotional devastation when all your electronic plans go to hell, but don't let it ruin your trip. A comparable analogy is a dead camera in the most photogenic setting you have ever seen. And don't let your journalistic endeavors prevent you from enjoying yourself. Unless you are getting paid for it, documentation, however cool, should come second to exploration. On my last trip I crashed the hard drive on my laptop when I fell in a Nigerian sewer, causing very deep despair. From that point on I got much more resourceful locating word processing and email facilities. I received flack from people who viewed my electronic tether to the world as an impediment to my foreign experience, and rightly so I suppose. However, documenting my travel provided a desirable focus for me, and contact with the world made information gathering on the fly possible. Communications with the near and dear were treasured as much as my postal mail pickups in capital cities, especially since two-way dialog was possible if I hung around for awhile.

ACOUSTIC COUPLERS

Veteran travelers report that even when they can't find a place to plug in their computers' phone cables, they can make a connection by using an acoustic coupler. This device, which conjures visions of the early days of computing, attaches directly to a telephone receiver. This means that any pay phone or international line can be a reliable hookup.

The Walkabout Travel Gear catalog (*http://www.walkabouttravelgear. com/*) offers a full line of accessories for the wired traveler and is an excellent place to learn about items you might need for your journey.

Walkabout Travel Gear
http://www. walkabouttravelgear.com/
Tips and accessories for wired travelers.

Walkabout sells the Telecoupler II ($145), which plugs into a computer's modem and attaches to virtually any telephone—including pay phones, cellular phones, and digital phones. Because you are not actually plugging into the line, you do not need an adapter for the telephone jack. The 1996 model of the Telecoupler weighed under 10 ounces and had a data/fax rate up to 14.4 Kbps (kilobytes per second).

FOR AOL USERS

Each of the online services offers ways to connect while traveling outside the U.S. If you're using AOL, type the keyword *aolglobalnet* to get a country-by-country listing of access numbers, connection speed, and additional hourly fee. This site has specific instructions which vary depending on whether you're using a PC or a Mac.

AOLGLOBALnet carries a $6, $12, or $24 per hour surcharge, depending on the country where you are connecting, in addition to normal hourly connect charges. For example, if you're calling in Adelaide, Australia, the surcharge is $6 per hour and the modem speed is 28.8 Kbps. If you're dialing in from Accra in Ghana, the surcharge is $24 per hour and the modem speed is significantly slower: 9,600 bps.

FOR COMPUSERVERS

For information about logging in to CompuServe from remote locations, see the Member Services area and click on Access Phone Numbers. Or go directly to Access Numbers and Logon Instructions (CIS: LGN-1). Click here to find one section on the U.S. and Canada, and another on all other countries.

A search for a list of U.S. connections at the highest speed (57.6 Kbps) gives the following list of phone numbers to call to log in;

```
CompuServe 57600 Baud Access Numbers


ST CITY             AC PHONE # MODEM
CA Irvine           714 261-0583 V120
CA San Francisco    415 982-0401 V120
GA Atlanta          404 814-9138 V120
IL Chicago          312 849-3457 V120
MA Boston           617 338-0093 V120
MO Kansas City      816 502-1098 V120
OH CompuServe       800 473-6282 V120
```

```
OH Dublin            614 717-9700 V120
TX Dallas            214 953-1152 V120
TX Houston           713 718-9541 V120
VA Fairfax           703 359-3916 V120
WA Seattle           206 269-0538 V120
```

By calling these numbers, you can log in from anywhere in the U.S., but if you're not close enough make one of these a local call, you should call the toll-free number. CompuServe also lists numbers for connecting from abroad.

MILES FROM NOWHERE, MINUTES FROM CONTACT

In 1994, as travel writer Jeff Greenwald approached his 40th birthday, he decided to travel around the world—without using airplanes. To get away from the rut of commuting, he chose to circumnavigate the globe with on-the-ground transport: trains, boats, cars, and, where none of those were available, on foot.

He acknowledged the irony of using the latest computer technology to get his dispatches to readers through the Travelers' Center of Global Network Navigator (this service went offline in late 1996). "The point of my trip was to forsake technology, so my reliance on technology and my presence on the Web became an ironic counterpoint to this journey. While my brain was telecommuting at the speed of light, my body was still compelled to travel at a snail's pace, face down in the sand."

Though GNN is no longer on the Net, Jeff Greenwald's dispatches are part of his book, *The Size of the World,* published by Globe Pequot.

There were days when Jeff cursed the wires, couplers, and laptop he dragged with him during his quest. One such day was during a festival in Oaxaca, Mexico. Mariachi bands played in the town square, children paraded in costumes down the street, and Jeff was stuck in

FIGURE 9-4
Jeff Greenwald on the road in Africa with his laptop.

the dank offices of Telefonos de Mexico trying futilely to get his dispatch to the travel editor back at GNN in California. Each successive attempt thinned his wallet, but not one dispatch got through. Months later when he was halfway around the world, Jeff realized that the entire travesty may have been due to his failure to flick a switch from tone to pulse dialing.

At other times, however, Jeff was ecstatic that as he traveled through Guatemala, Istanbul, Nepal, and more than a dozen other countries he could share his adventures—almost instantaneously—with friends, family, and fascinated followers half a world away. "I had this sense of being almost on fire, that the excitement and heat of my journey was providing me was something I could broadcast in no time at all," he says. "It was a very giddy feeling."

Occasionally, as events with international ramifications broke before his eyes, Jeff's dispatches abruptly changed tone from the insightful, often amusing observations of a traveler to the more objective accounts of a news reporter. He arrived in Tibet shortly after President Clinton agreed to "de-link" China's human rights record from its application for Most Favored Nation status. "The Chinese were gloating about the way they were oppressing the Tibetans even more now that they felt America had stepped away from the fight," he wrote. "I felt a real sense of responsibility and privilege to be able to convey that information."

THE LOSS OF A LAPTOP

Carrying a laptop can be ideal if you want to compose long letters or business documents on a train or plane and zip them off when you can find a connection. However, a laptop will add extra pounds to your pack or carry-on bag, and it can also be a target for thieves. When Jeff was in Nepal, his state-of-the-art laptop was stolen on an overnight bus ride.

> *I was devastated, more depressed than I'd ever been in my life. The laptop, more than merely the most useful tool I was carrying, had become a companion to me. I was pouring my emotions into it—all the best things I was doing on my trip, the best writing, the best feelings, the best observations were all being confided to that machine, which became a companion, almost in the way an android, like Data from Star Trek, would be a companion. I just really respected the machine's ability and its incredible versatility and portability; it was almost my little therapist.*

TIPS FOR TRAVELING WITH A LAPTOP

Here are some key tips from Ellen Brewer, who has traveled extensively with a laptop. Ellen emphasizes that these tips apply to the type of travel that she does and may not be completely applicable to all travelers.

Prove you own it

Carry some proof that this computer was purchased in the U.S. and that you have the right to have it with you. We xeroxed the purchase papers and brought copies with us. Two copies is probably best: one with the computer and one somewhere else to show its value if it's stolen. In Europe, the point is to show that you're not planning to sell it there; on re-entering the U.S., the point is to show that you didn't buy it abroad. There's a complicated document called a carnet that you can get for computers. We did that last sabbatical when the MacPlus went with us.

Secure it

Never leave your computer unsecured, and keep it with you whenever you can. We each have a Kensington security cable (much better than the generic one the UI Computer Center sells) and we used them all the time (except when we took a trip of several days: then I put my laptop in its case and hid it, hoping any thief who noticed my manuals would think I'd taken it with me). A cable isn't serious security, but it's a lot better than nothing.

Watch out for carry-on baggage ripoffs

Snapping up computer cases (or hand baggage that might have a computer in it) at airport security checkpoints is now a common scam. I've seen separate warnings this year for both U.S. and European airports. Try not to get in a situation where you're delayed at the metal detector, either by people ahead or by your own metal items. Unfortunately, proximity alarms that go off if your bag gets too far from you are not allowed in airports. It was easier for us, with two people. The main thing is to be alert to the possibility.

European flights have smaller baggage limits

The limit for cabin baggage on intra-Europe flights is 5 kg (11 pounds) for economy/tourist class. While this weight limit isn't usually enforced, it can be. The size limits are smaller too, and these are what make them take one look at our carry-on bags, which just meet the U.S. cabin baggage size limits, and insist that we check them. So be prepared to carry your computer case as your only carry-on baggage or get a minicase that'll fit in a backpack or something. Check with the airline you'll be using to be sure what limits apply to you.

Back up before flying

You should back up your data before each flight and keep your backup disks separate from your computer. Ideally you should have a separate backup that stays while you fly, at least for critical data, so that it could be sent on later if necessary. We bought a ZIP drive, which came with backup software. It's made backups easier for us. I've bought ZIP cartridges in England and in Denmark to add to what we brought with us. They're more expensive in Europe than in the U.S.

Printing

A small portable ink-jet printer is a very useful item to have. I advise bringing extra ink cartridges. When I turned off the power before the little green light went out on my portable Stylewriter and the ink cartridge died, I was glad I had extras. You may also want to bring U.S.-size paper and envelopes, depending on what you'll be doing over there. The printer manual was useful to have along.

Power supplies and cables

Be sure all the power supplies are the "universal" kind. Mac Powerbooks all come with such, but Stylewriters don't, and neither do ZIP drives. They can be ordered and they're not very expensive. This is a much better approach than trying to use a Radio Shack (or similar) transformer. I think the easiest plan if you have more than one piece of computer hardware is to buy (or borrow) a good power strip with an on-off switch in the country you're staying in; then plug adapters for the U.S. to that country into the power strip. You should bring such adapters with you unless you're sure they'll be available there. You can get them at hardware stores (brand is Franzus) or from Radio Shack. A cable check to be sure you've got all the different kinds of cables you need is a good idea when packing.

STAYING WIRED WITHOUT A COMPUTER

During the past couple of years, veteran traveler John Labovitz has sent his travel stories to his friends via email and postings to a Web site (*http://www.meer.net/~johnl/trip/*). For his summer 1996 trip, he chose to leave his little computer at home and file dispatches from wherever he could find a connection as he traveled across the U.S. and on to Eastern Europe.

Following is an excerpt John wrote as he prepared to embark on this trip:

PERSONAL ACCOUNT
John Labovitz
johnl@meer.net

On past trips, I have lugged around a computer of some sort, either a tiny palmtop machine on which I can type with two fingers and squint at my words, or a laptop that seems to grow heavier and heavier with each letter entered. Using a modem and an acoustic coupler with which I can communicate on any telephone, I have been able to send swift and timely dispatches to folks who are interested in my wanderings.

This time, not wanting to worry about expensive microelectronics or infinitely heavy plastic contraptions, I have forsaken any portable electronics. Instead, I am utilizing simply pen and paper, taking notes while in motion, and occasionally stringing together the prose you see here.

At least on the cross-States leg of this journey, nearly every friend I am visiting has a computer with which I can do simple word processing, and most have Internet accounts. In some cities, I will look for cafés, libraries, and universities that have some sort of Net access, and attempt to send back my dispatches from these borrowed nodes. As I compromise on ease of access to computer and Net, I hope to be able to fine-tune my writing, and learn something of the state of Net access around the world. Not to mention taking a weight off my back muscles.

I'm sure there are cybercafés in Los Angeles, but my friends here are students, so I do the scam of borrowing their accounts. It works well; the Bruin Computer Lab at UCLA is remarkably lax about using their computers. I simply find a blank disk, create a "preferences" setup, and— voila—I am online, with Netscape, Telnet, Eudora, etc. While Douglas is off eating Chinese food for breakfast, I read and write email.

As John shows, travelers need not carry a laptop and a tangle of wires to use the Net while on the road. At a Net café, all the equipment is configured—users don't have to worry about how to connect. And if there's a technical problem, a café employee may be able to lend a hand.

ESCAPING A CAGE OF WIRES

Some have asked what the big deal is—why bother with a Net connection when you can just as easily write a letter? In addition to the convenience and cost efficiency of email, electronic communication offers something letters can't: immediacy and the ability to let the folks back home share in your adventure.

Just ask Greg Elin, who during the fall of 1995 embarked on a transcontinental motorcycle ride across the U.S. that he called "Silicon Alley to Silicon Valley." (Silicon Alley is New York City's high-tech hub and Silicon Valley is the locus of computer companies south of San Francisco.)

Greg set out to prove that people could access the vast stores of electronic information without remaining chained to their desks. Using a Connectix camera mounted to his motorcycle helmet, he routinely broadcast images to his Web site. When he was transmitting images, Greg sent a new image every minute or so.

PERSONAL ACCOUNT
Greg Elin
elin@interport.net

"Until now, the legacy of the information age—which has given the individual access to vast amounts of knowledge and power—has been a type of bondage," he said just before the trip. "Bondage to the terminal, to the telephone, to the fax machine. With this landmark tour, we hope to not only honor the developers of the Internet, but to demonstrate that technology has escaped its cage of wires."

During his trip, sponsored by Total New York (*http://www.totalny. com*), Greg found time to visit his parents in Chicago, hook up a new computer for them, and get them on the Net. A week and a half later, Greg pulled his motorcycle to the side of the road, took a digital photo of a stunning sunset, and quickly uploaded the image to his Web site. Within minutes, his mother and his girlfriend (and anyone

FIGURE 9-5
Greg Elin stayed wired while motorcycling across the U.S., transmitting images from a Connectix camera mounted on his helmet.

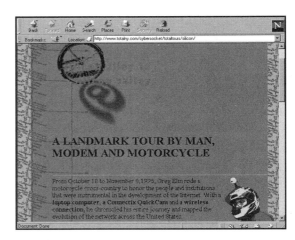

else with a Net connection) could see an image of the sunset Greg had just witnessed.

"It has the potential to be so personal," he says. "All I needed was a computer, the Net, a phone, and a camera, and they were seeing live pictures from my motorcycle in New Mexico."

Next time out, Greg hopes to gather together a few fellow travelers and anyone else with too much time on their hands in August 1997 for the first "Alley to Valley Rally," a bring-your-own-vehicle cross-country digital road rally to promote mobile and wireless connectivity. As they travel, participants will collaborate on creating and updating a Web site. Contact Greg at *elin@interport.net*.

Over and over, travelers who take the Net with them emphasize how outstanding a tool it is for making personal connections. "The Net is not this faraway vision of cyberspace, but real people you can visit," Greg says. And keeping that connection alive leads to making more of those connections as one travels, leading to sublime encounters that make a journey rewarding and memorable.

How Travel Agents Use the Net

10

The Internet is forcing professionals in many industries to take a fresh look at how they do business. The Net is toppling information oligarchies, and the travel profession is not immune. In the previous chapters we discussed how some people who once used travel agents are arranging trips for themselves using the Net. The obvious question arises: are travel agents about to go the way of the blacksmith? The answer may surprise you. Travel agents and agencies that embrace the Net can cut their costs and increase their customer base. In fact, the only travel agents who have to worry about the Internet are those who fail to integrate it into their business.

- ▶ Transforming Crisis into Opportunity
- ▶ Getting Online
- ▶ Your Web Site: An Interactive Brochure
- ▶ For the Corporate Travel Manager
- ▶ Destination Sites

TRANSFORMING CRISIS INTO OPPORTUNITY

With the emergence of the Internet, many travel agents fear their clients will abandon them and do all their trip planning on the Net. But lots of travelers simply don't want to mess around with the details of trip planning. And even those who want to make their own arrangements will often seek the expertise of well-informed travel consultants.

A summer 1996 study of 2,400 travelers by the American Society of Travel Agents (ASTA) stated that 86 percent of those who used online travel services still had their travel agent make some or all of their purchases. "The results of this survey clearly illustrate that the traveling consumer is continuing to kick the tires of the travel products offered online, but they aren't buying through this medium," says ASTA President and CEO Jeanne Epping. For more on the study, see *http://www.astanet.com/www/astanet/news/press/press_96/pr082296. html*.

Ten-IO

http://www.ten-io.com

Ten-IO maintains a list of travel agents. For details about how to get on the list, see this site.

Dennis Coffey, CEO of the Ten-IO, which creates Web sites for travel agents, says the Net will reorient the travel agent's role, but will not make agents obsolete. "There are a small number of people who want to spend five hours on the Net to save $2, but they are not a large part of the populace. When people book their trips, they want a level of confidence provided by planning their trips with someone who's more knowledgeable than they are." Travel agents can use the Net to strengthen their relationships with clients, Dennis adds, by providing added value through email consultation, references to Web sites, and tips about how travelers can use online resources to enhance their trips.

John Clifford

Senior International Consultant, All Around Travel

netravel@ix.netcom.com

http://www.allaroundtravel. com

John Clifford, director of International Travel Management in San Diego, says that while Internet access "does empower the consumer to be better educated and make more informed purchasing decisions, it doesn't automatically make the layman an expert at planning travel. Just like being able to view real-time, open-heart surgery on the Web does not make me instantly a heart surgeon."

And of course there are people who would have no problems navigating the Net's travel resources, but who simply consider trip planning a royal pain. They like having a travel agent handle the routine details—booking tickets, reservations, car rentals. It's not that these people don't use the Net; many of them do. But rather than a trip-arranging tool, they view the Net as a giant automated travel brochure.

FIGURE 10-1

All Around Travel's Home on the Web (http://www.allaroundtravel.com) helps travelers make better decisions.

They like flipping through the pages looking for interesting destinations, but when they find one they like, they call or email their travel agent and say, "Book it."

That's not to say that travel agencies, like almost every other service industry, will not have to adjust to this new information technology. In the past, access to airline reservation databases or other travel booking systems was restricted to those "in the business." The pre-Information Age business model depended largely on belonging to the travel information cartel. Being a member let travel agents, in essence, resell this information to their customers. That's not to say that personal service wasn't important—it was the other half of the equation.

But those days are over. Now most of the information travel agents had exclusive access to is available free on the Net. Integrating this new reality means agents must recognize, whether they like it or not, that this information is going to be available to their customers. Rather than pretending these resources don't exist, agents should actually encourage their customers to use them.

"Nothing will replace personal service," says Annette Sorscher of Annette's Travel in Boca Raton, Florida. "I don't think the Net will put anyone out of business unless they don't offer personal service. Loyalty depends on how you treat your clients."

But to provide such service in this new environment means travel agents need to get connected to the Net themselves. Travel agent Sally Lewis, marketing manager for 1travel.com, says agents can help their customers and save them time by monitoring the reams of travel information published both online and off.

Annette Sorscher
CLIA Master Cruise Counselor, Annette's Travel & CruiseBase
cruisebase@emi.net
http://www.emi.net/ ~cruisebase

Sally Lewis
Marketing Manager,
1travel.com
slewis@ptd.net
http://www.1travel.com

"Today, coupons and special deals change by the instant. Agents with their fingers on the pulse can save you lots of money." Lewis is mystified that agents will spend thousands of dollars to advertise locally, but hesitate to spend some money to get online. "You can get a huge return on your investment," she says.

Getting connected doesn't mean just surfing travel sites on the Web; it means putting one up as well. A travel agency can use its site to manage links to other useful sites, thereby creating a default travel page for their customers—a starting point, if you will, for their Net trip-planning excursions.

Simply putting up a Web site and leaving it unattended like a billboard ad is not a winning strategy. "Just because a travel agent puts up a Web site doesn't mean people will be knocking on their door. You have to be set up to respond quickly," Sally says. In other words, if you have an online presence, check your email every day—several times a day in fact—because clients expect rapid replies to their email queries.

In the introduction to this book, travel editor Morris Dye notes that before the dawn of online travel services, agents sold two things: access to reservation systems and expertise about travel planning. As the Net has become more widespread, selling access, for example to a CRS (computer reservation system), has become less important. What agents continue to sell is their expertise—consumers will always need informed travel counselors.

Sally Lewis agrees: "If you're a smart business person and an aggressive salesperson, you can make this work. A lot of travel agents are ordertakers—they're not used to going out there and actively selling. You need to do that on the Net."

USING NEW TOOLS

Competition greases the wheels of commerce. The Internet has raised the competitive stakes for travel agents. If travel agencies can't or won't find the best deals for Net-savvy travelers, travelers will do it for themselves. Traveler Jane Nowlin found a package deal that was considerably less expensive than the best price her agent offered. "I printed the offer and took it to my agent. She did not have Internet access and thus couldn't look it up herself, although I thought she should have."

Listen carefully to what Jane says here: she didn't seem to be upset that she found a better deal than her agent found, but she *was* miffed that the agent didn't have the tools to find her the best deals in this new competitive environment. Jane, like many other travelers, now expects agents to learn to use the tools that even Net newcomers are already comfortable with.

While some agents are intimidated by the new technology, they actually are ahead of professionals in many other fields, because they know how to use a CRS. "Travel agents are not thought of as technically sophisticated, but people don't realize how knowledgeable they are," says travel agent and round-the-world specialist Edward Hasbrouck. The travel agents' global network of reservation systems has many similarities to the Internet, he says, "but the two worlds don't talk to each other."

Edward Hasbrouck
Sundance Travel Time
ehasbrouck@igc.apc.org

The Net is "revolutionizing our industry at a lightning-fast pace. And those who don't adapt will either survive in a very specialized, 'boutique-like' agency with their particular specialties, close, or be bought out by a bigger player," says John Clifford, who has been selling travel over the Net since 1995.

By learning how to employ the Net, agents can expand their repertoire of sources, whether that means finding a Web page that tells more about a destination than any brochure, making a post to a newsgroup that leads to a key connection for a client, or simply being able to quickly respond to a customer's email message.

EXPANDING YOUR CLIENT BASE

While many agents view the Net as a threat, savvy agents see the tremendous opportunity inherent in getting themselves and their agency plugged in to this resource.

PERSONAL ACCOUNT
Nancy Zebrick
All Destinations Travel
nzebrick@ix.netcom.com

Nancy Zebrick, of All Destinations Travel in Cherry Hill, New Jersey (*http://www.alltravel.com*), says about 20 percent of her business comes to her through the Net, and this figure is growing rapidly. Nancy advises agents to use their expertise to specialize and aggressively promote that specialty. The Net has changed the orientation and nature of her business, Nancy says, giving it access to clients around the world.

> *I don't consider us local anymore. I consider us global. Right now I'm working with a client from Oslo, Norway, arranging a trip to Club Med and Disney World here in Florida. He found us through the Net. We also get*

referrals through the Net. Word of mouth is the best thing—that shows we'll keep growing.

I used to be a dietitian and I got into this business to do my own ticketing. Right after I became a travel agent (spring 1995) the caps were instituted (limiting commissions). So I looked into my crystal ball and saw that the Net was the way to go. Because I hadn't been in the business for years, I didn't live off the fat of commissions, so I survived when suddenly commissions diminished.

People who make it on the Net are really specialized. Because of my background in diet and fitness, I'd been to 39 fitness spas. Some were real spas—others just a resort with a massage therapist on duty. I knew which were the real spas and used this expertise to build my business.

It wasn't like I just opened a site and business came through the door. I had to develop the trust and confidence of clients. To do that, I got back to each one within 24 hours with a price and recommendation. The key to making it is to follow up quickly and work the leads. We don't just send email—we call to develop a more personal bond.

Also, we don't accept any advertising on our site. I give honest opinions, tell people what's good, what's bad, and what's ugly. So when they see that I've recommended a spa, they know it's truly one of my favorites.

Nancy says there's no magic formula to success on the Net. Like just about any business, it's a lot of hard work. Some leads are good; others are "junk," she says, but her agency follows up on each one, just as it would follow up on phone inquiries.

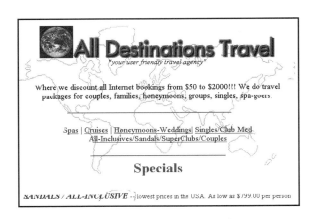

FIGURE 10-2

All Destinations Travel (http://www. alltravel.com) offers discounts through its Web site.

For the next couple of years, knowing how to use the Net will put agents at a significant competitive advantage over their Luddite competitors. Further on down the road the knowledge they gain about the Internet, its demographics, and developing subculture will make the difference between survival and failure. Before the end of the decade, understanding how to navigate through the Net will be considered as essential as knowing how to employ a CRS system.

GETTING ONLINE

As more and more workplaces get wired to the Net, more "white collar" travelers expect to be able to make their travel arrangements with the same tools they use to do their job. Rather than pick up the phone and get put on hold for an agent, they'd much prefer to shoot their questions to their agent via email. And email saves time and money for agents as well.

"Using email, I can transmit a message with little or no chance of misunderstanding to a client I might never meet, at a cost lower than using the telephone," says Bob Ensten of American Made Travel Adventures in Novato, California. Through email, agents can give thoughtful consideration to each part of the client's message, respond comprehensively, and even include referrals to online documents, such as a useful Web page.

Bob Ensten
American Made Travel Adventures
BobAMTA@aol.com

Bob also uses the Web to research trips for clients. "Recently, a client wanted to plan a trip to Croatia. Not knowing anything about Croatia, I searched the Web for any articles/information about that country—and found several," he says. "I also use AOL for information, for

FIGURE 10-3
Welcome to Croatia (http://vukovar.unm.edu/wtc/wtc.html) is an example of the thousands of Web sites travel agents can use to find destination information for their clients.

example, the Weissmann Travel Reports, a great source of information in an easy-to-use format."

Net-savvy agents are using Web sites to reach clients outside their local areas. John Clifford, for example, has been able to attract business for those interested in trips to San Diego and Mexico.

It has been helpful in bringing in some excellent bookings, the largest being a $13,000 trip from a business owner in Minnesota. He was going to Mexico with his girlfriend and wanted everything first-class. Overall, I'd have to say we've sold about $75,000+ (not in commissions) of business in about a year and a half of growing Net participation.

ITN

http://www.itn.net

ITN is an airline booking service that allows travelers to buy airline tickets over the Net—all purchases are routed through travel agents, with the agent keeping the commission. ITN charges a $3 fee for routing the booking to the agent.

What does that participation entail? For John, it means communicating with customers via email, joining mailing list discussions, and having his Web site (*http://www.allaroundtravel.com*) listed on several major online travel centers. John also has an independent Web page tailored for gay and lesbian travelers, (*http://www.geocities.com/WestHollywood/1993/*). "The Net has allowed me to develop selling to niche markets, like gay and lesbian clients, or those planning extensive trips to Australia, Europe, Costa Rica, and elsewhere," John adds.

Sally Lewis agrees that finding your niche is the best way to go. "Agents have been squeezed by airline caps—airlines themselves are heading toward direct distribution. Many travel agents see the light and know that they need to niche themselves as some sort of travel expert online to survive. No matter how electronic we become, there will always be a need for expert advice in certain categories of the travel business, just like there are consultants in any business who can say "been there, done that, don't do this, go here."

SPECIALIZING ON THE NET

Using the Net, travel agents can carve out a virtual niche market by specializing in a particular kind of travel. Capitalizing on the cruising craze, Internet Cruise Travel Network (*http://www.cruisetravel.com/*), created by a Florida travel agency, serves up a full menu of cruise line offerings, their sailing itineraries, and ship and cabin layouts. ICTN agents will take reservations online and handle all bookings and billing.

By using the Net, agents reach travelers in their chosen medium. In Chapter 1, honeymooner Leslie Camino-Markowitz told how she used the Net to find a travel agent on the Spanish island of Ibiza.

Because the agent, James Benjamin of Festive Travel & Tours, lived at this destination, he was familiar with the best accommodations and made her honeymoon trip a delight.

Here's how James got started:

> When we decided to start a site on the Net, we really had no idea what to do. We started late in the season and just put a few pages together to try to promote the area. In no time at all, we were receiving email with requests from all of Europe. We were very excited by the response. We rented hotel rooms, rental cars, apartments, villas, flights, and the requests continue to roll in. Living in a place does help in the planning of a holiday there.

When Leslie and her new husband arrived in Ibiza, James met them at the airport, showed them to their hotel, and then shared a bottle of sangria to congratulate the newlyweds. So, in this case the Net facilitated both a strong business relationship and led to a new friendship. And as Leslie told her story about how helpful the agents were and how beautiful the island is, this powerful online word of mouth advertising convinced others to follow.

THE POWER AND PROFIT OF EMAIL

You don't need to create your own Web site to begin reaping the benefits of the Net. For $10 to $20 a month, you can get an account with an Internet service provider such as Netcom or America Online. This account will allow you to browse the Net, monitor and post to newsgroups, and, most importantly, send and receive email.

James Benjamin
festinfo@festivetravel.com
http://www.festivetravel.com/

TIP

To subscribe to the "Travel-Agents" listserv, send email to Joe Goodman at *goodmanj@voicenet.com*. This mailing list is strictly limited to travel professionals.

Edward Hasbrouck says, "I do 30 percent of my business through email. The agents who are doing well are those who have made effective use of email." Geoff Zamboni of Deluxe Travel Professionals International of Tampa, Florida, is a case in point. Geoff was able to stay in touch with clients and close a couple of big sales during a recent Christmas vacation.

PERSONAL ACCOUNT

Geoff Zamboni
Deluxe Travel Professionals
International
deluxejeff@aol.com
*http://www.1travel.com/
deluxe*
*http://www.1travel.com/
rainbow*

My laptop has a fax program and a modem. So I can access email and Internet consolidator programs as well as a freestanding consolidator program on the PC, which I update via modem for latest fares.

With the reservation system loaded on a laptop, I can dial in to the agency, hook up to their LAN [local area network], and then gain access as though I were in the office or at home.

Our Internet presence gains us clients all over the world with our "virtual" storefront available to people in Tokyo, Sydney, and some guys in France, with whom I am working now. The Internet is a great expansion of client demographics.

How does email business come to travel agents? Several ways: some potential clients see agents' postings in the travel newsgroups; others see the email address in agents' literature. And of course some come through email referrals. It's easy to forward an email address to a friend and recommend an agent who is online. Participating in the newsgroups or listservs can be key—by answering a question online, you can show your knowledge of a particular specialty and encourage travelers to seek your services.

"Newsgroups can be wonderful for agents," says Annette Sorscher, the Florida-based agent who specializes in cruises. "You get to see what people are thinking about different lines, cruises, trips." One complaint won't dissuade her from recommending a cruise line, Annette says, but if she sees a pattern, she becomes wary and may not suggest that cruise or company. What's the greatest benefit of the newsgroups? "We get to hear what the public thinks, not just what the cruise lines tell us."

Mailing lists and newsgroups can also be good sources for attracting new clients. While blustery announcements promising great deals are ignored (or worse—resented) by most people, answering someone's question can lead to a new client relationship.

Says Kimberly Barker, a former travel agent who publishes the Fam Connection Web site and companion newsletter:

> When people post in newsgroups, answer their questions with timely and useful information. Be a consultant. Show your stuff by offering genuine help. The same person who asked the weather question may come to you when it's time to plan that trip. Being there to offer guidance and experience as an agent may not guarantee you business, but finding your niche in these places and offering your services can often pay off in spades. You haven't spammed the group with all your ads about what a wonderful agency you have and how you're the best travel agent for outdoor adventure travel. You have merely offered your experience and knowledge to a consumer who is seeking help. And voila! You have begun a very discreet marketing campaign by simply lurking and speaking up when you have something genuine to offer.

PERSONAL ACCOUNT

The Fam Connection
http://www.redshift.com/ ~talisman/FamConnection. html

For more information about the newsletter, mail Kimberly at *ldpdl@redshift.com.*

TIP

"Spamming" means widely and/or inappropriately distributing advertising online, for example, trying to sell air travel in the *rec.travel.cruises* newsgroup. While it may be appropriate to post this notice in *rec.travel.marketplace*, posting in unrelated newsgroups is considered bad "netiquette." The penalty for spamming is typically nasty email responses in your mailbox.

YOUR WEB SITE: AN INTERACTIVE BROCHURE

In the retail business, they call advertising signs "silent salesmen." A Web site can be seen as an interactive version of an advertising sign. It's not only an inexpensive way to get a travel agency's message out—it's also a way to leave the office open 24 hours a day, 365 days a year.

"Traditionally, planning and booking a cruise with a client would only be done during my office hours, making it convenient for me and my staff but not necessarily for the client," says Gordon Merritt, a Miami agent who specializes in cruise travel. "By going online, we are able to receive and send messages from and to clients any time of

Gordon Merritt
Internet Cruise Travel Network
gordon@cruisetravel.com
http://www.cruisetravel. com/

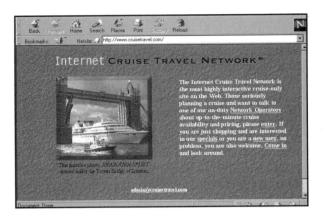

FIGURE 10-4

The Internet Cruise Travel Network site (http://www.cruisetravel.com/) is much more versatile than a printed brochure.

the day or night. We respond rapidly to our clients and potential clients, many times within the half hour."

Gordon's site serves as an interactive travel brochure, yet it does far more than any printed brochure could do—and it can be easily updated with new specials or features. The Cruise Travel Network is a smartly organized site which tells potential clients about cruise types, itineraries, special deals, and monthly features. While many may come solely for the information, Gordon's mentality is like that of any smart merchant: get 'em into the store, and they just may buy something.

"We're receiving a good response to our site and have sold many cruises as a result," he says. "It's already paid for itself many times over." Gordon, however, is going a step further than most online agents. He's planning to support his site with a team of network operators who will be available 16 hours a day to answer questions over his Web site's chat channel. In other words, rather than sending email back and forth, a client and operator can have an online dialogue, typing questions and answers in real time. Like email, there's no additional charge for this service; once you've paid for basic Net access the rest is free.

PERSONAL ACCOUNT
Robert and Chrys Longley
Cruisin
longleyr@pop.tiac.net
http://www.asource.com/cruisin

Rob and Chrys Longley brought their Cruisin site (*http://www.asource.com/cruisin/*) online in February 1995. While the Longleys don't have a walk-in agency, they have "five virtual offices throughout the U.S. with more on the drawing board." Why do customers visit? They can check the electronic brochures, learn about special deals, and request quotes about cruises, all from the comfort of their own home, anytime they want.

They have been so successful selling cruises through their Web site that they had to upgrade their computer systems to keep pace.

> *We found out recently that you can outgrow a virtual storefront. We actually got to a point where we were having a difficult time keeping up with both our clients and agents. That and the server was crashing every three or four days. We increased the size of the site, reallocated where requests were going, and we will probably double in size before the end of the year. Very exciting.*

The Longleys are averaging $60,000 in business each month through their storefront on the Web. They also have an email list of several thousand people, so if they come across a special deal they'd like to publicize, they can send email directly to their customers. Many agents create specialized lists; the Longleys, for example, could have a list of clients interested in Caribbean cruises—if they come across a special Caribbean cruise they could notify those on this list.

By using email, agents don't have to wait for their clients to stop by their site—they can take the initiative and notify them directly. Be aware, though, that sending email to past or prospective clients should be done judiciously. Early in the relationship, you should ask them whether they want to receive travel alerts and other information via email. Otherwise your well-meaning email alert may more than likely be viewed as junk email. Even with permission, use this tool carefully. Wise cyberagents send mail occasionally, when it's warranted, as a service rather than an intrusion. Rob says he occasionally posts travel specials on cruising-related newsgroups, though "that gets overused too much as it is."

TIP

Travel agents can learn about travel specials through mailing lists such as TravelHub's Specials and Wholesale-Promos (see *http://www.travelhub.com* for more information). Some major airlines send weekly lists of discount fares, such as American Airlines' NetSAAvers (*http://www.americanair.com/aa_home/ net_saavers.htm*). Other lists apply to specific types of travel. To find email lists for a specific topic, see Liszt (*http://www.liszt.com*), where you can search for listservs by topic.

Key Resources for Travel Professionals

Just as there are Web sites for travelers, there are also Web sites that specialize in circulating information to and among travel agents. Following is a sampling of some of the best resources for travel professionals:

Travel Weekly News (*http://www.traveler.net/two/twpages/twnews.html*)

An offshoot of the extensive Travel Weekly reviews page, TWN has synopses of key stories relevant to the travel industry. If you're in the travel business, you'll want to check this site weekly. Also see Travel Weekly's main site (*http://www.traveler.net/two/*), which reviews more than a thousand other travel sites. The Travel Weekly sites come from Reed Elsevier, one of the world's largest independent suppliers of travel information products.

ITN's Travel Agent Resources (*http://www.itn.net/cgi/get?itn/resources/agents*)

ITN is an excellent place to get oriented. It lists key links for agents ranging from ASTA to Travel Weekly. If you want a tutorial of the Web, just spend some time browsing these links. ITN is also a good place to list your agency as it provides referrals to agents from ITN clients. Joe Witherspoon of ITN maintains Travel and Tourism Industry Resources (*http://www.waveconcepts.com/tawww*), a superb set of links including industry organizations, travel industry services, and travel-related newsgroups. Other good starting points include Webcrawler's Travel Agent Resources (*http://webcrawler.com/select/trav.agent.html*) and Dr. Memory's links for travel agencies (*http://www.access.digex.net/~drmemory/agents.html*).

ASTAnet (*http://www.astanet.com/*)

Home of the American Society of Travel Agents. You'll find a solid digest of travel industry news, a list of Net travel resources, travel tips, and ASTA's event calendar. Wondering what it takes to become a travel agent or interested in the outlook for the industry? See *http://www.astanet.com/http://www/astanet/whatis/becomeag.html*. You'll find a directory of travel associations at *http://www.astanet.com/www/astanet/news/trvassoc.html*. A searchable list of ASTA's 25,000+ members rounds out the site.

MUCH MORE THAN A FLYER THAT GLOWS

Tom and Mary Kay Aufrance run Aufrance Associates, a South Lake Tahoe, California, company that designs Web sites and offers software. They specialize in creating sites and systems for local clients, such as Lake Tahoe's High Sierra Web Site (*http://highsierra.com/*).

PATAnet (*http://www.pata.org/patanet/*)

The Pacific Asia Travel Association calls itself the voice of Pacific-Asia travel and tourism. The site has travel news for the region, and information about relevant events and conferences. The home page is a clickable map of the region with links to a page for each country. Click on Malaysia and you reach Malaysia's Home Page (*http://www.jaring. my/*). The site is graced by Russell Johnson's photos, in a collection called "Jewels of the Mekong." You'll also find a page on PATA's Green Leaf program, promoting sustainable development in the region.

TravelASSIST Magazine (*http://www.travelassist.com/mag/mag_home.html*)

This is a general interest publication, focusing on a different theme each week. Usually the theme is a destination, but some of the monthly issues focus on a specific type of travel, such as cruising. Travel agents will finds plenty of useful nuggets in each issue. TravelASSIST also includes "Ask the Agents," where you can seek advice from other agents, tour companies, or vendors. Travel agents can sign up to participate as advice-givers, which could lead to getting known on the Web and eventually to sales. Also see the TravelDEALS section with late-breaking bargains you can pass on to your clients.

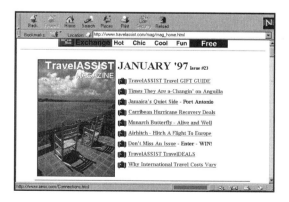

FIGURE 10-5

TravelASSIST is an online magazine that takes you around the world.

Tom and Mary Kay believe that marketing a Net site begins at home. As Web site providers, they have some suggestions about what a travel professional should expect from an Internet service provider. "Before anything else, your site must be able to be found," they say,

FIGURE 10-6

*Lake Tahoe's High Sierra site
(http://highsierra.com/) highlights the region's
top attractions, such as Emerald Bay and
ski resorts.*

meaning your site must be registered with the 15 or more major Internet search directories, such as AltaVista and Yahoo. "And if your link doesn't come up on the first few pages of each directory, then get your Web developer to work on improving your position."

The ISP you choose for hosting your site should be reliable, they advise, meaning that your site "should be online and not out of commission due to technical difficulties. If potential customers can't get to your site, it's like getting a constant busy signal on the phone!"

TEN COMMANDMENTS FOR A SUCCESSFUL WEB SITE

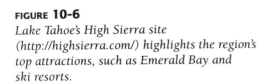

PERSONAL ACCOUNT

Tom and Mary Kay Aufrance

Aufrance Associates
tmaufr@highsierra.com
http://highsierra.com

Tom Aufrance

After the top two important components Tom has just mentioned, Tom and Mary Kay offer the following ten commandments for a successful Web site:

1. The site should prominently identify the travel company, services, and how to make contact with you (such as your company's 800-number).

2. Right on top, you need an attractive photo that allows the reader to imagine, "That's me there in that exotic place! Where do I sign up?!"

3. Make sure your call to action is interspersed throughout the text ("Click here to make your reservation request, now!"). This "Click here" button should lead to a reservation request form that includes all the information you need to replace that first phone call, such as name, address, phone number, email address, desired service, and arrival/departure times. You need to

get all the information you can, in order to respond and close the sale on each lead.

4. Your request form should send you an email message (which means you need your own email account) so that you or your staff can respond within 24 hours, before the lead goes stale. If you don't, some other travel site will respond quicker and get that lead instead of you.

5. Ideally, your request form will not only send you an email message, your requests should also go into a Microsoft Office-compatible database, which you can use later for promotional mailings or marketing analysis. Why Microsoft Office-compatible? Because it is what most office staffs know how to use for mail merges or other marketing programs.

6. You should be able to make changes to your own Web site, so that you can add specials or try experimenting with new offers for your Internet customers. You should not have to wait for your Web designer to get around to it.

7. A "Search" on your site is like a magnet for readers. So get one! Our High Sierra site logs show the most readership is on pages that are titled "Search for Your Dream Vacation" or something like that. People love the interactivity, and also the ability to customize their search criteria to fit their personal desires. And, if you can fill someone's desire for that "two bedroom condo near Heavenly Valley ski area over Christmas," then you've made a sale.

8. Sell the sizzle of your vacation area! For example, create a clickable map of area golf courses, and intersperse your call-to-action all over it, for example, "Click here to make your reservations near this golf course."

9. As soon as you can, get Internet commerce to work on your site. Take credit cards and make reservations. (If you have to, include a disclaimer that your confirmation will follow within 24 hours, by phone or email.) Get ready to let your Web site actually make those sales for you!

10. Finally, start to think of the Internet as a big computer on which you can put your own big reservations system! If you do, you'll realize that you should expect much more than just an online "flyer that glows." You can expect to do more business due to your Internet presence.

WALK BEFORE YOU RUN

As mentioned earlier, the best way to start is to get an Internet connection and get to know this new neighborhood. Browse travel sites in your areas of expertise. When you get your Net connection you get an email address along with it. Hopefully you don't have a closet full of old business cards and stationery, because you need to get that email address printed on your literature as soon as possible, especially on your business cards.

Then make sure your staff begins to routinely ask clients if they have an email address; start communicating with clients electronically whenever it's appropriate.

The next logical move is to get listed on the major Internet travel agent directories. Two of the best such directories are ITN (*http://www.itn.net*) and TravelHub (*http://www.travelhub.com*). These directories let travelers book over the Net and direct these bookings to certified travel agents. By listing on these sites, you get Web exposure without having to invest in building your own site.

TravelHub organizes agents by specialty. So if your niche is adventure tours, a traveler interested in whitewater rafting in Costa Rica would be the type who is directed to your site. To check it out, I visited TravelHub's site and clicked on Adventure and then entered the search term *Costa Rica*. The search came up with Global TravelNet in Greenville, South Carolina, which specializes in Costa Rican adventures. TravelHub listed the agency's address, toll-free number, and had a button labeled Request Travel, where a potential client can input name, email, phone number, and destination. Clients can also sign up to receive email bulletins about travel specials in their area of interest.

FIGURE 10-7

TravelHub (http://www.travelhub.com) helps travelers find the right type of agency for their specialized trips.

"The writing is on the virtual wall," says Miguel Castaneda, Travel-HUB's CEO and Webmaster. "It seems like every airline, hotel, and cruise line is looking to bypass travel agencies with direct bookings on the Web. TravelHUB exists to help remind the Internet public of the enormous advantages of using certified, professional travel agents."

ADVICE FROM WIRED AGENTS

What do fellow agents have to say about getting up to speed on the Net? "Surf, surf, surf," says John Clifford. "See what others are doing that you think could apply to selling the unique products that you specialize in. And yes, *specialize*. Nobody can be an expert at everything. You have to show the Net-surfing consumer that you're better at what you sell than anybody else. Otherwise, why would they use you?" John also recommends getting on mailing lists such as Travel-Agents and communicating online with others in the agent community.

Bob Ensten echoes John's advice. "Play with the Net. Try new things every day and don't be afraid of it," he says. "Ask others for their input and assistance—hands on is the best way to learn."

One of John's specialties is gay travel. He has used the Net to market this expertise throughout the U.S. and beyond by making sure his site is properly listed on all the key search directories. So when someone searches for the term *gay travel*, John's site will be among those that pop up.

"I'm a self-taught guru, and I haven't read one book on building a Web site, marketing on the Net, or anything," he says. "I learned by *doing*."

Bob and John are among the growing number of agents who can't imagine doing business without the Net. And part of the benefit they cite is quick and easy electronic access to other agents and travel suppliers throughout the world.

Many of these travel agent "early adopters" taught themselves the ropes by just diving in, using the Net to see what others were doing, and then trying to improve and expand on it. In the early days this meant learning HTML coding, the tags embedded in a Web page document that tell the browser how to display it on a user's screen.

But today that job has gotten a lot easier as dozens of automated HTML coding programs have hit the market. These programs let you

Submit It
http://www.submit-it.com/
A quick and efficient way to list your site on most of the main search directories, Submit It will simultaneously list your site to more than a dozen search engines and directories.

decide how you want your Web page to look and prepare the HTML coding. Many of these programs can be downloaded directly off the Net and range in price from $99 to free. The Netscape Gold browser has a built-in HTML editor, which enables even novices to become Webmasters.

FOR THE CORPORATE TRAVEL MANAGER

Corporate travel managers aren't just working for the executives for whom they're booking travel. They're also expected to meet the needs of their companies, which means booking employees on preferred airlines and at hotels where the company has a corporate agreement. Sometimes corporate travel managers get caught between the desires of an employee and the mandate of the company.

Thankfully, there are several products that have recently been released to help make it easier for corporate travel planners to do their jobs well. These range from specialized software systems from small, privately held companies to the highly anticipated product from Microsoft and American Express. The package, slated for release in mid-1997, offers access to myriad reservation systems, destination information, negotiated discounts, and travel advice. These systems let travel managers set parameters, such as which airlines and hotels are preferred or required. Then business travelers can reserve and purchase their travel from their desktop computers, within the limits set by the corporate travel manager.

This saves time for the corporate travel manager and money for the company. Rather than serving as a booking agent for employees, the travel manager actually manages the system. And these systems give corporations more leverage in negotiating preferred rates with travel suppliers because companies can more easily direct their employees to specific travel suppliers. Through these systems, companies can more clearly track and document their employees' travel patterns.

Internet Travel Network (*http://www.itn.net*) has a similar system called Internet Travel Manager. Say a traveler wants to go from Houston to Chicago. If the company he works for has corporate agreements with Hyatt and American Airlines, the traveler will be shown these travel suppliers first. Or a company could take a more rigid approach and show only options on American Airlines and with Hyatt.

The system can be set up to book the travel at preferred rates negotiated with travel suppliers. So if a company has a special deal with Hyatt, those rates will be reflected. ITN's system lets a travel manager monitor what is being spent and then instantly works within that framework to bring costs down, says ITN's Joe Witherspoon.

TIP

For a demonstration of ITN's Internet Travel Manager, see *http://www.itn.net/xyzcorp*.

The new systems are about "using tools to move market share into areas that are more favorable for a corporation," says Rick Lifsitz, vice president of marketing for E-Travel Systems. He cites a major media company based in New York that cut a $50 million travel budget by 13 percent after it began using one primary carrier (instead of three) for the bulk of its air travel.

Major online travel suppliers are causing other changes in the way corporations book travel. TravelNet and Pegasus planned to launch a system to enable corporate travel buyers to link directly to hotel reservation systems, cutting CRSs out of the loop. New systems are letting travelers directly access a live hotel inventory, customized to reflect special rates negotiated between the hotel and corporation.

TravelNet President Randall Malin says he expects similar systems for car rental companies by mid-1997. By late 1996, many hotel chains and a few car rental companies had put their reservation systems on-line. What is new about these corporate systems is the customizable feature, enabling corporate employees to book their own travel within the guidelines set by the company. In several systems these guidelines will be different for employees at different levels in the company. For example, the CEO may be permitted to book a first-class flight and $250 suite, while a middle-level manager could travel business class and stay in a room costing up to $150. For more on corporate travel systems, see Chapter 5, "For the Business Traveler."

DESTINATION SITES

The Web has also become a mecca for Web sites dedicated to promoting specific destinations, from national tourist boards to finely crafted local sites, such as the Virtual Yakima Valley (*http://www. yakima.net*). Dedicated to providing up-to-date information on events and activities for Washington state's Yakima Valley, this extensive and well organized site is a service to those interested in the area as well as to those who want to publicize local attractions.

PERSONAL ACCOUNT
Pablo M. Supkay, MBA
INCOMMAND Interactive
pablo@in-command.com .
http://www.in-command. com

Following is an (email) interview with Pablo Supkay of Incommand Interactive, an Internet provider in Yakima, who created and maintains the Yakima site. Pablo's comments serve as a primer for others interested in creating a regional Web site, though many of his ideas contain good advice for any travel pro who wants to build a successful Web site.

How do you get the word out to potential clients? How do you get people to know that you exist on this crowded Web?

> Our page targets a specific group of people who have
> an interest in the Yakima Valley. Local exposure
> was achieved by establishing a relationship with
> local media and sending various press releases over
> an extended period of time. On the Internet, the
> main thrust of our promotional efforts was directed
> at submitting our URL to all major search engines
> and directories. We have also placed an emphasis on
> getting linked from regional and tourism-related
> indexes. Many links have been created by
> individuals with an interest in the Valley without
> our intervention.

What are the components of a successful site?

> — Timely and dynamic data: repeat usage occurs when
> rapidly changing data is available and kept up-to-
> date.

> — Comprehensive information: a site is
> differentiated from other sites on the same subject
> based on the completeness of the information. We
> have not charged for placing community information
> or links to Yakima-related Web pages on our site.
> As a result, we have the largest collection of
> Yakima links and information on the Web and have
> developed a reputation for being the front-runner
> in this niche.

> — Intuitive navigation: users must be able to
> quickly and efficiently find information they are

seeking. We have incorporated a local search engine
to help users find info based on keywords.

— Pleasant design: the site must be easy to read,
functional and professional in appearance.
Simplicity is often a key design component in
accomplishing these goals.

How did you build your site?

We have used WebSite webserver software on our NT
machine since early 1995. It has done a good job in
serving our pages over this time period.

TIP

WebSite 1.1 and WebSite Professional are award-winning Web
server software packages for Windows NT/Windows 95.
WebSite provides easy-to-use solutions for people who want to
publish on the Internet. For more information, see WebSite
Central (*http://website.ora.com/*).

Our success has hinged on providing free
development and hosting for community-based
organizations and information. We have invested the
time to promote the use of information technology
in our community and, as a result, have secured
involvement by all the major institutions in the
Valley.

Initially, we input a great deal of local
information and linked to every site that we could
find about Yakima. After achieving "critical mass,"
the site has grown on its own as individuals and
organizations have asked to be linked from our
site. We see ourselves as the catalyst for the
development of electronic information in the
Valley. We have grown the market for Web
development in the Valley while helping to promote
Yakima.

At some point in the near future, enough viewers
will exist in our region to help justify local
advertisements on our site. When the market is
there, we will be positioned to charge for banner
advertising.

What advice would you give others who are just starting up?

— Be prepared for a long-term return on investment. "Get rich quick" schemes do not normally succeed on the Net. It takes time and effort to establish a presence.

— Identify the target market and its information needs. Research competitive offerings and write a list of site features needed in order to establish your site as the clear leader in contention for your target market. Once a leadership position is achieved, maintain and widen the gap by continually adding info and features.

— Zealously promote your site using the most cost-effective means to reach your target segment. Rely on the press as a source of invaluable advertising.

— Don't put a site up for the world to see until it meets some minimum requirements for completeness. There is nothing more irritating to users than a site that promises tons of unavailable information and is "under construction" for an extended period of time.

IN A NUTSHELL

Whether you simply want to get Net access and email to communicate with clients or take the full plunge and establish your own Web site, one thing is clear: you can't afford not to get online. Clients will soon expect you to communicate by email, but more importantly, the Web offers an almost limitless array of information and tools for agents. As the competition among agents intensifies, you'll have to employ every tool at your disposal to remain competitive. Both your prospective customers and your competitors will be using the Net. If you're not, you may be out of the game.

Most of the agents profiled above jumped online for common sense business reasons. But after they got on the Net they found a whole new world had opened to them, a world that included new ways to attract clients, novel methods for researching destinations, and broader connections with their colleagues. So while many agents rightly feel they must get online to survive, there are lots of side benefits to being on the Net. Don't wait too long to share in this adventure.

NetTravel Toolbox
Useful Web Sites Listed by Subject

ADVENTURE TRAVEL

Cyber Adventures
http://www.cyber-adventures.com
Tales and tips from adventurous travelers.

The Doc's Favorite Travel Stories
http://www.access.digex.net/~drmemory/sow.html
Travel guru Dr. Memory selects his favorite travel stories.

2 Chicks, 2 Bikes, 1 Cause
http://www.2chicks.org
Two women tour Australia (1997) and the U.S. (1996) by bicycle to raise awareness about breast cancer.

The Russian Chronicles
http://www.f8.com/FP/Russia/index.html
A 5,000-mile journey, traveling through remote regions in Russia, documenting the outlook and opinion of contemporary Russians.

Mountain Travel Sobek
http://www.mtsobek.com
One of the world's premier adventure tour companies.

Outside Online
http://outside.starwave.com/
News from *Outside* magazine and much more.

Himalayan Explorers Club
http://www.abwam.com/himexp
Tips for travelers to the Himalayas, including where to visit, selecting a guide, and how to help the local people.

Lonely Planet's Thorn Tree
http://www.lonelyplanet.com/feedback/thorn.htm
A computer bulletin board organized by region, this site can help you find adventurous traveling companions.

Great Outdoor Recreation Pages (GORP)
http://www.gorp.com
A bible for those who love the outdoors.

The Climbing Archive
http://www.dtek.chalmers.se/Climbing/index.html
Tips for climbers and links to potential climbing partners for wherever you plan to go.

Nomadic Research Labs
http://www.microship.com

The original technomad shares his wired journeys bicycling across the U.S. and his plans to develop a fully wired ship.

Webcrawler's Travel Adventures
http://webcrawler.com/select/trav.advent.html

A superb list of links to adventure and ecotourism sites.

John Labovitz's Travel Stories and Resources
http://www.meer.net/~johnl/trip

John writes about his Green Tortoise adventure in the U.S. and his journey through Eastern Europe, and provides links to other funky travel sites.

ADVISORIES

U.S. State Department Travel Warnings
http://travel.state.gov/travel_warnings.html

Background on crime, medical treatment standards, and embassy locations.

CIA World Factbook
http://portal.research.bell-labs.com/cgi-wald/dbaccess/411

Basic geography, current environmental issues, population figures, and ethnic makeup.

U.S. Customs Service
http://www.customs.ustreas.gov

Find out what you can legally bring back from the countries you visit.

World Travel Watch
http://www.ora.com/ttales/editorial/wtw

A global roundup of events that affect conditions for travelers.

AIRLINE SCHEDULES AND RESERVATIONS

Travelocity
http://www.travelocity.com

Extensive destination information, hotel and car rental access. Email updates on airfare bargains for the routes you select.

Preview Travel
http://www.reservations.com

Airline schedules, reservations, and destination information.

Expedia
http://expedia.com

Easy-to-find schedules and fares, hotel directory, Fare Tracker email alerts about bargain flights to destinations you select, bonus frequent flyer miles.

ITN
http://www.itn.net
Low graphics mean quick loading; personal service because ticketing is through a travel agent, Java-based low-fare ticker.

Flifo
http://www.flifo.com
Fare Buster feature looks for cheaper flights around the same time as the one you selected.

TISS
http://www.tiss.com
Cheap consolidator flights.

PC Travel
http://www.pctravel.com
Destination information, discounts for members.

AIRLINE SITES

Airlines of the Web
http://www.itn.net/airlines
Links to hundreds of airlines, frequent flyer programs, airport information, and more.

Delta Airlines
http://www.delta-air.com

United Airlines
http://www.ual.com

American Airlines
http://www.americanair.com

USAirways
http://www.usair.com

Southwest Airlines
http://www.iflyswa.com

AROUND THE WORLD TRAVEL

Round-The-World Travel Guide
http://www.solutions.net/rec-travel/rtw/html/faq.html
Key advice for long-term travelers, such as how to find work and how to stay in touch with the homefront.

Around-the-World Airfare Builder
http://www.highadv.com
Dozens of possible RTW routes and fares, some under $1,500.

ARRIVAL TIMES FOR AIRLINES

Flyte Trax
http://www.weatherconcepts.com/FlyteTrax/
This site can tell you when a flight that's in the air is due to arrive—it even shows a map pinpointing the current location of the flight.

BARGAINS

Arthur Frommer's Outspoken Encyclopedia of Travel
http://www.frommer.com
"Secret" deals uncovered by the world's leading travel guidebook writer.

Expedia Fare Tracker
http://expedia.com/pub/faretrkr.hts?
Expedia will send you news of bargains on the routes you select.

American Airlines Net SAAver fares
http://www2.amrcorp.com/cgi-bin/aans
Last-minute discount on flights.

USAirways E-Savers
http://www.usair.com/travel/fares/esavers.htm
Email alerts on discount flights.

Click-It Weekends
http://www.travelweb.com/thisco/clickit/common/hotels.html
Last-minute deals on hotel rooms.

Electronic Travel Auction
http://www.etauction.com
Bid on unsold airline seats, package tours, and more.

Shoestring Travel
http://www.stratpub.com/
Where budget travelers trade tips to help one another save money.

Budget Travel
http://www.budgettravel.com/
Reams of listings for cheap flights around the world.

1travel.com
http://www.1travel.com/
A compendium of bargain airfares, cruises, and hotel rooms. With Consolidators Online, you get access to fares from more than 50 consolidators throughout the world.

Interactive Travel Guide
http://www.developnet.com/travel/
This site started as "Clever Ways to Travel for Free or Little Cost," and while the site has broadened its focus, it's still a good source for bargains, for example, tips on where to change money in Europe or how to get a driveaway vehicle.

Travel Deals
http://www.travelassist.com/mag/a50.html
If you know where you're going, check Travel Assist's Travel Deals before you leave.

Discount Lodging Directory
http://www.ios.com/hotels/hotels.html
State-by-state lists of hotels that offer discounts for federal employees.

Traveler's Net
http://www.travelersnet.com
Cut out the middleman and save up to 7 percent off airfares and other travel arrangements.

TravelBids
http://www.Travelbids.com
A site that rewards you for booking it yourself.

The Savvier Traveler
http://www.savtraveler.com
Discounts on cruise bookings and more.

BED & BREAKFAST DIRECTORIES

InnSite
http://www.innsite.com
Browse among the thousands of B&Bs or search for B&Bs by region.

Bed and Breakfast Inns of North America
http://cimarron.net/
A well organized and extensive listing of inns, with images.

The Inn Traveler
http://www.inntraveler.com/
Extensive directory of B&Bs and inns.

America's Best Bed & Breakfasts, Country Inns, and Small Hotels
http://www.virtualcities.com/~virtual/ons/0onsadex.htm
A guide to U.S. B&Bs and inns.

Along the Way
http://www.flinthills.com/~atway
An online guide to bed & breakfasts in the Midwestern U.S.

BOOKSTORES

The Adventurous Traveler
http://www.AdventurousTraveler.com/
Includes book excerpts, browsing by location or activity, and keyword searches.

The Travel Bug

http://www.swifty.com/tbug/

Guidebooks and travel accessories.

Book Passage

http://www.bookpassage.com

Features a wide selection and has a knowledgeable staff ready to answer travelers' questions.

BUSINESS TRAVEL

Biztravel

http://www.biztravel.com

Articles and tools for the business traveler.

Business Travel Resource Center

http://www.travelweb.com/thisco/bustravl/bustravel.html

Catch up with the news through the online versions of the *Wall Street Journal* and *Barron's*, get a package sent to you overnight through FedEx, or arrange ground transportation to your hotel.

QTW Corporate Travel

http://www.quinwell.com/business.html

Information about airfares, baggage allowances, and business travel services, such as preferred car rental rates.

The Business Travel Pages

http://www.mcb.co.uk/apmforum/travel/welcome.htm

Focusing on Asia, this site recommends hotels, has tips for restaurants, and articles about Asian business and management.

Banks of the World

http://www.wiso.gwdg.de/ifbg/bank_2.html

If you're traveling to an overseas hotel and wondering where you'll be able to find an ATM that takes your bank card, check this site for links to banks organized by country.

Association of Business Travellers

http://www.hk.linkage.net/markets/abt/

ABT offers a comprehensive free online hotel reservation service, savings and discounts on hotel rooms, savings at restaurants, and lost luggage tracing.

The Executive Woman's Travel Network

http://www.delta-air.com/womenexecs/

Advice on safety, tipping, and planning for your trip.

CAR RENTALS

Hertz
http://www.hertz.com

The Avis Galaxy
http://www.avis.com

Alamo's Freeways
http://www.freeways.com

Budget Rent a Car
http://www.budgetrentacar.com

Dollar Rent A Car
http://www.dollarcar.com

COURIER FLIGHTS

International Association of Air Travel Couriers
http://www.courier.org
Learn how to fly for next to nothing by carrying packages for others.

Worldwide Courier Association
http://www.courier.org
Tips on finding the right courier flight.

CRUISE LINES AND BOOKING CRUISES

Royal Caribbean Cruise Lines
http://www.royalcaribbean.com/

Carnival Cruise Lines
http://www.carnival.com

Cunard Line
http://www.cunardline.com/

Norwegian Cruise Line
http://www.ncl.com/

Princess Cruises
http://www.awcv.com/princess.html

Freighter World Cruises
http://www.gus.net/travel/fwc/fwc.html
For an unconventional cruise experience.

Windjammer Barefoot Cruises
http://wheat.symgrp.com/symgrp/windjammer
An informal way to cruise in tall ships.

Internet Cruise Travel Network
http://www.cruisetravel.com/
Research and book your cruise over the Net.

The Cruise Web
http://www.cruiseweb.com
Organizes listings by cruise line and by destination and has a section for bargain cruises.

Cruisin
http://www.asource.coum/cruisin
Cruise counselors who do all their business on the Net.

CULTURAL EVENTS AND FESTIVALS

CultureFinder
http://www.culturefinder.com
Input the name of your destination and the dates you'll be there, and this site will deliver a list of events, including art exhibits, operas, plays, and classical music performances.

Festivals.com
http://www.festivals.com/welcome.htm
Updated listings, feature articles, and a search directory to help you find festivals at your destinations.

DINING

DineNet
http://www.menusonline.com
U.S. restaurant listings.

The Essential Restaurant Guide
http://www.epicurious.com/e_eating/e03_restguide/guide.html
Part of the Epicurious site.

World Wide Sushi Restaurant Reference
http://wwwipd.ira.uka.de/~maraist/Sushi/
An international guide to sushi restaurants.

World Guide to Vegetarianism
http://www.veg.org/veg/Guide/index.html
An indispensable guide for vegetarians.

Koshernet
http://www.koshernet.com
To find restaurants that adhere to Jewish dietary laws.

The Gumbo Pages
http://www.gumbopages.com/
For a taste of New Orleans.

DIRECTORIES AND DESTINATION SITES

NetTravel
http://www.nettravel.com

The companion site to this book, NetTravel is a gateway to the world of online travel.

Travel Weekly
http://www.traveler.net/two/

A dozen categories, including cruises, railroads, and theme travel, as well as the standards: air travel, hotels, and tours.

Yahoo Travel
http://www.yahoo.com/Recreation/Travel/

Yahoo's travel directory is an extensive list of travel links well organized by category—an excellent place to browse or search for a specific site.

Webcrawler
http://webcrawler.com

Webcrawler organizes links by subject and gives a brief description of sites.

The Travel Channel
http://www.travelchannel.com/

A comprehensive source for city profiles and much more.

Arthur Frommer's Outspoken Encyclopedia of Travel
http://www.frommer.com

An outstanding resource for information on more than 200 cities, this site also includes terrific bargains on air fares, cruises, and much more.

World Travel Guide
http://www.wtgonline.com/

An easy-to-navigate site. The "A-to-Z Country Factfinder" enables users to click on any region of interest for information of lodging, history, and maps.

/travmag/
http://www.travigator.com/travmag/for/direct.htm

A useful listing of more than 3,000 sites by subject. This site has a search directory and up-to-date, Net-related travel news.

Rec.Travel Library
http://www.solutions.net/rec-travel/

A fine selection of travel sites organized by subject and by region. Also information on packing well, driving while traveling abroad, and travel clubs.

CNN Travel
http://www.cnn.com/TRAVEL

A nice roundup of links to useful travel resources as well as travel-related news.

City.net
http://citynet.com

Detailed city information including ideas for quick tours in hundreds of cities throughout the world.

DISABLED

Global Access
http://www.geocities.com/Paris/1502/
Disabled travelers report on what hotels and tourist areas are accessible.

Travel Source
http://www.access-able.com/
Accessible tours; has a search directory that lets you type in a destination and search for a type of trip.

Disability Travel Services
http://www.dts.org
Online newsletters, travel guides, travel agents that specialize in serving special needs populations.

The Able Informer
http://www.sasquatch.com/ableinfo
An online newsletter of resources for the disabled.

AccessAbility Travel
http://www.disabled-travel.com
A travel agency specializing in trips for the disabled.

Accessible Journeys
http://www.disabilitytravel.com/
Accessible vacations exclusively for slow walkers, wheelchair travelers, their families, and their friends.

Environmental Traveling Companions
http://www.hooked.net/users/stuarth/ETC/
A San Francisco-based group offering whitewater rafting and sea kayak trips for disabled people.

Getaway Cruises
http://www.cruiseaway.com/
Escorted cruises for the disabled.

ECOTOURISM

Ecotourism
http://www.podi.com/ecosource/ecotour.htm
A guide to the ecotourism marketplace and tour information.

El Planeta Platica: Eco Travels in Latin America
http://www.planeta.com
A guide to Latin American ecotourism.

EDUCATIONAL VACATIONS

Learning Vacations
http://www.learningvacations.com
Trips ranging from sailing schools to safaris.

Earthwatch
http://gaia.earthwatch.org
Join a field research team.

Hospitality Net's Virtual Job Exchange
http://www.hospitalitynet.nl/job
Opportunities to work in foreign countries for those in the hospitality business.

EarthWise Journeys
http://www.teleport.com/~earthwyz
Alternative travel adventures.

EMAIL

Hotmail
http://www.hotmail.com
Web-based free email.

Juno
http://www.juno.com
Free email with more than 400 telephone numbers throughout the U.S. for computer access.

NetAddress
http://www.netaddress.usa.net
Web-based free email.

FAMILY TRAVEL

Disney Travel Ideas
http://www.disney.com/News/docs/travel.html
Park maps, hours, show schedules, ticket information, and special events. Disney also includes links to directions, local weather, and traffic reports, and lets you know about hotels and campgrounds.

Parent Soup
http://www.parentsoup.com
See the travel section of this family-oriented site for tips on what the kids might enjoy.

The Exploratorium
http://www.exploratorium.edu

San Francisco's hands-on science museum—this site is worth a visit even if you don't have plans to visit the city by the Bay.

The Hilton Vacation Station
http://www.hilton.com/^8393346789720/programs/families.html

An online game room for kids, complete with lists of supervised activities at various Hilton hotels.

Family Cruises' Big Red Boat
http://www.familycruises.com/big_red.html

Cruises with activities for kids.

FREQUENT FLYERS

Web Flyer
http://www.insideflyer.com

Features from *Inside Flyer* magazine, FAQs about frequent flyer programs, and hundreds of ways to earn miles without leaving the ground.

How Far Is It?
http://www.indo.com/distance/

Point-to-point distances between cities throughout the world.

GAY AND LESBIAN TRAVEL

Q-Net
http://www.q-net.com

An extensive guide for gay and lesbian travelers.

Mi Casa Su Casa
http://www.well.com/user/homeswap/

An international home exchange network for gay and lesbian travelers.

QTCompanion
http://www.bures.com/qtc/

Information for gay travelers.

Alyson Adventures
http://www.channel1.com/alyson/

Bicycling, hiking, skiing, and diving tours for lesbians and gay men.

Gay Key West
http://www.gaykeywestfl.com/

Guesthouses and inns catering to a gay clientele.

Gay Las Vegas

http://coyote.accessnv.com/kmess/gayvegas.html

An extensive list of things to do on and off the strip.

Lesbian and Gay London

http://www.users.dircon.co.uk/~zzyzx/tourist/glguide/glguide.htm

Tips for finding the perfect local pub, gay- and lesbian-friendly hotels and restaurants, and links to other sites for travelers to London.

m2m|w2w vacations

http://www.geocities.com/WestHollywood/1993

Vacation packages and useful links for gay and lesbian travelers.

GUIDEBOOKS

Lonely Planet

http://www.lonelyplanet.com

This budget backpacker's guide has gone mainstream and offers a tremendous amount of information online.

The Rough Guides

http://www.hotwired.com/rough/

For people who still seek a sense of adventure when they travel.

Fodor's

http://www.fodors.com

With Fodor's "Personal Trip Planner," you can create a personal guide to dozens of cities, complete with listings customized to reflect your interests and needs.

Moon Publications

http://www.moon.com

Innovative travel guides that often take the road less traveled.

Let's Go

http://www.letsgo.com

Budget travel by and for students and others traveling on a shoestring.

HEALTH INFORMATION

CDC Travel Information

http://www.cdc.gov/travel/travel.html

A comprehensive site from the Centers for Disease Control, smartly organized by region.

Travel Health Online

http://www.tripprep.com/

Health information, country descriptions, entry requirements, and embassy and consulate locations.

Staying Healthy in Asia, Africa, and Latin America
http://www.moon.com/staying_healthy/

Includes the full text of Moon's book by the same name and has a feature that lets travelers search for a specific disease or region.

Lonely Planet's Pills, Ills, and Bellyaches
http://www.lonelyplanet.com.au/health/health.htm

Remedies for those nasty road bugs.

Healthy Flying
http://www.flyana.com/

Helps travelers reduce the risk of getting sick en route.

HOME EXCHANGE

International Home Exchange Network
http://www.homexchange.com

Trade your home for a place to stay at your destination, or host visiting travelers.

World Wide Travel Exchange
http://www.wwte.com/

Exchange your home with other vacationers or rent out your place.

The Travel Exchange Club
http://www.travex.com/travex/home.html

Similar to IHEN, but does not charge to list your home.

Jewish Travel Network
http://www.jewish-travel-net.com

Home exchange and hosting for Jewish travelers.

Mi Casa Su Casa
http://www.well.com/user/homeswap/

An international home exchange network for gay and lesbian travelers.

HOSTELS

The Internet Guide to Hosteling
http://www.hostels.com

Thousands of hostels around the world, a hosteling FAQ, a conferencing area where you can ask questions or share your experiences, and reviews of budget guidebooks.

American Youth Hostels
http://www.iyhf.org

More than 5,000 hostels in 77 countries.

HOTELS

TravelWeb
http://www.travelweb.com
Search or browse through thousands of listings of hotels around the world.

All the Hotels on the Web
http://www.all-hotels.com/
An index of more than 10,000 hotel sites around the world, organized geographically.

The Hotel Guide
http://www.hotelguide.ch
An international guide with more than 50,000 hotels in its database. The beauty of this guide is that you can use a series of preferences to focus your search.

Hotel Anywhere
http://www.hotelanywhere.com
Links to thousands of hotel sites, airlines, cruise lines, and travel agents.

The Vacation Rental Source
http://www.vrsource.com/
Listings for villas and condos available in the U.S., Hawaii, and the Caribbean.

Hilton Worldwide
http://www.hilton.com

Hyatt Hotels & Resorts
http://www.hyatt.com

Radisson Hotels
http://www.radisson.com/

INTERNET CAFÉS

Yahoo's list of Net cafés
http://www.yahoo.com/Society_and_Culture/Cyberculture/Internet_Cafes

Internet Café Guide
http://www.kuwait.net:80/~notish/fun/Cafes/
Somewhat slow but this site may help you find a café at your destination.

Cyber Café Guide
http://www.cyberiacafe.net/cyberia/guide/ccafe.htm
May not be up-to-date, but offers listings for cafés.

LANGUAGES

Travlang's Foreign Languages for Travelers
http://www.travlang.com/languages/
Click on the language you need to learn, and select from "Basic Words," "Directions," or "Times and Dates," among other categories.

MAGAZINES

Condé Nast Traveler
http://travel.epicurious.com/travel/g_cnt/home.html
Travel stories and an online concierge to help you choose a destination.

The Connected Traveler
http://www.travelmedia.com/connected
Personal impressions and photos of exotic and down-home destinations.

Mungo Park
http://mungopark.msn.com/
Adventure travel stories and reports directly from the field.

No S—tting in the Toilet
http://www.magna.com.au/~nglobe/nsitt/contents.html
An irreverent look at the inevitable hardships of real-world travel.

Monk
http://www.neo.com/Monk/
A mobile zine from two guys traveling across the U.S.

MAPS

Perry Castañeda Library Map Collection
http://www.lib.utexas.edu/Libs/PCL/Map_collection/Map_collection.html
City and country maps from throughout the world and featured maps of political hot spots.

MapQuest
http://www.mapquest.com
Zoom in on your destination, find directions, local hotels, restaurants, and more.

MapBlast
http://www.mapblast.com
Create your own maps of U.S. destinations.

NEWSGROUPS AND LISTSERVS

DejaNews
http://www.dejanews.com
Search for newsgroups or specific postings on topics of interest.

Liszt
http://www.liszt.com
Find listervs (mailing lists) on specific subjects.

NEWSPAPERS

Newslink
http://www.newslink.org
Links to more than 1,500 regional news sites throughout the world.

The New Century Network
http://www.newcentury.net/
A network of major metro dailies.

PACKAGE TOURS

SunTrips
http://www.suntrip.com
Air-hotel packages to prime vacation spots in Hawaii and Mexico.

Club Med
http://www.clubmed.com
Not just for singles, Club Med offers trips for couples and families.

PARKS AND CAMPGROUNDS

National Park Service
http://www.nps.gov
Official information for U.S. national parks.

Great Outdoor Recreation Pages (GORP)
http://www.gorp.com
A superb resource for anyone interested in hiking information, adventure stories, or outdoor gear.

The Campground Directory
http://www.holipub.com/camping/director.htm
A guide to private campgrounds.

PEOPLE FINDERS

Yahoo's People Search
http://www.yahoo.com/search/people
A good place to find a long-lost friend.

Four11
http://www.four11.com
A database of telephone numbers, addresses, and email addresses.

Internet Address Finder
http://www.iaf.net
Email addresses.

Bigfoot
http://bigfoot.com
This site says it has the largest and most accurate "white page" listings on the Net.

ROAD TRIPS

American Automobile Association
http://www.aaa.com/
Preview AAA tourbooks, locate AAA offices, and find lodgings and other places where AAA members receive discounts.

Route 66 Collection
http://www.kaiwan.com/~wem/
A traveler's guide and maps.

MapQuest
http://www.mapquest.com
Directions to where you're going; you can also use this site to find hotels and restaurants, among other services.

The WWW Speedtrap Registry
http://www.speedtrap.com/speedtrap/
Organizes traps by state and country, based on tips from readers.

Adventures in a VW and Other Interesting Things
http://coyote.accessnv.com/wayback/
Follow one traveler's excursions in his VW bus to the Grand Canyon, southern Utah, and Death Valley.

SENIORS

Elderhostel
http://www.elderhostel.org
For people who know they're never too old to learn.

ElderTreks

http://www.eldertreks.com/

Adventures for people over 50.

SeniorNet

http://www.seniornet.org

An all-around guide for seniors on the Net, which often offers good travel information.

On-Call Vacations

http://www.on-call.com/

Last-minute deals on cruises, hotel rooms, and resort vacations for seniors 55 or over who belong to United Airlines' Silver Wings Plus.

SKIING

GoSki

http://www.goski.com

GoSki uses the ultimate resource, its readers, to cover more than 1,500 resorts in 25 countries. Avalanche warnings, gear reviews, weather updates—it's all here.

SkiMaps

http://www.skimaps.com/

Maps of more than 100 ski resorts around the world.

Ski Colorado

http://www.aescon.com/ski/index.html

More than a solid list of the state's ski areas and lodges, Ski Colorado offers advice on staying healthy at high altitudes, telemarking, tuning your skis, and more.

Madnordski

http://danenet.wicip.org/madnord

An essential resource for cross-country skiers, this site focuses on the Madison (Wisconsin) area, but has a superb list of links to other cross-country skiing sites.

Western Canada Ski Guide

http://softnc.com/waveworks/Guide.html

A guide to the stunning, jagged peaks of Western Canada—includes a clickable map of the region.

TOURISM BUREAUS AND EMBASSIES

Tourism Office Worldwide Directory

http://www.mbnet.mb.ca/lucas/travel

Addresses and phones for tourism offices around the globe; if an office is online, the directory provides a link.

Travelsearch
http://travelsearch.com/tourism.htm
A listing of U.S. state and regional tourist bureaus.

The Electronic Embassy
http://www.embassy.org
A list of most of the embassies in Washington, D.C.

The Embassy Page
http://www.embpage.org
A source for embassy information and links.

TRAINS

Eurail
http://www.eurail.com
Information and sales of Eurail passes.

Cyberspace World Railroad
http://www.mcs.com/~dsdawdy/cyberoad.html
Worldwide timetables and information.

Subway Navigator
http://metro.jussieu.fr:10001/bin/cities/english
Information, directions, and maps for 60 metro train and subway systems in 29 countries.

Rail Europe
http://www.raileurope.com/
Fares and timetables for the 1,500 most traveled routes in Europe.

Amtrak
http://www.amtrak.com
The official source for the U.S. rail service.

The Great Little Trains of Wales
http://www1.roke.co.uk/WHR/gltw.html
Train trips from a simpler age.

TRAVEL AGENTS ONLINE

Travel Weekly's list of travel agents
http://www.traveler.net/two/twpages/twagents.html

ITN's list of travel agents
http://www.itn.net/cgi/get?itn/members

Worldwide Agency Locator
http://agencylink.sys1.com
Search by city, country, or agency name.

TRAVEL AGENT RESOURCES

Travel Weekly News
http://www.traveler.net/two/twpages/twnews.html
Synopses of key stories relevant to the travel industry.

ASTAnet
http://www.astanet.com/
A solid digest of travel industry news, a list of Net travel resources, travel tips, and an event calendar for the American Society of Travel Agents.

ITN's Travel Agent Resources
http://www.itn.net/cgi/get?itn/resources/agents
An excellent place to get oriented, this site lists key links for agents ranging from ASTA to Travel Weekly.

PATAnet
http://www.pata.org/patanet/index.html
Home page of the Pacific Asia Travel Association: travel news for the region and information about relevant events and conferences.

TravelASSIST Magazine
http://www.travelassist.com/mag/mag_home.html
A general interest publication, focusing on a different theme each week.

TravelHub
http://www.travelhub.com
List your travel specials and see what others are offering.

Ten-IO
http://www.ten-io.com
Ten-IO maintains a list of travel agents. For details about how to get on this list, see this site.

Submit It
http://www.submit-it.com
Submit It lets you list your site with all the major search engines.

TRAVELING WITH THE NET

TeleAdapt
http://www.teleadapt.com/
Detailed technical instruction about how to hook up in dozens of countries.

GeoAccess
http://www.geoaccess.com
Dial a local access telephone number in most countries and then pay $3 per hour for Net access (plus a 25-cent connection surcharge). The registration fee is $25.

i-Pass Alliance

http://www.ipass.com/

This service enables Internet service providers to offer their customers local dial-up access in most of the world's countries.

Walkabout Travel Gear

http://www.walkabouttravelgear.com

A full line of accessories for the wired traveler and an excellent place to learn about items you might need for your journey.

WORK AND STUDY ABROAD

studyabroad.com

http://www.studyabroad.com

Hundreds of overseas study listings and links.

Council on International Educational Exchange

http://www.ciee.org/

International education and volunteer opportunities.

Sensational Sabbatical Suggestions

http://omni.cc.purdue.edu/~alltson/sabbat.html

Essential advice for those planning a sabbatical.

Global Travel Apartments' Comfort Zone

http://www.globaltrvlapt.com/

Find a place to stay for an extended travel assignment or relocation.

Basic Internet Training

To get the most out of your Internet connection, you have to develop some basic Net skills. As you spend more time online, you'll find a host of other resources and tools you can adopt. But for now, you should focus on the core skills required to get you on your way.

In this book, we talk about email and the Web. In this appendix, we'll discuss how they work and how to use them. We'll also discuss two other key Net tools, the Web browser and the newsreader. For those who like interaction with other Net users, we'll explain IRC, or Interactive Relay Chat. And finally, we'll briefly talk about constructing and publishing your own Web pages.

If you've already been on the Net, this appendix may not interest you. But if you've never seen a Web page, you may feel frustrated by all the new terminology. If you're new to the Net, you may need to re-read a section of this material or come back later to look up a term. Don't let this discourage you, as you'll soon get the hang of it once you're on the Net.

- ▶ Choosing Your Tools
- ▶ Nuts and Bolts of Email
- ▶ Joining Mailing Lists
- ▶ Newsgroups
- ▶ Interactive Communication Tools
- ▶ Using the World Wide Web
- ▶ Web Publishing

CHOOSING YOUR TOOLS

There are many sources for Internet tools. Some are available for free online, others may come with an Internet account or be purchased as a kit. For example, Eudora is a favorite email program, and Netscape is the most popular Web browser. You can download versions of these programs off the Net or purchase commercial versions (that come with end-user support) in software stores.

Here are some other ways you can connect to the Internet and get the tools you need:

- A commercial online service (such as America Online or CompuServe) provides Internet access and an integrated set of tools for using email and browsing the Web.
- A local Internet provider will provide instructions for you to connect to their service and download free versions of tools.

In other words, there are different tools for accessing the Internet, but all share a common set of basic functions. The purpose of the following tutorial is to introduce you to these basic functions.

AN OVERVIEW OF INTERNET SOFTWARE TOOLS

These tools provide you with the ability to communicate online:

Dialer (or dial-up networking)

This program, required only with dial-up Internet accounts, establishes a connection to an Internet service provider. Once you have the connection, your computer is on the Internet and you can use the programs described in this section. The dialer is used to make the connection as well as terminate it when your Internet session is completed. Windows 95 comes with a built-in dialer that works with its Web browser, called Internet Explorer, or other browsers like Netscape's. If you don't already have a dialer on your computer, most ISPs will provide you with a freeware dialer program.

Email (electronic mail) program

An email program is a software tool for sending and receiving email messages. When you get an Internet account, you get an email address that anyone online can use to send you mail. In order to send a message, you need to know the email address of the person you want to communicate with online.

Two of the most popular mail programs are Eudora and Pegasus. You can download the freeware Eudora Light for Windows or Mac (*http://www.qualcomm.com/quest/products.html*) or Pegasus Mail for Windows or DOS (*http://www.cuslm.ca/pegasus/*). Both are free for non-commercial use, although QualComm also sells a more full-featured version of Eudora called Eudora Pro. And many browser programs contain an integrated email program.

Web Browsers

A Web browser is used to retrieve the pages from Web servers and display them on your computer screen. (A Web server is a computer on the Internet using a common programming language). Most Web pages today include graphics and text, with an increasing amount of multimedia data as well (audio, animation, and video). The pages usually contain hyperlinks to other documents or images. In addition, a Web browser can get information from other types of servers, including FTP for downloading files and programs. Many ISPs will give you a freeware Web browser, which will get you online. The most popular browser is Netscape Navigator, which can be downloaded at *http://www.netscape.com* once you're online. Others are Microsoft's Internet Explorer and NCSA's Mosaic. Netscape integrates other tools into its Web browser so that you can use it for email and as a newsreader.

Hyperlinks
Also known as hypertext links or simply "links," hyperlinks connect a given document to information within another document. The links are usually represented by highlighted words or images. When the user mouse clicks on the highlighted link, the user automatically connects to the linked document.

Newsgroups

Usenet newsgroups provide yet another way for people on the Internet to communicate with each other by posting news on a distributed bulletin board system. "News" is a vast collection of daily postings on almost every subject imaginable. At last count, the number of individual newsgroups was approaching 20,000. You can subscribe to various subject-specific newsgroups and read the news in each group using a newsreader. You can also use the newsreader to create your own postings.

Netscape Navigator provides a newsreader, but most other newsreaders are public domain programs that use command line interfaces rather than a graphical interface. We cover newsgroups in Chapter 8.

Chat

Chat, or Internet Relay Chat, allows a group of users to talk to each other at the same time. This method of direct, real-time exchanges permits useful conversations, but it can be an annoying and confusing way to communicate. Nonetheless, it is very popular, especially

Real time

Synchronous communication. For example, talking to someone on the phone is in real time whereas listening to a message someone left on your answering machine is not (asynchronous communication).

Server

A computer that runs software enabling it to offer information to other computers on the network.

with young people. Travelers seem more involved in mailing lists and newsgroups, because they don't have to be online all the time to participate in the discussion.

Chat is a text-oriented application, and users type in their remarks, which are shown to everyone in a chat room or channel. New, more graphical Chat programs are beginning to emerge.

Before the World Wide Web became a dominant application, there were several other programs that performed useful functions for Internet users. These programs are still in use, but are quickly being replaced by the Web and its software.

FTP

FTP is an acronym for File Transfer Protocol. An FTP archive is a set of files made available on a server for other users on the Net to download. FTP is also a program used to send or retrieve files from an archive. You can now use a Web browser to get files from an FTP archive.

Gopher

Gopher isn't used much anymore. It is an information server that organizes online information in easy-to-navigate hierarchical menus—which was handy before graphic browsers came along. Although still available, Gopher is no longer widely used as a means of serving information now that the Web has overtaken its functions. But you may run into a Gopher server now and then, especially on some government sites.

Telnet

Telnet is a program that allows you to log in to another computer on the Internet and have a terminal session, if you have an account on the remote computer.

Web browsers and email software are the most widely used Net tools. Since you'll probably spend most of your online time exchanging email messages and using the Web to access information and create your own Web pages, this tutorial concentrates on describing how to use these two tools.

NUTS AND BOLTS
OF EMAIL

Earlier, we talked briefly about using email as an essential Internet communication tool. In addition to simple text notes, you can also use email to send large documents, pictures, sounds, and programs as attachments. Virtually anything that's been reduced to digital data can be attached to an email message. When creating the message, you use the "Attach" function to select the file you wish to send. The user who receives the message must have the program required to read or view the file once it is detached from the email message.

TIP

Check to make sure that the person receiving your attached message has compatible software to read what you send. Also, some commercial services don't allow you to attach files and send them to people outside of their service, and some limit the size of the email and its attachments. You can still exchange messages with people using commercial service; you just may not be able to attach all documents.

BASICS OF EMAIL ADDRESSING

Your email message needs an address for the person you're trying to reach and a return address to show who sent it. A typical address consists of two parts separated by the @ symbol: the user's name and the domain where the user is known:

username@domain name

The domain name usually identifies the host name of an organization, which could be a commercial business, a network provider, or an educational or government institution.

My address is:

shapiro@songline.com

shapiro is the username and *songline.com* is the domain name.

Most host names end in a three-letter identifier. These three letters indicate the type of entity they are. For example, *netscape.com* is a commercial entity, while *pata.org* is the domain name of the Pacific Asia Travel Association.

.edu	education
.gov	government
.mil	military
.net	network resource
.org	non-profit organizations
.com	commercial organizations

TIP

An address must have all of its parts spelled correctly for it to reach the right person. An improperly addressed message will bounce back to you. When possible, cut and paste email addresses to avoid misspellings.

Bounce

A bounced message means that it is returned to your email address and does not reach the addressee. Bounced messages contain information about why the message did not reach its destination.

The users on your local network share the same domain, so you don't have to use the domain name with local email. For example, if I want to send email to my editor (*stevep@songline.com*), I can send it to just "stevep"—I don't need to attach the domain.

THAT EMAIL LOOK

The email arriving in your box may look strange to you at first. There can be a lot of verbiage at the top before you get to the meat of the message. These lines are called message headers, and most email programs give you the option of seeing the full header or just the important sender and subject information.

A barebones header is shown in Figure B-1.

When you create a new message, you must supply the "To" field and, optionally, the "Subject" field and the "CC" field. The mail program will automatically supply the "From" and "Date" fields when you send the message. There are often more than five fields in a message header, but those are the most useful ones.

A full header can be a truly impressive block of text because it includes all the routing sites the message hit before arriving. Since the Net routes with no regard to distance, an email message sent from

your neighbor across the street may get routed through three servers thousands of miles away, and each will be listed in the full header. And the message probably will go through different routes every time you send it.

The header includes information about the sender, when it was sent, the subject of the message, for whom it was intended, and where the sender wants you to reply to the message. Sometimes you might send email from your home Internet account but want the recipient to reply to your office email account. So occasionally the sender address and reply address will be different.

After the header comes the body of the message:

```
My wife and I enjoy touring Europe without a
schedule or itinerary—and without the hassle of a
car. We just purchase a train pass. But the last
time we did this we had depended on local advice
and broken-English instructions from train
conductors which was sometimes right, sometimes
wrong.

So on our most recent trip I decided to see if
there were any Italian train schedules on the
Internet—and there was a great site that allowed me
to choose the city I was leaving, the destination
point, and the date of travel. It would return me a
page showing the departure and arrival times all
day, ticket prices, and travel time.

This allowed us to list all the towns and cities we
wanted to see. Then I plugged them into the Web
site and printed out the schedules the site
generated. Since it was free I printed out every
possible combination of departure and destination
points. We packed the printouts in our luggage and
they proved invaluable on our trip.
```

Following the text of the message is the attachment box, which looks as follows:

```
Attachment Converted: C:\DOWNLO~1\RELEAS~2.DOC
```

With a mouse click on Attachment Converted a dialog box pops up on my computer, asking me where on my computer hard disk I want to put the attachment.

And finally, the user's designated signature file tags the message:

```
Stephen P. Pizzo
Sr. Editor,
707-829-6512
Lack of skill dictates economy of style.
```

Email signatures typically include phone numbers, postal addresses, Web site addresses, and whatever else may be important for others to know. Most email programs provide a way to create a signature so that it's automatically inserted at the end of every message.

HANDING OUT YOUR BUSINESS CARD

The email signature is also a way to make sure people get essential information about you in every email message you send. It's like giving the reader your business card every time they read your mail.

You can raise or lower the aggressiveness of your signature's tone, but as you will discover, the signature block is a widely used email device to make sure people remember you and can respond to you without having to search around for numbers and addresses.

Some consider it poor netiquette to have an email signature more than a few lines long. This was a bigger concern when modems were slow and long signatures only slowed down your connection. But there's still no reason to have a long signature that risks triggering the ire of other readers.

JOINING MAILING LISTS

One way to learn about the latest travel trends or to find bargain fares is to join mailing lists or listservs. I'll briefly discuss the basics of mailing lists below, and in Chapter 8 you can see how travelers use them.

A mailing list doesn't appear out of nowhere. An organization or individual has to create it. The process involves contracting with an ISP to handle the technical aspects of list maintenance, leaving the substantive work of managing the list to its sponsor.

There are three widely used list-management software packages—*listserv, listproc*, and *majordomo*—but the basic principle of each is the same. Once the software adds a subscriber to the list address, any message sent to that address will be forwarded to subscribers within a matter of minutes.

The creator of a list also determines its structure. This takes one of three forms:

- **Open.** This a list where subscription requests are approved automatically and where participants post messages without anyone screening them in advance.

- **Approved.** This is a list where the manager receives all subscription requests for approval. Once approved, list members can post messages without interference, as with an open list. The catch is that the list manager can "unsubscribe" people without their consent and refuse to approve their return if they begin to cause problems.

- **Moderated.** This is a list where the manager not only approves subscriptions, but screens every message before the group receives it.

Once you join a mailing list, you can throw in your two bits on a subject or "lurk" in the background until you feel compelled to contribute. Sometimes you find endless (and ultimately useless) discussions, while other times you hear about travel news or tips. Generally, like all human interchange, these lists are a mixed bag. With some messages you'll read a few words and hit the Delete key as you get the sense that the subject is of no interest. Others you'll save to read later, and some you'll read carefully and answer immediately. Generally, however, if you're careful about which mailing lists you join, you can cut down on the junk mail you receive.

The Net has spawned thousands of email-connected mailing lists and newsgroups on just about every subject imaginable.

Mailing List
A conference/discussion group on a specific topic where all messages are sent to one email address and then redistributed to the email boxes of the list's subscribers. If the list is moderated, someone will review the messages before redistributing them. Mailing lists are commonly called "listservs" after one type of mailing list software.

TIP

To find a listserv or mailing list you might be interested in subscribing to, check out *http://www.liszt.com/* to search by keyword.

These groups are quickly replacing the old computer bulletin board (BBS) groups that were a mainstay of veteran travelers and others groups—such as Grateful Dead fans—with similar interests. Monitored lists like Infotec Travel, maintained by Marcus Endicott, tend to be ones that draw participants willing to stick to serious subjects; there are many others with specific subject matters ranging across the travel spectrum.

Whatever kind of group you decide to join, a word to the wise: learn how to unsubscribe at the same time you first follow the instructions for subscribing to the list. Since email distribution of these lists is automated, getting stuck on a list you decide you hate can develop into a real pain. Even if you like the water you get from a particular mailing list, there are times when you want to turn it off or suspend it (when you go on vacation, for instance). Usually, when you join a list you automatically receive instructions for unsubscribing or suspending your mail. If you have an easier time keeping track of paper, print a copy of this list and keep in a folder called "Unsubscribe." Then, because paper has a way of getting lost, make a copy and keep it on your computer in a file where you'll (hopefully) know where to look for it later.

LURK BEFORE YOU LEAP

Netiquette
Polite and considerate Internet communication; following the generally accepted guidelines for Internet use.

The netiquette for participating in Internet forums says you should stand quietly in the background to get the flow of things before expressing your views. If you come upon a technical interchange between veterans, it doesn't make sense to write back, "Hi, people, what are you talking about?"

If the mailing list is active, it won't take you long to get the feel of the group. You'll see what comments draw heated discussion, which draw ire, and what is ignored. Wait until you have something worthwhile to add, and you won't be embarrassed. Besides, since you're not standing up in front of anyone, it's easier to add your two cents in a discussion group than it would be in a crowded room of opinion-ated travelers. Even if you never say a word, chances are you'll learn from the exchange of others.

TIP

Any good email program allows you to compose whole messages offline before connecting to the Internet. You can save these messages and send them later when you are online. This feature can save you time and money by limiting the time you spend online.

NEWSGROUPS

Newsgroups (also referred to as Usenet news) are like mailing lists in that they make it possible to send a message many people can read and respond to. But unlike mailing lists, newsgroups rely on news-group software, not your email program. With newsgroups, you use a newsreader program to read messages sent to the newsgroup. Newsgroups resemble large bulletin boards that address specific ar-eas of interest.

You can read and respond to these messages on the Internet. Most newsreader programs will "thread" newsgroup messages; that is, group responses to a single posting in order so you read back through the "thread" of the conversation. When you reply to a news-group message, you have the option of replying to the entire news-group by selecting the Post Reply button, or you can send a private email to the person who posted the message.

HOW CAN NEWSGROUPS HELP ME?

Many of the same reasons you would want to use mailing lists apply to why you would use newsgroups. Travelers use them for everything from seeking information about a destination to finding tips about the best travel bargains.

To read and respond to newsgroup messages, you must have a news-reader. As with email programs and Web browsers, the type of Inter-net connection you have determines what kind of newsreader software you may use. You may have a newsreader built into your Web browser; look for a toolbar or menu option that says News (for

For information on finding and using newsgroups, see Chapter 8, particularly the section on DejaNews (www.dejanews.com), which has a search directory for newsgroups.

<table>
<tr><td>

Which to choose: a newsgroup or a mailing list?

</td><td>

Some people prefer newsgroups, some like mailing lists, and some use both for slightly different purposes. Here are a few tips to help you decide which might be best for you.

- If you don't like dealing with a lot of mail, use newsgroups.
- If you want to make sure others know you have posted a message, use mailing lists.
- If you want to see what others have had to say about a topic recently, use newsgroups.
- If you want more control over which messages you choose to read, use newsgroups.
- If you want to follow a discussion without having to go looking for relevant messages, use mailing lists.
- If you can't find a mailing list of interest, look for a newsgroup (and vice versa).

</td></tr>
</table>

example, Netscape has newsreader software incorporated in its browser).

READING NEWS

As mentioned above, newsgroup messages are organized in *threads*. This means that a message and all its replies are linked together in a way that makes it easy to follow an entire discussion. This threading is visible in Figure B-2, which shows a typical newsreader program screen. All the groups subscribed to are shown on the left, the *headers* of messages are shown on the right, and the text of the currently highlighted message is shown at the bottom.

There is another important difference between mailing lists and newsgroups. Recent newsgroup messages are available online for anywhere from a few days to a few weeks, whereas mailing list messages are not automatically stored anywhere online (although some mailing lists maintain archives of old messages). This means you can find a newsgroup that might be of interest and immediately read recent messages posted to the group. This serves two important purposes: it tells you if the newsgroup is appropriate for your interests, and it shows whether the question you want to ask has recently been asked and answered.

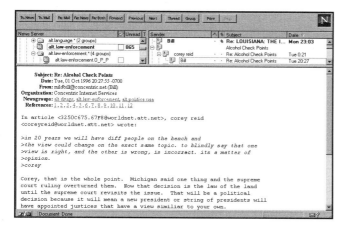

TIP

If you're looking for newsgroup messages on a particular topic, DejaNews (*http://www.dejanews.com/*) lets you specify the text you want to search for, whether you are interested in recent or older messages, and so on. You can even limit your search to messages in specific groups or from a specific author.

GETTING THE FAQS

Almost all newsgroups and some mailing lists have FAQs (Frequently Asked Questions) and their answers. If you have questions about the

FIGURE B-3
This DejaNews search of the term "beach resorts" found hundreds of newsgroup postings.

newsgroup, such as how it works and the topic it addresses, check the FAQs before posting a message. Many newsgroups routinely post their FAQs, while others just make them available for downloading. You'll find a copy of most FAQs at *ftp://rtfm.mit.edu/pub/usenet/news. answers/*.

SOME WORDS OF CAUTION

When you hear all the hoopla about indecent material and pornography on the Net, the material in question is frequently found in newsgroups. In particular, there are a large number of *alt.sex* newsgroups that exist specifically to discuss and exchange photographs and text on adult topics. It's quite easy to avoid these groups because the name says it all. But, nevertheless, it's possible to run across foul language in almost any newsgroup. That's part of the freedom of the Net.

INTERACTIVE COMMUNICATION TOOLS

You may have noticed that all the tools discussed so far allow communication between people outside of "real time." That is, the communication isn't interactive, like a phone call. While this is usually fine, there may be times when you want to communicate directly with people who are online at the same time you are. The tools generally used for this purpose are discussed briefly in this section.

CHAT (INTERACTIVE RELAY CHAT OR IRC)

Internet Relay Chat (also known as IRC, or more generally, Chat) is a multi-user, multi-channel chatting network. It allows people all over the world to talk to (or at) one another in real time. Each Chat user uses a nickname, and all communication with other users is either by nickname or by the channel that they or you are on. To use Chat, you either need to be using Internet access software with Chat capabilities built in, or you need a Chat program on your computer.

CU-SEEME

CU-SeeMe is a free videoconferencing program (under copyright of Cornell University and its collaborators) available to anyone with a

Macintosh or Windows and a high-speed connection to the Internet (the program is choppy over telephone line modems). By using a reflector, multiple parties at locations anywhere in the world can participate in a CU-SeeMe conference, each from an individual desktop computer.

CU-SeeMe is intended to provide useful conferencing at minimal cost. To participate as a viewer requires only the free CU-SeeMe software and an audio-capable computer with a screen that can display 16 shades of gray. To generate your own video stream requires the same, plus a camera. The cheapest camera is produced by Connectix and costs under $100. Video quality is fair, but it is free video-conferencing. Since the sound quality can be variable, many users continue to talk over the phone while they use CU-SeeMe for the video.

There are people using CU-SeeMe all over the world. You can read about some of them in an online document called "In the Eye of the Reflector" (*http://cu-seeme.cornell.edu/EyeofReflector.html*).

For more information and to download the CU-SeeMe software, go to *http://cu-seeme.cornell.edu/*.

Internet telephones, which allow you to dial up directly from your computer keyboard, may well become a favorite tool for you, especially if you have large phone bills from calling all around the world. Check out Internet telephones at *http://www.Netspeak.com*.

FIGURE B-4
CU-SeeMe opens a small video screen on the user's computer.

USING THE
WORLD WIDE WEB

The Web consists of documents containing links to other documents on the Internet. You navigate the Web by following these links, moving backward or forward from one document to another. You can also browse directories that organize Web sites, much as a card catalog system does, and keep your own list of "bookmarks" you can use to go directly to favorite sites. Table B-1 defines the most common Web terms.

Browser	A user tool that displays Web documents and launches other applications
Home Page	The starting point for the set of pages available for a person, company, or organization; also, the first page your browser displays when you start it
HTML	HyperText Markup Language: the language in which World Wide Web documents are written
Hypertext	Documents that contain links to other documents; selecting a link automatically displays the second document
Image	A picture or graphic that appears on a Web page
Link	The text or graphic you click on to make a hypertext jump to another page
Search Directory	A Web site that indexes or searches Web pages and allows you to search for terms you specify
Site	The location of a Web server
URL	The address that uniquely identifies a Web resource

TABLE B-1
Basic Web terminology

LOCATING DOCUMENTS ON THE WEB

Each document on the Web has a unique global address that allows it to be retrieved directly. This unique address is called a URL or Uniform Resource Locator. Just as individuals have email addresses that locate a person within a specific domain, documents have addresses that locate them in a specific server domain.

A URL has three parts: the protocol identifier, the domain or hostname of the server, and the document's pathname. This follows the syntax for URLs:

protocol://domain name/pathname

On the World Wide Web, HTTP (or HyperText Transfer Protocol) is the *protocol* or language that browsers use to talk to servers. All URLs for Web sites begin with *http://* (although some Web sites are now supporting *http* and *shttp*, which incorporate encrypted files). Most Web browsers will communicate using other Internet server protocols, such as Gopher and FTP. Thus, you might see a URL that starts with *gopher://* or *ftp://*.

The next part of the URL is the *server* name. This might be as simple as the domain name, but usually it is preceded by *www*. This prefix is merely a naming convention that many follow, but it is not a requirement to be on the Web. For instance, either of the following URLs will take you to the default page for the Songline Studios Web server:

http://songline.com/

or

http://www.songline.com/

The final part of a URL is the pathname. This tells the server where you want to go on the server, just like you may tell your own computer where to go to get a file. If you have the pathname for a specific document, you can supply it and go directly to that page of the Web site. Otherwise, you can begin at the default home page and navigate to the document using links.

It's often possible to guess the right URL. Almost every URL starts with *http://www.*—commercial site URLs generally end with *.com*, government sites end with *.gov*, and educational sites end with *.edu*. A travel agency called World Travel may have the URL *www.worldtravel.com*. Similarly, the URL for the White House is *http://www.whitehouse.gov*.

A WINDOW ON THE WEB

A Web browser gives you a window to view the Web. Figure B-5 shows a Web browser that starts at its own home page. This figure indicates the parts of the browser window. The menu bar allows you to access all the functions of the browser from pull-down menus. Under the File menu, you will find Open URL or you can use the Open Location box on the browser screen to enter a URL for a document you'd like to view. Next is the Toolbar, a set of graphic and text icons that provide easy access to most common functions, such as accessing your home page, moving back and forth from one document to another, and so on. One of the most important icons is the Stop button. This allows you to interrupt any document transfer, which is useful if you find that a document is taking too long to load.

Next, you will find the Location or URL field. It displays the URL of the current document. You can also use this field on most browsers to enter URLs directly. The URL that is displayed in this field may not always be exactly what you typed, as some Web servers translate a simple address into a more complex one.

On Netscape, there is a row of directory buttons, two of which are labeled NetSearch and NetDirectory. These buttons will take you directly to the most popular directories and search engines.

The largest part of the browser's window is occupied by the document viewing area. This has a scrollbar which you use to view documents that are longer than what can display on the screen. Below the viewing area is a status bar. In this area, you will see messages about

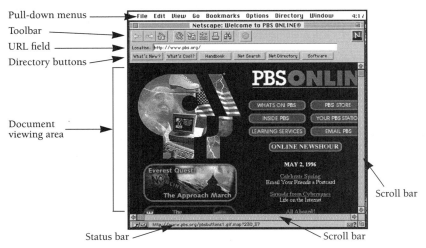

FIGURE B-5
Parts of a Web browser

the document's status, including when it has finished downloading. Also, if you move the cursor over a hypertext link, the URL will be displayed in the status bar, which is handy if you want to know where you'd be going if you click on the link.

Most browsers allow you to select which of these areas are displayed, so be sure to check the Options menu to see which areas are enabled or disabled.

TIP

Remember that Web pages are constantly changing. Several months will have passed between the time these illustrations were produced and the time you read this book. In what might be called "Web time," several months usually means a myriad of changes and improvements to a Web site.

GOING TO A SPECIFIC PAGE

To get to a particular Web page, there are a variety of ways to enter a URL:

- Use a menu option or keyboard shortcut. Look for a menu option such as File/Open, File/Open Location, or File/Open URL. Often, there are keyboard shortcuts assigned to the options, such as CTRL-O or COMMAND-L.

- Type in the URL directly. Most browsers have an area that displays the URL of the page you are currently viewing. Type the URL of the page you want to go to and press ENTER or RETURN.

TIP

A useful feature of Netscape is its ability to "build" a URL from partial information. For example, if you want to go to the URL *http://www.companyname.com*, you can type *companyname* as the location you want to go to. Netscape adds *http://www.* and the *.com* automatically. If there is nothing found under *.com*, it will try *.gov*, *.edu*, and so on. But sometimes it helps speed your connection if you include at least the *www.* in front of the *companyname.com*.

Toolbar buttons to go to a specified URL

Click on a toolbar button. Many browsers have toolbars that provide quick access to the most common browser tasks. Figure B-6 shows a few examples of the buttons different browsers use that let you specify a URL to open.

TIP

An important point to remember is that URLs are case-sensitive past the domain name. For example, if you type *http://worldtravel.com* or *http://WorldTravel.com*, you will go to the same place. But if you type *http://worldtravel.com/COLLECTIONS.html* instead of *http://worldtravel.com/collections.html*, you may receive an error message that such a page doesn't exist.

IT'S NOT WORKING!

Sometimes when you type in a URL, you'll receive an error message indicating that the server is not available. After you check the URL for accuracy, wait a few seconds and try it again, as it may now work. Another solution for a particularly long URL is to delete part of the URL and go to the next directory. For example, say the URL you have is *http://www.access.gpo.gov/su_docs/aces/aaces002.html*. If you receive an error message, try *http://www.access.gpo.gov/su_docs* or *http://www. access.gpo.gov*. This will send you to the next directory up (or page) where you can see the links available. The creators of the pages may have changed the page so that your particular link no longer works. Scrolling down on the home page *http://www.access.gpo.gov/*, you find a variety of options, including the one you tried to reach with the first URL.

DEALING WITH IMAGE FILES ON A DIAL-UP ACCOUNT

Graphics can take a long time to load through a regular telephone service Internet connection. But not all sites have a special view of their pages without graphics. If you are tired of waiting for images to download, you can do a couple of things to solve the problem:

- Turn off the images in your browser menu bar. While this solves your download problem, no images will reach you, just text. Sometimes the images are important.

- As the images are downloading, you can begin reading, using the scrollbar to the right to move you down the page.

- Hit the Stop button on your browser. When you do, the images will stop downloading. This trick is especially helpful when you know the information you want resides on a different page: the link is there, but you're still waiting on the graphics. As soon as you hit stop, the page's graphics will stop loading and the rest of the text will usually appear. If you decide you need the graphics, you can always select reload (or an Images button on some browsers), and the browser will request the page again from the Web site and retrieve it for your computer.

MOVING BACK AND FORTH BETWEEN PAGES

Once you've loaded the pages to your memory or hard drive (this means you've gone to the page by putting in the URL or selecting it through a hypertext link), you can navigate back and forth without waiting a long time. All browsers provide some way for you to move back and forth among the Web pages you viewed in your current session. As with opening a page, there are usually several ways to do this:

- Use a menu option or keyboard shortcut. Look for a menu option such as Navigate/Back and Navigate/Forward or Go/Back and Go/Forward.

- Click on a toolbar button. Many browsers have buttons on their toolbars that look like arrows facing left and right. The left arrow steps you back through pages you have viewed and the right arrow steps you forward.

BOOKMARKS AND HOTLISTS

If you go to a page that you want to return to, your Web browser will let you add it to a list so you don't have to remember the URL or write it down. Some common names for these lists of saved URLs are bookmarks, favorites, and card catalogs.

Washington attorney John Maxwell, Jr., highly recommends the use of bookmarks to simplify your time on line:

> *Use Net browser bookmarks. Most Net browsers support the use of bookmarks. Learn to use these to save time. A bookmark allows you to save the location of a favorite site, and when you activate the bookmark you will go directly to that site instead of the long route you may have taken to find the site in the first place. Usually the bookmark feature is one of the main menu items and you just select "add bookmark" or some similar selection to add it to your list of sites. The bookmarks then are accessible as a list that you can scroll down and choose from. It's a very handy time-saving device.*

No matter how your browser works, be forewarned that your URL list can easily grow so large as to be almost useless. Most browsers allow you to organize your favorite URLs into folders by subject. Also, you should go through your bookmarks from time to time and delete those URLs that once seemed important, but are now either defunct or no longer relevant to your interests.

SEARCH DIRECTORIES: FINDING INFORMATION ON THE WEB

What if you don't know the URL for a page you want to visit? Maybe you read about it somewhere and didn't keep the reference. Or you know your subject (say "beach resorts"), but aren't sure what's out there. Search directories can help you find what you seek.

Internet search directories periodically scan the contents of the Web to rebuild their massive indexes of Web pages. Some search titles or headers of documents; others search the documents themselves, and still others search indexes or directories. When you request specific keywords, the engines search the indexes they have built for those words. Your keyword search is not a live search of the Web, but a search of that directory's index.

There are two types of ways to search the Net: directories and Web robots. Directories (or indexes) are collections of resources that you can easily browse or search. Yahoo (*http://www.yahoo.com*) is one of the best known directories. People create and maintain these directories by combing other sites, organizing the information on their Web pages, and making sure the links to the other sites remain accurate. Web robots (or search engines) depend on software, rather than people, that automatically searches the Web for new material.

The distinction between directories and robots is blurring. Directories are incorporating search engines and search engines are incorporating indexes you can browse. And not all search engines are created equal. That is, different engines find different pages, even when you give them the same search terms. Search engines differ in how they index and store the information in Web pages. If your first search doesn't turn up the information you're looking for, try another search engine. If none of them locates what you want, try using different search terms.

Two features will probably influence your choice of a favorite search engine. One is ease of use: it should allow you to customize searches without offering so many options that using it is confusing. Second, a good search engine should be accurate: if properly configured, it will return a reasonable quantity of fairly precise results.

There are several indexes and directories on the Net that are both search engines and collections of resources you can easily browse or search. Some, such as Yahoo, are large collections organized alphabetically by subject. Though new ones are being added regularly, here are some of the most popular:

Yahoo
http://www.yahoo.com
Yahoo features a hierarchically organized subject tree of information resources. It offers limited search options, but is often a useful starting place because of its large database of authoritative sources.

Webcrawler
http://webcrawler.com
Webcrawler offers an extensive travel section and other resources organized by subject.

Internet Sleuth
http://www.isleuth.com
The Internet Sleuth is less well known than the Webcrawler, but it offers a wide variety of specialized searches by category and links you to some of the top search engines and people finders.

SEARCH ENGINES

Web robots depend on software that automatically searches the Web for new material.

AltaVista
http://altavista.digial.com
AltaVista has become so popular that it logs more than 2 million visitors a day. If you want a lot of return hits for a query, Alta Vista is the choice—but be prepared to wade through a lot of clutter to find a few nuggets.

Webcrawler
http://webcrawler.com

Webcrawler, a search engine as well as a directory, is fast and returns a weighty list of links. It analyzes the full text of documents, allowing the searcher to locate keywords which may have been buried deep within a document's text. Webcrawler is a good choice if you are looking for a company or organization's home page since it returns fewer hits to sort through than Alta Vista.

Lycos
http://www.lycos.com

Lycos is named after a quick and agile ground spider. It searches document titles, headings, links, and keywords, and returns the first 50 words of each page it indexes for your search. Its search engine is more configurable than Webcrawler.

Excite
http://www.excite.com

Excite contains searches of millions of Web pages and several weeks of Usenet news articles and classified ads, as well as links to current news, weather, and more. It presents results with a detailed summary to provide you with an annotated selection.

PUSHING THE ENVELOPE

Most of the hottest Internet development these days revolves around the Web. Audio, video, virtual reality, animation—it's hard to keep up. Here are some locations for more information on some of the latest trends in Web development:

RealAudio™
http://www.realaudio.com

The RealAudio home page lets you listen to music, news, talk shows, and more while you are browsing the Web. If you have a 28.8 modem, you can download and use the latest release of RealAudio. If your modem is slower than that you will have to use RealAudio1. But, like so much of the Net these days, support for these older "version 1" technologies is rapidly disappearing. Soon a 28.8 modem will no longer be a luxury, but a necessity.

Java™
http://java.sun.com/

Java is a programming language that lets Web page developers add software applications, games, animation, and other features to their Web pages.

Shockwave™
http://www.macromedia.com/

Found on the Macromedia home page, Shockwave enables the playback of high-impact multimedia on the Web.

The VRML Repository
http://www.sdsc.edu/vrml/

Virtual Reality Modeling Language (VRML) is a developing standard for describing interactive three-dimensional scenes delivered across the Internet.

Web Review™
http://webreview.com
Songline Studios produces this online magazine, Web Review, that keeps up with Web technologies and the people who use and create. Clicking into Web Review weekly will keep you current.

WEB PUBLISHING

If you're feeling ambitious and thinking about building your own Web site, you may be considering whether you should build it yourself or let someone else do it for you. You may want to only skim the following section if you're not sure that you want a Web site.

But you should know one thing: anyone, from large corporations to young kids, can create and manage a Web site. It is this great equalizing capability of the Web that has fueled its incredible growth. The question is whether or not you can budget the time to manage a Web site properly by yourself. If not, what you learn here will help you shop wisely for a service provider to do it for you.

Here's an introduction to the basics of Web publishing, along with pointers to sites where you can learn more on the Web itself.

HTML—THE LANGUAGE OF THE WEB

When Web technology was first designed, the goal was to develop a way to describe the elements of a page's structure without specifying how the page should actually be displayed. In other words, the Web page specifies *what* to display, and different browsers decide *how* to display it. For this reason, the same Web page is available to anyone on the Net, whether they're using UNIX, DOS, Windows, Mac, OS/2, or any other operating system. If there is a browser that runs on that system, users of the system can view the page.

You don't need to understand HTML to use the Web, and if you're certain you'll never code your own Web page you can skim the following section. But if you want to create your own Web page in the future, you need to first understand some basics.

Every Web page is a plain text file that contains "tags" or codes. These tags tell the browser how to display the file. The codes represent instructions written in HTML (HyperText Markup Language). You can use any text editor (such as word processing programs) to create or modify HTML documents.

TIP

You can learn how others code their Web pages. In Netscape, once you have a page up on your screen, select "View Source" from Netscape's View menu. That will show you a text version of the page, including all the HTML codes. This is a great way to learn how to get your page to look like one you admire.

HTML codes specify heading levels (as in an outline), paragraph styles, inclusion of images and sound, addresses of pages to link to, and anything else the browser needs to know. For example, Figure B-7 shows how a browser displays a Web page (in this case, the home page for Travelocity (*http://www.travelocity.com*).

Figure B-8 shows the text and HTML codes that make up the first part of the Library of Congress page.

Here are a few codes commonly used on Web pages:

- <html> specifies the beginning of the document.
- <img src= specifies a graphic to display, along with text ("alt") that should be displayed if the browser can't display graphics.
- <p> specifies a new paragraph.
- <a href= specifies that the text from here to </a> is a hypertext link to the Web page in quotes. The Web page between the code can be a document you've created or a link to a URL on someone else's computer.

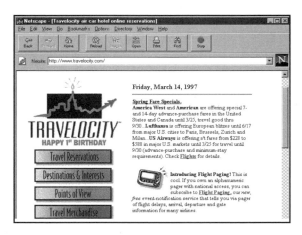

FIGURE B-7
How a page may look onscreen.

```
<!doctype html public "-//W30/DTD WWW HTML 2.0/EN">
<html>
<head>
<title>Library of Congress World Wide Web (LC Web) Home Page</title>
<base href="http://lcweb.loc.gov/homepage/lchp.html">
<head>
<body bgcolor="#ffffff">
<a href="http://lcweb.loc.gov/homepage/lchp_txt.html">[text-only]</a>
<!—begin imagemap for head–>
<p align=center>
<a href="http://lcweb.loc.gov/homepage/lchp.html">
<img src="/homepage/images/homehead.gif"
border="0" alt="[Library of Congress World Wide Web

(LC Web) Home Page - Header]"></a><br>
<!—end imagemap–>
<p>
```

FIGURE B-8
Text and HTML codes.

At first, HTML authoring was similar to the state of word processing about 15 years ago—you inserted codes into your document to indicate formatting styles and didn't know what the finished document would look like until you printed it out. Today, just about every word processor prides itself on being WYSIWYG (What You See Is What You Get). The latest generation of HTML editors emulates a WYSIWYG environment for HTML authoring.

These "structured editing" products let you create Web pages without having to insert the HTML codes manually. Some of these tools are free. Most of the ones that require payment have demo versions available that you can download (copy to your hard disk) and try. Then, if you like it, you can buy it. Also, some are add-ons to word processors such as Microsoft Word, letting you author HTML from within the word processor.

The following sites contain pointers to reviews of a number of HTML editing tools:

The Stroud List
http://cws.iworld.com
One of the Internet's most popular and respected sites for reviews of, and links to, Windows 95 and Windows 3.x Internet programs of all kinds. Choose HTML Editors from the main menu.

Yahoo's Macintosh HTML Editor List

http://www.yahoo.com/Computers_and_Internet/Software/Internet/World_Wide_Web/HTML_Editors/Macintosh/

List of links to a variety of HTML editors for the Macintosh.

At the following sites, you can obtain HTML editing software. Note that some of the software is only for particular operating systems:

Adobe" PageMill™

http://www.adobe.com/

Adobe PageMill Web page authoring software provides an integrated authoring tool and preview browser.

Netscape Navigator Gold™

http://www.netscape.com/

Netscape Navigator Gold integrates the features of Netscape Navigator 2.0 with Internet publishing capabilities, making it easy for you to see exactly how your page will look in Netscape while you are editing it. Netscape also provides storage locations for your pages.

Bare Bones Software BBEdit™

http://www.barebones.com/bbedit.html

One of the most popular text editors for HTML authors working on a Macintosh. Extensive HTML tools and extensions are available for BBEdit.

HotDog WebEditor from Sausage Software

http://www.sausage.com

Developed by an Australian, this URL will bring you to HotDog's site, where you can buy the popular Web editor. It's a simple-to-use HTML editor that sells for under $50.

FrontPage from Microsoft

http://www.microsoft.com/frontpage/

Since it's from Microsoft, it's compatible with Microsoft Office and has the company's "wizards" to help you with any problems. The product is designed for the nonprogrammer and has WYSIWYG editing.

Home Page from Claris

http://www.claris.com/

You can download trial software from this site and, if you want, buy it retail for under $100. They have versions for both the Mac and Windows.

MAKING YOUR PAGES AVAILABLE ON THE NET

Once you write your page, you have to put it on a Web server where the world can access it. If you want, you can have your own computer server connected to the Internet, but this can be costly and involves technical issues that only the computer-savvy should attempt. The simplest is to store your pages on someone else's Internet server (usually on your Internet provider's computer) in a particular directory. The document can then be referenced by a URL unique to your site.

A Guide to the Online Services

Though the Web is becoming ever more prominent, lots of travelers still find what they need through online services such as CompuServe and America Online. The Web certainly offers more information, but online services tend to organize and select some of the best sites, and provide an easy-to-use format that new users appreciate. While there are other services out there, AOL and CompuServe are by far the two largest, so we'll concentrate on them. Following is a guide to the most useful areas and forums in these two services. The other prominent online service is Microsoft Network. See *http://www.msn.com* for more information. If you want to learn more about Prodigy, see *http://www.prodigy.com*.

Note: Some of the best travel areas on the online services also have homes on the Web. If we've already discussed the Web sites, we won't go into detail in this appendix—we'll merely mention the site and refer you back to the chapter where you can find more information about each of these sites.

- ► CompuServe
- ► America Online
- ► Microsoft Network

COMPUSERVE

Air Information/Reservations
Service: FLIGHTS

Air Information/Reservations contains easySABRE, the Official Airline Guide Electronic Edition Travel Service, and Worldspan. Each offers complete schedule and fare information for all commercial flights throughout the world. When using any of these products, you will be asked for your departure and destination cities and your date of travel. All systems offer reservations and ticketing options as well as other travel information.

California Forum
Service: CALFORUM

Enjoy online sunshine with the California Forum. Join the daily happy hour or the weekly poolside chat in the forum's conference sections. Find out the latest happenings in every corner of California, from the redwoods to San Diego. Discuss politics, touring, and sports with California natives and California lovers.

Canada Forum
Service: CDNFOR

Whether you want to learn more about Canada, discuss issues in Canadian culture and politics, or plan a trip to Canada, the Canada Forum is the place to visit. Canada Forum members discuss business, sports, recreation, travel, the arts, and Canada's role in world politics. There are also message areas for each province and territory.

Pacific Forum
Service: PACFORUM

Australia and New Zealand are just a few of the locations you can visit in the Pacific Forum. Come discuss the culture, business, politics, and travel destinations in your favorite port-of-call or the place you call home. The Pacific Forum offers library and message sections packed full of hardware/software support, travel details, naturalist information, sporting news, and entertainment. So if you want to enjoy the laid-back lifestyle of Australia and New Zealand, come visit the Pacific Forum.

FIGURE C-1

CompuServe's Web site
(http://www.compuserve.com).

Department of State Advisories

Service: STATE

The United States Department of State's Citizen Emergency Center maintains a continuously updated information service for Americans traveling abroad. Advisories and warnings cover conditions such as warfare, political unrest, hotel/motel shortages, currency regulations, and other information of interest to the globe-trotting traveler. Updated constantly by the Department of State.

easySABRE

Service: SABRE or SABRECIM

easySABRE, the travel reservation system from American Airlines, provides flight schedules for almost all commercial airlines, information on more than 45 million airfares, and access to more than 27,000 hotels and 52 car rental agencies. You can use easySABRE to find the fastest route to a destination, check weather reports and AAdvantage travel awards, and take advantage of the lowest airfares with the Bargain Finder feature. After confirming airline, hotel, and car reservations online, you can arrange to receive your tickets through a travel agency, city ticket office, corporate travel office, airport, or by U.S. mail. Save up to 25 percent on vacation travel and up to 65 percent on short-notice travel. Updated continually. You can access easySABRE through the standard format at "SABRE" or the graphical CompuServe Information Manager at SABRECIM.

European Forum

Service: EUROFORUM

The European Forum provides general information on PCs, communications, business opportunities, and travel of interest to members traveling in Europe. Additional sections are dedicated to different European languages and regions, including Italian, French, Spanish, Nordic, German, Swiss, Austrian, Dutch, Flemish, Eastern European, Hungarian, and Irish. Members can post questions and discuss issues important to European members.

European Railway Schedule

Service: RAIL

If you are planning to travel by train in Europe, you will want to consult the electronic timetable information provided by the Deutsche Bahn AG. You'll find information about European-wide train connections and fares, and you can order your tickets.

Florida Forum

Service: FLORIDA

The Florida Forum allows residents, vacationers, or anyone with an interest in Florida to share information about the Sunshine State. You can talk with the residents to find the best places to stay, eat, or visit if you're planning a Florida vacation. Find information on sporting and recreational activities or events/attractions of interest. Access the Disneymania section for topics about Disney World such as cartoon characters, attractions, and vacation packages.

FTM Airmax

Service: AIRMAX

FTM AirMax, the only interactive and automated database in the travel industry, is available for downloading. Frequent Travel Management, Inc., developed and owns the FTM AirMax database. The company updates the database daily (updates are also downloadable) and monitors most frequent flyer programs based in North America. To use the database, members need to enter their travel date, city pairs, and indicate whether a hotel or car rental will be needed at each destination. FTM AirMax will generate in seconds specific program information and calculate the exact reward mileage for all bonus rewards.

Good Pub Guide

Service: UKPUBS

Looking for a good watering hole for your next trip? Consult the Good Pub Guide. You'll find detailed descriptions of more than 1,300 pubs, all of which have been visited and commented upon by the Good Pub Guide's team of anonymous inspectors. Descriptions include general information as well as other features such as whether children are welcome and whether the pub has a no-smoking area. Approximately 4,000 shorter entries contributed by users are also available, as well as an area allowing you to recommend that your own favorite pub be included in the guide.

Hotel Information

Service: HOTELS

You'll find menu options for finding information on accommodations when traveling in the U.S. and around the world.

Lanier's Bed & Breakfast Guide Online

Service: BED

Lanier Publishing's Bed & Breakfast Guide Online provides information on more than 9,000 inns in the United States and Canada. Based on the best-selling *Complete Guide to Bed and Breakfasts, Inns, and Guesthouses in the United States and Canada*, this service has everything you need to get started or to continue your exploration of this wonderful form of travel. Bed & Breakfast Guide Online contains such necessary data as location and phone number for inns, as well as listings of amenities, types of meals served, accessibility for the disabled, accommodation of children and pets, and price range. So if you would enjoy a change from the routine of hotel chains, access the Bed & Breakfast Guide Online to learn about the B&Bs in the areas you plan to visit.

Lanier's Inn and Lodging Forum

Service: INNFORUM

Want to start your own Bed and Breakfast? View pictures of inns all over the world? Locate favorite inn recipes? Access Lanier's Inn and Lodging Forum to talk about Bed and Breakfast travel with other inn enthusiasts and hospitality professionals around the world.

Magellan Geographix Maps

Service: MGMAPS

Whether you need a map for business, education, or personal use, turn to Magellan Geographix maps online. Basic Maps offers maps of the seven continents and a frequently updated Specialty Map. Maps of the World offers more than 600 maps that span the globe, including some geared toward current and special events.

New York Newslink

Service: NEWYORK

New Yorkers and visitors can have a link to the current happenings in and around the Big Apple in the New York Newslink Forum. The forum, an electronic extension of the daily Gannett Suburban Newspapers, provides discussion topics ranging from off (or nearly off) Broadway to the New York Giants.

Travel Britain Online
Service: TBONLINE

Who's playing in London's West End theaters? Which are the most popular pubs in London? Where and when are Britain's liveliest festivals? Answers to these and other questions can be found in Travel Britain Online. A database of events provides information on British festivals, exhibitions, shows, and sports events. Users can also access a listing of some of London's best pubs and check out the latest tourist news on Travel Britain News.

Travel Forum
Service: TRAVSIG

The Travel Forum allows you to exchange travel stories, ideas, and information with other forum members who are interested in traveling. Talk with others who have already been to your destination to find out the best (or worst) restaurants and hotels. Learn about the customs in foreign countries and other important information. And find out about destination spots, cruises, academic travel programs, and rail travel. Leave questions for others or share your experiences.

UK Forum
Service: UKFORUM

The UK Forum focuses on a variety of United Kingdom cultural and social themes such as politics, sports, business, TV/film, hobbies, photography, and U.K. travel. The forum includes the ever-popular Rovers Return Club where members can participate in the kinds of forthright discussions associated with British pubs.

UK Travel
Service: UKTRAVEL

For local help with planning your business and leisure time in the United Kingdom, visit UK Travel. This site has databases covering U.K. travel needs: each of the databases is equivalent to one of their popular printed guides. AA Accommodations and AA Restaurants incorporate only those establishments that have been awarded an AA rating by an independent AA inspector. AA Golf Courses gives you complete details of more than 2,000 U.K. golf courses. AA Days Out provides more than 2,000 ideas for places to go and attractions to see for the entire family. Travel Britain Online is a guide to events and attractions taking place all over the U.K. The What's On Guide is a complete guide to entertainment and events.

United Connection
Service: UNITED

Access the same extensive and up-to-the-minute fare and schedule information available to travel agencies and airlines in the United Connection. Look up the latest information on more than 550 airlines, 50 car rental companies, and 200 hotel companies worldwide. Members can also make reservations and purchases, check United Mileage Plus account balances, get gate information on United and United partner flights, choose how to receive their ticket, and more.

VISA Advisors
Service: VISA

VISA Advisors is a passport and visa expediting firm located in Washington, D.C., providing visa and passport requirements and documents. They will assist you in visa and passport processing and legalization of documents. VISA Advisors charges a service fee per document and will hand-carry your documents to the embassies or consulates involved. Visa and passport requirements are updated monthly.

Weather Reports
Service: WEA

For United States locations, the National Weather Service features short-term state, zone, and local forecasts, extended state and national forecasts, severe weather alerts, precipitation probability, state summaries, and daily climatological reports. For non-U.S. locations, current conditions and three-day forecast reports are provided by Accu-Weather, Inc.

World Community Forum
Service: WCOMMUNITY

The World Community Forum provides a special opportunity to meet and chat with other CompuServe members from all over the world. Members can use this communication-oriented service to discuss general topics of common interest, obtain and share diverse opinions on current events and issues (on both local and global levels), and learn more about any region of the world, its people, culture, and languages. To facilitate truly global communication, the World Community Forum is offered in English, French, German, and Spanish. Computer translation technology software maintains a separate version of the forum for each language.

WORLDSPAN Travelshopper (CIM)
Service: WORLDCIM

CompuServe and Worldspan Travelshopper provide this new interface to the Worldspan Reservation System for members who use CompuServe Information Manager (CIM). Worldspan Travelshopper allows you to navigate easily through flights, fares, fare restrictions, and flight details. In addition, store your flight search criteria, passenger information, and personal profile data online to save time and money when making a reservation or simply browsing flights.

Zagat Restaurant Survey
Service: ZAGAT

Want to find out about a restaurant before you visit it? Whether you are seeking French cuisine or deep-dish pizza, access the Zagat Restaurant Survey. The survey features thousands of reviews based on annual surveys of restaurant patrons just like you. Search for old and new restaurants in more than 20 cities and regions across the United States by restaurant name, location, type of cuisine, or price. While online, find out how to become a Zagat restaurant reviewer.

AMERICA ONLINE

Here you'll find descriptions of more than 20 top AOL travel areas. AOL also has sites for major country and city destinations ranging from Mexico to Paris. For a comprehensive, updated listing of AOL travel sites, type the word *travel* into the search engine of the AOL directory. To reach the AOL directory, click on the FIND button at the top right of the main AOL screen.

The Independent Traveler
Keyword: Traveler

You could consult dozens of guidebooks and still not find as much useful information as you can uncover here to become the quintessential Independent Traveler. From last-minute travel bargains to packing tips, the Forum is the place to go to make the most of your vacation or business trip. The Travel Resource Center offers tips to get the most bang for your buck on the road, such as insightful advice for how to get the best exchange rates. In the Bargain Box, you can find the latest and greatest airline ticket deals with updates on airfare wars and promotions.

Digital City
Keyword: Digital City National

Planning a trip to a major U.S. city? Check into the Digital City of your choice for up-to-the-minute weather, entertainment listings, and much more. The national Digital City directory is your guide to dozens of profiled cities in the U.S. and abroad. It's organized by region for easy reference and has a link to the international directory. When you get to the city of your choice, you'll find ways to connect with local people, a photo library, and places to shop.

Arthur Frommer's Secret Bargains
Keyword: Arthur Frommer

Legendary travel writer Arthur Frommer scours the globe for the best travel deals: airfares, hotel rooms, restaurants, and more. You can find bargains typically only known to travel agents, such as unadvertised budget airfares. In Best of the Bucket Shops, learn how to get great deals from consolidators. In Cost-Cutting Clubs & Companies, you can find the "Poor Man's Spa" and discover "foam-rubber bus travel."

Travel Channel
Keyword: Travel Channel

The Travel Channel is AOL's window on the world. Whether you're planning a family vacation, thinking about a romantic cruise, or thinking about buying airline tickets, the Travel Channel can help with your plans. To help you get a clearer picture of a dream vacation, the Fantasize section has suggestions on all kinds of trips based on your interests. You can buy airline tickets online with a link to Preview Travel Reservations. Fellow travelers share their stories and tips on various message boards, with hints on the most secluded spots for a romantic weekend or the best adventures for the entire family. So before you pack your bags, hop over to this area for some solid travel guidance.

Time Out Guide to New York
Keyword: Time Out New York

The Empire State Building, sidewalk hot dog vendors, world-class museums, and entertainment that lasts all night long. It's big, bustling, and brimming with boisterousness, though sometimes it can be a bit overwhelming. This is where Time Out New York can help: a clear and concise guide to the Big Apple with information on sights, theater, sports, and hotels.

Europe Through the Back Door
Keyword: Rick Steves

Rick Steves has spent the past 20 summers exploring Europe, taking careful notes and sharing his off-the-beaten-track discoveries. Regardless of your age or budget, you can explore Europe with confidence, and avoid looking like the stereotypical clueless tourist. The site has a quick and easy search tool, to aid in hunting down information on your destination. Europe Through the Back Door helps travelers steer clear of tourist traps and discover the true face of Europe. This area not only guides you to out-of-the-way vacation destinations, it offers valuable Travel Tips, complete itineraries, and advice for countries throughout Europe—just click on the flag of the country you plan to visit.

Global Citizen

Keyword: Global Citizen

If you're looking for advice for the international traveler, Global Citizen (sponsored by American Express) helps you book travel reservations, peruse heaps of vacation offers, and get travelers checks online. For business travel, bring your suitcase over to the Business Traveler where you can find culture bytes on nearly every country in the world. You could soon be shaking hands and nodding yes to deals with the best of them, with these foreign etiquette tips in your bag of tricks. And in The Road Warrior, people who call the globe their office share crazy stories of traveling horrors and obstacles they've overcome.

Weather News

Keyword: Weather

Weather News has forecasts, satellite images, and the latest weather information from earthquakes in California to hurricanes battering the Eastern seaboard. You'll also find international forecasts, long-range forecasts, a recreation weather planner, and satellite images.

ExpressNet

Keyword: American Express

Frequent travelers on the move like to get where they're going in a hurry. ExpressNet offers a wide range of travel and financial services from American Express to jet vacationers and business people to their destinations posthaste. American Express Cardmembers enrolled in ExpressNet can get up-to-the-minute information about accounts, access Membership Rewards points balances, find out about exclusive offers and events, use the ExpressNet Shopping Service, and even purchase travelers checks online. Airline, car, and hotel reservations can also be conveniently made online.

Travel Corner

Keyword: Travel Corner

The insider information here can turn an ordinary trip into an exceptional journey. U.S. and international profiles, dispatched by a network of correspondents in more than 220 countries, provide concise, accurate, and frequently updated information on your destination. For each major city, Travel Corner provides the must-sees and must-dos and gives you the addresses and phones of major attractions. In Top Ten Picks, you can get lists for the best scenic drives, museums, ecotourism destinations, and city parks. You'll also find the Top Ten Overrated Destinations, the Top Ten Family Destinations, and more.

Globalnet

Keyword: AOLGlobalnet

AOLGlobalnet is AOL's new international access network. In this area you can find the locations, numbers, and instructions on how to start using AOLGlobalnet. This service is available in nearly 200 cities within more than 75 countries. More cities worldwide are being added all the time, many with 28.8k bps access.

Family Travel Network

Keyword: Family Travel

The Family Travel Database lets you search for family-friendly vacation destinations. Talk to other parents and kids about different trips. Find out What's Cool, or take a Virtual Vacation to some exotic and far-off land. There's the Travel Library, deals, vacation packages, and more. Parents and kids send in details about their experiences, so you can benefit from stories of hits and misses of their trips.

Travel America…Online

Keyword: TAO

Whether you're looking for campgrounds in the state next door or four-star hotels in Hawaii, you'll find plenty of quality information on travel for all 50 states. With TAO's handy State Travel Directory, you can always get what you need from listings of visitor bureaus, transportation information, and travel advisories. Get the skinny on America's favorite national parks, with a state-by-state directory for all 369 national parks, provided by the National Park Service.

Lanier Family Travel Guides

Keyword: Lanier

This area offers advice from how to eat well while on the road to finding seasonal travel packages at bargain prices. Vacationers with specific questions and concerns about how-to issues, such as how to plan a bike trip with youngsters, will find the advice in this area both plentiful and helpful. Also look here for information about bed and breakfasts, hostels, hotels, motels, and inns.

Bed & Breakfast Guides by Lanier

Keyword: B&B

The guide includes location and phone numbers, amenities, types of meals served, accessibility for the handicapped, accommodations for children and pets, and price range of more than 14,000 inns worldwide. Search by state or look for inns by specialty. Inn News and Message Center highlights the Inn of the Week, inns that focus on romance, sports, and contests. The best-loved, most requested recipes from every region and for every season, including brunch and tea time treats, are cataloged in the Inn Recipes section.

Over the Rainbow

Keyword: Over the Rainbow

This site lists gay-friendly areas of American and international cities and gay-owned hotels and stores to help keep you on that yellow brick road. Most of the writers contributing reviews to the area are residents of the cities they cover, so you get insider information not usually available to a travel writer who just breezes in for the weekend. Restaurants, sites and attractions, cultural events, and shopping centers that cater to the gay community are profiled, with addresses and phone numbers.

Cruise Critic

Keyword: Cruise Critic

Thinking of sailing the seven seas? Cruise this site before you book your stateroom. It provides candid reviews of more than 100 ships, including a Top Ten list, in Editor's Picks. The Cruise Selector allows you to match several variables (cruising region, budget range, and lifestyle) to choose a package that suits you. Cruise Tips offers information on a range of topics, including how to select a cabin, when to tip, and what to do while ashore in various ports. Scan the Cruise Board for comments from recent travelers or post your own travel notes.

AAA Online

Keyword: AAA

The American Automobile Association is more than just emergency breakdown service. Pick a pleasure cruise with confidence, obtain a good map of the national parks, or get simple advice on driving from Boston to Bethlehem (Pennsylvania, of course).

Travelers Advantage

Keyword: TA

Travelers Advantage offers discounts, travel agent services, and specials to its members. TA has information on money savings programs; for example, you can save 5 percent off your purchase price if you book it yourself. The site also offers hotel discounts of up to 50 percent and a 24-hour reservations hotline. If you're looking for information on travel, cruise, hotel, or resort packages, TA features vacation specials. For information on what to do when you get there, TA has weekly events focusing on popular travel destinations.

Outdoor Adventure Online

Keyword: Outdoor

Have you ever dreamed of backpacking through the Carrizozo Lava Flow in New Mexico, sailing around the Hauraki Gulf of New Zealand, or catching a sight of pilot whales swimming off the coast of New England? Before choosing a new adventure, check here first for advice from the old hands. Consult the directory of Guides and Tours so your family isn't let loose in some strange land like the Brady Bunch was in Hawaii. Based on the sport or activity you want to pursue on your vacation, you can find the right location from the Destination and Resort directory. Lodging prices, special attractions, and safety tips are included with the addresses and phone numbers listed in the profiles. Make the Going Places section your checklist for gathering customs information, car rental information, and financial advice.

Backpacker's BaseCamp

Keyword: Backpacker

Want to know where to camp? What gear to buy? How to get the most out of your outdoor experience? Find out at Backpacker's BaseCamp, where you can learn from fellow campers and hikers, as well as the magazine's outdoor-savvy editors. Tap into the Gear Connection for extensive gear-related information, including annual gear guides, gear tests, image libraries, and advice on the best footwear for scaling rocky mountains.

Zagat

Keyword: Zagat

Let a jury of your peers decide where you dine out tonight. Zagat restaurant reviews are made up of surveys completed by people like you, not professional reviewers. Every year, Zagat survey participants rate the food, atmosphere, service, and cost of restaurants all over America, including your neighborhood. Zagat recently added a survey of hotels, resorts and spas.

Destination Florida

Keyword: Florida

Tips on visiting Disney World and discount tickets to top attractions throughout the state. This is a rich site that can help you plan your trip to one of the world's leading vacation areas. Whether your interest is planning a trip to Orlando, finding a resort in Key West, or just seeing what Dave Barry has to say, this is the place to start.

The following AOL areas also have Web sites which have been discussed in the body of this book. We'll list them here with brief descriptions and let you know what chapter to see for more information.

Preview Travel Vacations

Keyword: Vacations

Check airline schedules or book your flight. For more, see Chapter 2.

Travel Advisories

Keyword: Travel Advisories

U.S. State Department warnings and consular information. For more, see Chapter 1.

InsideFlyer Online

Keyword: InsideFlyer

The source for frequent flyers with tips on how to get the most for your miles. For more, see Chapter 2.

MSN (MICROSOFT NETWORK)

Note: MSN's main sites are available through the Web.

Expedia

http://expedia.com

An all-in-one site featuring booking for airlines, hotels and car rental, this site has lots of destination information. Expedia's Fare Tracker sends email alerts for bargain flights.

Mungo Park

http://mungopark.com

An adventure magazine spearheaded by Richard Bangs, Mungo Park features best-selling authors writing about their journeys and takes viewers on virtual trips ranging from remote rivers in Africa to astronaut John Grunsfeld writing dispatches while traveling aboard the space shuttle Atlantic.

Index

279

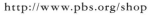
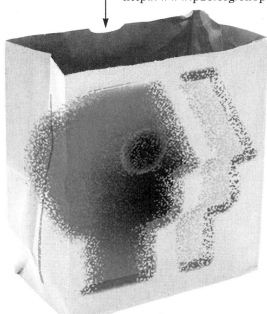 

More Titles from O'Reilly

Songline Guides

Net Lessons: Web-based Projects for Your Classroom

By Laura Parker Roerden
1st Edition March 1997
306 pages, ISBN 1-56592-291-3

Net Lessons features 70 K-12 classroom-tested lesson plans that harness the unique potentials of the Web, plus hundreds of extensions and ideas for all subject areas. The book also includes curriculum frameworks for creating your own successful web projects, assessment tools, and the advice of teachers who have used the Web in their classrooms.

NetResearch: Finding Information Online

By Daniel J. Barrett
1st Edition February 1997
200 pages, ISBN 1-56592-245-X

NetResearch teaches you how to locate the information you need in the constantly changing online world. You'll learn effective search techniques that work with any Internet search programs, present or future, and will build intuition on how to succeed when searches fail. Covers America Online, CompuServe, Microsoft Network and Prodigy, as well as direct and dial-up Internet connections.

NetSuccess: How Real Estate Agents Use the Internet

By Scott Kersnar
1st Edition August 1996
214 pages, ISBN 1-56592-213-1

This book shows real estate agents how to harness the communications and marketing tools of the Internet to enhance their careers and make the Internet work for them. Through agents' stories and "A day in the life" scenarios, readers see what changes and what stays the same when you make technology a full partner in your working life.

NetTravel: How Travelers Use the Internet

By Michael Shapiro
1st Edition April 1997
312 pages, Includes CD-ROM
ISBN 1-56592-172-0

NetTravel is a virtual toolbox of advice for those travelers who want to tap into the rich vein of travel resources on the Internet. It is filled with personal accounts by travelers who've used the Net to plan their business trips, vacations, honeymoons, and explorations. The author gives readers all the tools they need to use the Net immediately to find and save money on airline tickets, accommodations, car rentals, and more.

Net Law: How Lawyers Use the Internet

By Paul Jacobsen
1st Edition January 1997
254 pages, Includes CD-ROM
ISBN 1-56592-258-1

From simple email to sophisticated online marketing, *Net Law* shows how the solo practitioner or the large law firm can turn the Net into an effective and efficient tool. Through stories from those who've set up pioneering legal Net sites, attorney Paul Jacobsen explains how lawyers can successfully integrate the Internet into their practices, sharing lessons "early adopters" have learned.

NetLearning: Why Teachers Use the Internet

By Ferdi Serim & Melissa Koch
1st Edition June 1996
304 pages, Includes CD-ROM
ISBN 1-56592-201-8

In this book educators and Internet users who've been exploring its potential for education share stories to help teachers use this medium to its fullest potential in their classrooms. The book offers advice on how to adapt, how to get what you want, and where to go to get help. The goal: To invite educators online with the reassurance there will be people there to greet them.

O'REILLY™

TO ORDER: **800-998-9938** • *order@oreilly.com* • *http://www.oreilly.com/*
OUR PRODUCTS ARE AVAILABLE AT A BOOKSTORE OR SOFTWARE STORE NEAR YOU.
FOR INFORMATION: **800-998-9938** • **707-829-0515** • *info@oreilly.com*

SONGLINE™
S T U D I O S

Songline Studios specializes in developing innovative, interactive content for online audiences.

Songline Studios mission is to create online programs that allow audiences to experience new people, places, and ideas in unique ways that can only be accomplished through the Web. "Users are not just looking for information online but are searching for rewarding experiences. We are focused on creating these experiences," notes Dale Dougherty, president and CEO of Songline Studios.

THE MEANING OF "SONGLINE"

Songline Studios derives its name from the Australian aboriginal concept of using songs to guide people through unknown territories. These oral maps or "songlines" depict events at successive sites along a walking trail that traverses through a region. This is evocative of Songline Studios' mission: to create resources and guides for online audiences as they seek out and experience new territories and new communities on the Internet.

You can visit the many online and print properties created by Songline Studios through their Web site located at *http://www.songline.com*

SONGLINE GUIDES

The Songline Guides book series connects people with their communities of interest on the Internet. They are non-technical guides, featuring the experiences of specific community members who are also early Internet adopters. These stories help the reader focus on what he or she might expect to gain from being online. Songline Guides can be found at your local bookstore or can be ordered directly from O'Reilly & Associates by calling **1-800-998-9938** or send an email message to **order@ora.com**. Look for Songline Guides for Realtors, Parents and other communities of interest in the near future.

For more information about Songline Studios, call 1-800-998-9973
or send email to: *info@songline.com*

TRAVELERS' TALES

TRUE STORIES OF LIFE ON THE ROAD

"*For* travelers who want a wider introduction to a country and its culture, Travelers' Tales is a valuable addition to any pre-departure reading list."

Tony Wheeler, Publisher ⤴ Lonely Planet Publications

TRAVELERS' TALES
FOOD
Edited by Richard Sterling

TRAVELERS' TALES
BRAZIL
Edited by Annette Haddad
& Scott Doggett

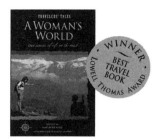

TRAVELERS' TALES
A WOMAN'S WORLD
Edited by Marybeth Bond

TRAVELERS' TALES
GUTSY WOMEN
TRAVEL TIPS AND WISDOM
FOR THE ROAD
By Marybeth Bond

TRAVELERS' TALES
HONG KONG
Edited by James O'Reilly,
Larry Habegger &
Sean O'Reilly

TRAVELERS' TALES
PARIS
Edited by James O'Reilly,
Larry Habegger &
Sean O'Reilly

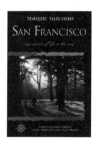

TRAVELERS' TALES
SAN FRANCISCO
Edited by James O'Reilly,
Larry Habegger &
Sean O'Reilly

VISIT
**TRAVELERS'
TALES
ON THE
INTERNET**

www.oreilly.com/ttales

OTHER TITLES IN THE SERIES:

TRAVELERS' TALES THAILAND
Edited by James O'Reilly, Larry Habegger & Sean O'Reilly

TRAVELERS' TALES SPAIN
Edited by Lucy McCauley

TRAVELERS' TALES FRANCE
Edited by James O'Reilly, Larry Habegger & Sean O'Reilly

TRAVELERS' TALES INDIA
Edited by James O'Reilly & Larry Habegger

TRAVELERS' TALES MEXICO
Edited by James O'Reilly & Larry Habegger

Check with your local bookstore for these titles or call O'Reilly to order:
800-889-8969 (credit cards only-Weekdays 6 AM -5 PM PST)
707-829-0515, 800-998-9938 (inquiries), or email to: order@oreilly.com

How to stay in touch with O'Reilly

1. Visit Our Award-Winning Web Site

http://www.oreilly.com/

★ "Top 100 Sites on the Web" —*PC Magazine*
★ "Top 5% Web sites" —*Point Communications*
★ "3-Star site" —*The McKinley Group*

Our web site contains a library of comprehensive product information (including book excerpts and tables of contents), downloadable software, background articles, interviews with technology leaders, links to relevant sites, book cover art, and more. File us in your Bookmarks or Hotlist!

2. Join Our Email Mailing Lists

New Product Releases
To receive automatic email with brief descriptions of all new O'Reilly products as they are released, send email to:
listproc@online.oreilly.com
Put the following information in the first line of your message (*not* in the Subject field):
subscribe oreilly-news

O'Reilly Events
If you'd also like us to send information about trade show events, special promotions, and other O'Reilly events, send email to:
listproc@online.oreilly.com
Put the following information in the first line of your message (*not* in the Subject field):
subscribe oreilly-events

3. Get Examples from Our Books via FTP

There are two ways to access an archive of example files from our books:

Regular FTP
- ftp to:
  ftp.oreilly.com
  (login: anonymous
  password: your email address)
- Point your web browser to:
  ftp://ftp.oreilly.com/

FTPMAIL
- Send an email message to:
  ftpmail@online.oreilly.com
  (Write "help" in the message body)

4. Contact Us via Email

order@oreilly.com
To place a book or software order online. Good for North American and international customers.

subscriptions@oreilly.com
To place an order for any of our newsletters or periodicals.

books@oreilly.com
General questions about any of our books.

software@oreilly.com
For general questions and product information about our software. Check out O'Reilly Software Online at **http://software.oreilly.com/** for software and technical support information. Registered O'Reilly software users send your questions to: **website-support@oreilly.com**

cs@oreilly.com
For answers to problems regarding your order or our products.

booktech@oreilly.com
For book content technical questions or corrections.

proposals@oreilly.com
To submit new book or software proposals to our editors and product managers.

international@oreilly.com
For information about our international distributors or translation queries. For a list of our distributors outside of North America check out:
http://www.oreilly.com/www/order/country.html

O'Reilly & Associates, Inc.
101 Morris Street, Sebastopol, CA 95472 USA
TEL 707-829-0515 or 800-998-9938
(6am to 5pm PST)
FAX 707-829-0104

O'REILLY™

TO ORDER: **800-998-9938** • **order@oreilly.com** • *http://www.oreilly.com/*
OUR PRODUCTS ARE AVAILABLE AT A BOOKSTORE OR SOFTWARE STORE NEAR YOU.
FOR INFORMATION: **800-998-9938** • **707-829-0515** • *info@oreilly.com*

Titles from O'Reilly

Please note that upcoming titles are displayed in italic.

WEBPROGRAMMING

Apache: The Definitive Guide
Building Your Own Web
  Conferences
Building Your Own Website
CGI Programming for the World
  Wide Web
Designing for the Web
HTML: The Definitive Guide,
  2nd Ed.
JavaScript: The Definitive Guide,
  2nd Ed.
Learning Perl
Programming Perl, 2nd Ed.
Mastering Regular Expressions
WebMaster in a Nutshell
Web Security & Commerce
Web Client Programming with
  Perl
World Wide Web Journal

USING THE INTERNET

Smileys
The Future Does Not Compute
The Whole Internet User's Guide
  & Catalog
The Whole Internet for Win 95
Using Email Effectively
Bandits on the Information
  Superhighway

JAVA SERIES

Exploring Java
Java AWT Reference
Java Fundamental Classes
  Reference
Java in a Nutshell
Java Language Reference, 2nd
  Edition
Java Network Programming
Java Threads
Java Virtual Machine

SOFTWARE

WebSite™ 1.1
WebSite Professional™
Building Your Own Web
  Conferences
WebBoard™
PolyForm™
Statisphere™

SONGLINE GUIDES

NetActivism   NetResearch
Net Law   NetSuccess
NetLearning   NetTravel
Net Lessons

SYSTEM ADMINISTRATION

Building Internet Firewalls
Computer Crime: A
  Crimefighter's Handbook
Computer Security Basics
DNS and BIND, 2nd Ed.
Essential System Administration,
  2nd Ed.
Getting Connected: The Internet
  at 56K and Up
Linux Network Administrator's
  Guide
Managing Internet Information
  Services
Managing NFS and NIS
Networking Personal Computers
  with TCP/IP
Practical UNIX & Internet
  Security, 2nd Ed.
PGP: Pretty Good Privacy
sendmail, 2nd Ed.
sendmail Desktop Reference
System Performance Tuning
TCP/IP Network Administration
termcap & terminfo
Using & Managing UUCP
Volume 8: X Window System
  Administrator's Guide
Web Security & Commerce

UNIX

Exploring Expect
Learning VBScript
Learning GNU Emacs, 2nd Ed.
Learning the bash Shell
Learning the Korn Shell
Learning the UNIX Operating
  System
Learning the vi Editor
Linux in a Nutshell
Making TeX Work
Linux Multimedia Guide
Running Linux, 2nd Ed.
SCO UNIX in a Nutshell
sed & awk, 2nd Edition
Tcl/Tk Tools
UNIX in a Nutshell: System V
  Edition
UNIX Power Tools
Using csh & tsch
When You Can't Find Your UNIX
  System Administrator
Writing GNU Emacs Extensions

WEB REVIEW STUDIO SERIES

Gif Animation Studio
Shockwave Studio

WINDOWS

Dictionary of PC Hardware and
  Data Communications Terms
Inside the Windows 95 Registry
Inside the Windows 95 File
  System
Windows Annoyances
Windows NT File System
  Internals
Windows NT in a Nutshell

PROGRAMMING

Advanced Oracle PL/SQL
  Programming
Applying RCS and SCCS
C++: The Core Language
Checking C Programs with lint
DCE Security Programming
Distributing Applications Across
  DCE & Windows NT
Encyclopedia of Graphics File
  Formats, 2nd Ed.
Guide to Writing DCE
  Applications
lex & yacc
Managing Projects with make
Mastering Oracle Power Objects
Oracle Design: The Definitive
  Guide
Oracle Performance Tuning, 2nd
  Ed.
Oracle PL/SQL Programming
Porting UNIX Software
POSIX Programmer's Guide
POSIX.4: Programming for the
  Real World
Power Programming with RPC
Practical C Programming
Practical C++ Programming
Programming Python
Programming with curses
Programming with GNU Software
Pthreads Programming
Software Portability with imake,
  2nd Ed.
Understanding DCE
Understanding Japanese
  Information Processing
UNIX Systems Programming for
  SVR4

BERKELEY 4.4 SOFTWARE DISTRIBUTION

4.4BSD System Manager's
  Manual
4.4BSD User's Reference Manual
4.4BSD User's Supplementary
  Documents
4.4BSD Programmer's Reference
  Manual
4.4BSD Programmer's
  Supplementary Documents
X Programming
Vol. 0: X Protocol Reference
  Manual
Vol. 1: Xlib Programming Manual
Vol. 2: Xlib Reference Manual
Vol. 3M: X Window System User's
  Guide, Motif Edition
Vol. 4M: X Toolkit Intrinsics
  Programming Manual, Motif
  Edition
Vol. 5: X Toolkit Intrinsics
  Reference Manual
Vol. 6A: Motif Programming
  Manual
Vol. 6B: Motif Reference Manual
Vol. 6C: Motif Tools
Vol. 8 : X Window System
  Administrator's Guide
Programmer's Supplement for
  Release 6
X User Tools
The X Window System in a
  Nutshell

CAREER & BUSINESS

Building a Successful Software
  Business
The Computer User's Survival
  Guide
Love Your Job!
Electronic Publishing on CD-
  ROM

TRAVEL

Travelers' Tales: Brazil
Travelers' Tales: Food
Travelers' Tales: France
Travelers' Tales: Gutsy Women
Travelers' Tales: India
Travelers' Tales: Mexico
Travelers' Tales: Paris
Travelers' Tales: San Francisco
Travelers' Tales: Spain
Travelers' Tales: Thailand
Travelers' Tales: A Woman's
  World

O'REILLY™

TO ORDER: **800-998-9938** • *order@oreilly.com* • *http://www.oreilly.com/*
OUR PRODUCTS ARE AVAILABLE AT A BOOKSTORE OR SOFTWARE STORE NEAR YOU.
FOR INFORMATION: **800-998-9938** • **707-829-0515** • *info@oreilly.com*

International Distributors

UK, EUROPE, MIDDLE EAST AND NORTHERN AFRICA (EXCEPT FRANCE, GERMANY, SWITZERLAND, & AUSTRIA)

INQUIRIES

International Thomson Publishing Europe
Berkshire House
168-173 High Holborn
London WC1V 7AA
United Kingdom
Telephone: 44-171-497-1422
Fax: 44-171-497-1426
Email: itpint@itps.co.uk

ORDERS

International Thomson Publishing Services, Ltd.
Cheriton House, North Way
Andover, Hampshire SP10 5BE
United Kingdom
Telephone: 44-264-342-832 (UK)
Telephone: 44-264-342-806 (outside UK)
Fax: 44-264-364418 (UK)
Fax: 44-264-342761 (outside UK)
UK & Eire orders: itpuk@itps.co.uk
International orders: itpint@itps.co.uk

FRANCE

Editions Eyrolles
61 bd Saint-Germain
75240 Paris Cedex 05
France
Fax: 33-01-44-41-11-44

FRENCH LANGUAGE BOOKS

All countries except Canada
Telephone: 33-01-44-41-46-16
Email: geodif@eyrolles.com
English language books
Telephone: 33-01-44-41-11-87
Email: distribution@eyrolles.com

GERMANY, SWITZERLAND, AND AUSTRIA

INQUIRIES

O'Reilly Verlag
Balthasarstr. 81
D-50670 Köln
Germany
Telephone: 49-221-97-31-60-0
Fax: 49-221-97-31-60-8
Email: anfragen@oreilly.de

ORDERS

International Thomson Publishing
Königswinterer Straße 418
53227 Bonn, Germany
Telephone: 49-228-97024 0
Fax: 49-228-441342
Email: order@oreilly.de

JAPAN

O'Reilly Japan, Inc.
Kiyoshige Building 2F
12-Banchi, Sanei-cho
Shinjuku-ku
Tokyo 160-0008 Japan
Telephone: 81-3-3356-5227
Fax: 81-3-3356-5261
Email: kenji@oreilly.com

INDIA

Computer Bookshop (India) PVT. Ltd.
190 Dr. D.N. Road, Fort
Bombay 400 001 India
Telephone: 91-22-207-0989
Fax: 91-22-262-3551
Email: cbsbom@giasbm01.vsnl.net.in

HONG KONG

City Discount Subscription Service Ltd.
Unit D, 3rd Floor, Yan's Tower
27 Wong Chuk Hang Road
Aberdeen, Hong Kong
Telephone: 852-2580-3539
Fax: 852-2580-6463
Email: citydis@ppn.com.hk

KOREA

Hanbit Media, Inc.
Sonyoung Bldg. 202
Yeksam-dong 736-36
Kangnam-ku
Seoul, Korea
Telephone: 822-554-9610
Fax: 822-556-0363
Email: hant93@chollian.dacom.co.kr

SINGAPORE, MALAYSIA, AND THAILAND

Addison Wesley Longman Singapore PTE Ltd.
25 First Lok Yang Road
Singapore 629734
Telephone: 65-268-2666
Fax: 65-268-7023
Email: daniel@longman.com.sg

PHILIPPINES

Mutual Books, Inc.
429-D Shaw Boulevard
Mandaluyong City, Metro
Manila, Philippines
Telephone: 632-725-7538
Fax: 632-721-3056
Email: mbikikog@mnl.sequel.net

CHINA

Ron's DataCom Co., Ltd.
79 Dongwu Avenue
Dongxihu District
Wuhan 430040
China
Telephone: 86-27-3892568
Fax: 86-27-3222108
Email: hongfeng@public.wh.hb.cn

ALL OTHER ASIAN COUNTRIES

O'Reilly & Associates, Inc.
101 Morris Street
Sebastopol, CA 95472 USA
Telephone: 707-829-0515
Fax: 707-829-0104
Email: order@oreilly.com

AUSTRALIA

WoodsLane Pty. Ltd.
7/5 Vuko Place, Warriewood NSW 2102
P.O. Box 935
Mona Vale NSW 2103
Australia
Telephone: 61-2-9970-5111
Fax: 61-2-9970-5002
Email: info@woodslane.com.au

NEW ZEALAND

Woodslane New Zealand Ltd.
21 Cooks Street (P.O. Box 575)
Waganui, New Zealand
Telephone: 64-6-347-6543
Fax: 64-6-345-4840
Email: info@woodslane.com.au

THE AMERICAS

McGraw-Hill Interamericana Editores, S.A. de C.V.
Cedro No. 512
Col. Atlampa 06450
Mexico, D.F.
Telephone: 52-5-541-3155
Fax: 52-5-541-4913
Email: mcgraw-hill@infosel.net.mx

SOUTH AFRICA

International Thomson Publishing
South Africa
Building 18, Constantia Park
138 Sixteenth Road
P.O. Box 2459
Halfway House, 1685 South Africa
Telephone: 27-11-805-4819
Fax: 27-11-805-3648

O'REILLY™

O'Reilly & Associates, Inc.
101 Morris Street
Sebastopol, CA 95472-9902
1-800-998-9938

Visit us online at:
**http://www.ora.com/
orders@ora.com**

O'REILLY WOULD LIKE TO HEAR FROM YOU

Which book did this card come from?

_____

Where did you buy this book?
- ❏ Bookstore
- ❏ Direct from O'Reilly
- ❏ Bundled with hardware/software
- ❏ Computer Store
- ❏ Class/seminar
- ❏ Other _____

What operating system do you use?
- ❏ UNIX
- ❏ Windows NT
- ❏ Other _____
- ❏ Macintosh
- ❏ PC(Windows/DOS)

What is your job description?
- ❏ System Administrator
- ❏ Network Administrator
- ❏ Web Developer
- ❏ Programmer
- ❏ Educator/Teacher
- ❏ Other _____

❏ Please send me O'Reilly's catalog, containing a complete listing of O'Reilly books and software.

Name _____ Company/Organization _____

Address _____

City _____ State _____ Zip/Postal Code _____ Country _____

Telephone _____ Internet or other email address (specify network) _____

Nineteenth century wood engraving
of a bear from the O'Reilly &
Associates Nutshell Handbook®
Using & Managing UUCP.

POST CARD

BUSINESS REPLY MAIL
FIRST CLASS MAIL   PERMIT NO. 80   SEBASTOPOL, CA

Postage will be paid by addressee

O'Reilly & Associates, Inc.
101 Morris Street
Sebastopol, CA 95472-9902